LUD
VIG
SEN KARL LUDVIGSEN

KARL LUDVIG SEN'S FAST FRIENDS

STARS AND HEROES IN THE WORLD OF CARS

DELIUS KLASING VERLAG

**FOR MY DEAR WIFE
ANNETTE
WITH LOVE**

CONTENTS

Even my 300SL was struggling at the high altitude at which this picture was taken – not in the Alps but in the Rocky Mountains. It was during an epic drive in the summer of 1959 with the Mercedes I bought in Germany and brought back to the USA.

Introduction

INTRODUCTION

I like to say that I've never had a job interview. I suppose there have been some exceptions. One might be when I was invited to meet Daimler-Benz export chief Heinz C. Hoppe in Manhattan when he was looking for a press manager for his American sales company. I was attracted but felt that my future still lay with General Motors.

Another might be my dinner with Bob Lutz in Detroit when he was chairman of Ford of Europe. We discussed a possible position there that eventuated as a vice presidency. But Bob and I had been friends for more than a decade so that doesn't really count.

Otherwise I was invited – sometimes out of the blue – to take up various positions in the world of cars. That included my magazine editorships and my jobs at GM, Fiat and Ford. The only common denominator was my passionate interest in automobiles, which I spiced up with my proven writing and research skills plus training in mechanical engineering and industrial design.

I took a big step into the unknown when I left GM in 1967, turning down several internal job offers. Could I support my family as a freelance writer? The same was true when I left Ford in 1983. Could I make the grade as the head of my own management consultancy specialising in the motor industry? Happily the answer in both cases was 'yes'.

The common factor for my employment choices was my deep curiosity about the whys and wherefores of automobiles, their users and their makers. High on my agenda was to gain knowledge of motor racing around the world, its history and its evolution. I tried to use my understanding of engineering and design to explain to an interested audience what was happening, why it was happening and who was making it happen. The latter turned out to be the most challenging to uncover!

I've had the pleasure and honour of meeting and working with many men and women in the course of my career, innovators to legends in their lifetime. As the biographer of such people as Juan Fangio, Giorgetto Giugiaro,

John DeLorean, Mario Andretti and Louise Piëch, I'm sharing the stories of some of the all-time greats of our automotive world. And if some of my other selections are people less renowned, I'm sure you'll find their stories equally intriguing.

Thank you for your interest in this perspective on the world of cars. These are some of the personalities who helped shape it and whose impact was truly transformative. Theirs is the automotive legacy we enjoy today.

Karl Ludvigsen
Hawkedon, Suffolk
June 2019

EXECUTIVES

Fa – as I called him – was always a smoker, cigarettes at first and then pipes in later life. He was always busy but we got to know each other better after he retired.

Executives

ELLIOT LEON LUDVIGSEN

I n 1922 the Fuller Manufacturing Company completed a handsome new pair of four-story factory buildings at the junction of Pitcher and Prouty Streets on the northern periphery of Kalamazoo, Michigan. Located 142 miles from both Detroit and Chicago by road or rail, Kalamazoo was well placed to serve the growing motor industry.

Enjoying the backing of notable local figures, the Fuller family had been in business in this bucolic western-Michigan city since 1888. By 1903 the Fuller brothers were producing the Michigan automobile. They stopped making cars in 1908, concentrating instead on producing their respected transmissions for cars and trucks.

This decision by the Fullers was in line with trends in the industry, which at the time saw many makers entering the fast-growing auto market by buying major components from suppliers to produce a vehicle which they assembled rather than manufactured themselves. Focusing on this through World War I, Fuller emerged with a strong reputation for its heavy-duty gearboxes. In 1923 Fuller phased out passenger-car units to concentrate on truck transmissions.

In 1928 a 25-year-old engineer at the Cleveland truck maker, White Motor Company, decided to stake his fortunes on Fuller, which had just been acquired by Chicago's Unit Corporation. Elliot Leon 'Lud' Ludvigsen was born of Danish parents in Jackson, Minnesota, where he attended high school. After a year at Wisconsin's Lawrence College, he 'had some thoughts about going to business school. But – I have to give my mother credit for this – she said, "Why don't you take up engineering? That's what you're mostly interested in anyway'."

Here, young Ludvigsen had remarkable antecedents. At their workshop in Jackson, his father and uncles had a bustling business manufacturing self-sharpening toe calks for horseshoes, whose design and production methods they patented. Sold in every state in the union, their products were made by specialised machinery they designed. Theirs was an example not to be overlooked.

'So when I went back in the autumn,' said Ludvigsen, 'I stopped off at the University of Minnesota and registered there in the engineering school.' Lud graduated with a Bachelor of Science degree in Mechanical Engineering in 1925. 'A guy by the name of F. T. Jones came up from the White Motor Company,' he recalled. 'The more we talked with each other, the more interest I developed in signing on for the one-year apprentice course.' That summer Lud joined White, which enrolled him in the firm's technical apprentice programme.

At Cleveland he encountered 'a great apprentice course – it was unbelievably good. We actually worked. I was in the heat-treating department for a month, and then engine machining and inspection, followed by axle inspection. I was in the sales engineering department for a while and then the order department. I got very much involved with the engine department where, for a period of time, I finally had charge of the dynamometer testing.' It led to Lud writing a shop man's textbook on metallurgy and heat treatment and to posts at White as quality inspector, engine test supervisor, and assistant to the chief inspector.

Lud's career took a fateful turn in the summer of 1928. Close observer that he was, he could see that White's 'costs were pretty much out of line, pretty high. If the quality had really justified it, it might have been all right, but I had a feeling that the quality wasn't quite there. I started looking around and one day I saw an ad in the *SAE Journal* for a sales engineer, mentioning truck design and components.' The ad was in the June 1928 issue, to which Lud responded with a two-and-a-half page letter on 11 June, stressing his interest and credentials in the field of sales. He got an immediate reply from the Fuller Manufacturing Company in Kalamazoo – After looking over this Fuller thing and its competitors, Lud decided that – it looked like a pretty narrow field – it had a chance to grow – and threw in his lot with Fuller.

As sales engineer, Ludvigsen 'covered the whole damn company. John Earle and I were the sales department, that's what it amounted to. John handled several accounts and I was sent out principally to contact potential customers. By 1930, having sold – several thousand transmissions – he was named sales manager for Fuller. Among his tasks was to sell strictly to truck makers, not to third parties, and to provide first-class service, rolling up his sleeves if necessary and putting his engineering know-how to good use.

Ray Armington, then superintendent of Euclid Road Machinery, recalled Lud's style when one of his off-highway vehicles struggled with a transmission and multiple-disc clutch produced by Fuller. 'As the transmissions were returned from the field for rebuilding,' said Armington, 'Fuller's sales manager, Elliot Ludvigsen, came out to our plant to help us out – and help us out he did. He was not just a salesman. He had the uncanny ability to get to the root of a problem. We soon had clutches that didn't lose their linings and transmissions that could be shifted without a crash.

'Lud's warm personality became influential with our customers,' Armington added, 'and indirectly he became a most effective salesman for Euclid hauling equipment. As Euclid's product line developed, Fuller transmissions were used exclusively – a direct result of Lud's painstaking care and follow-through ability.'

Supported by strong service-parts sales, Fuller weathered the depression years but other parts of the company went under, leading to receivership and new management in 1934. With fresh designs, Lud achieved a sale to International Harvester, 'the biggest thing that ever happened to us.' But he had to sharpen his pencil and then some.

'I battled the price situation with Harvester and we finally took the job for our manufacturing costs, which was what it amounted to. And materials, labour and manufacturing overheads. We did it for that because we figured if we could get this by them, this would bring our overheads down. It was a good concept, a really good concept. Normally you don't talk about your costings, but I did. I figured that was the only way I was going to be able to establish credibility for the future with them. So we got the job.'

Promoted to vice president and general manager by 1937, Lud had to deal with Harvester, as it accounted for 40 to 50 per cent of Fuller's sales. 'This worried the directors,' he related: '"We've got too many eggs in one basket," they said. But when you've got that many eggs in one basket you just live with it. You just make good deliveries and good quality and that's going to hold true in the truck business. That gave us our real comeback.'

In World War II Fuller was making transfer gearboxes and heavy transmissions for tank transporters under Government control, with Lud a member of a transmission committee in Washington that allocated output. Coming out of the war, Lud was testing heavy truck transmissions on the tough Ridge Route between Los Angeles and San Francisco when he had a brain wave. To get ten forward speeds, drivers had to operate both a five-speed transmission and a two-speed auxiliary 'splitter' that gave ratios between the five principal speeds. This required drivers to manipulate two shift levers to go back and forth between both boxes as they progressed.

Lud realised that it might be possible to have a two-speed auxiliary gearbox whose ratio step was so great that it covered the full range of the five-speed transmission. The driver would shift up through five gears, then activate the auxiliary when shifting back to first gear, and finally go through the five gears again. 'I had my secretary witness it when I got back,' said Lud about his notes on the idea, 'and I got Tom Backus down and I said, "Let's go to work on this thing, see how we can do it".'

Lud shared a patent on the concept with chief engineer Tom Backus, which when proven was marketed as the RoadRanger; a Ludvigsen idea. It required some gizmos of the kind distrusted by truck operators. The shift in the auxiliary box was made by a microswitch triggering a solenoid valve, which controlled a cylinder – either vacuum or compressed air – that made the shift. Both auxiliary ratios were synchronised by multiple-disc clutches. Fuller experimented with Porsche's ring-type synchromesh for this job but it didn't have the blocking function that this application needed.

'The drivers loved it,' Lud said, 'once they knew what they had.' This helped them over some teething troubles, after which RoadRangers were marketed in several torque capacities. Others who wanted to build something similar, like Leyland in the UK, paid Fuller a four per cent royalty on the idea.

By 1948 Lud Ludvigsen had climbed the ranks within the Fuller Manufacturing Company to become president. This was the man whose son – namely me – went down to the plant with him on Saturdays when Lud wanted some quiet time to catch up in his office. I looked through the *SAE Journal*, *Commercial Car Journal* and *Automotive Industries*, auto-making bibles. These and my experiences at Fuller had a lot to do with my growing passion for automobiles.

We would tour the quiet plant, which in my earliest visits still had huge overhead shafts and pulleys driving the machine tools through long belts. It was an exciting place with its own drop-forging presses, heat treatment and foundry. Digging through bins of scrap I found interesting pieces to take home.

Between my third and fourth years of high school I worked at Fuller during the summer. Under the patient tutelage of Gil Hulme, I was given a board in the drafting office, its big windows facing north from the main building. My main activity was inking drawings. The engineers would complete their component and assembly drawings in pencil, but for a permanent record, Fuller needed ink drawings on vellum. I was good enough at this to make myself useful.

Gil welcomed me back in the summer of 1952, in the hiatus between my high-school graduation and starting at MIT in the autumn. This was an exciting time at Fuller. It was offering new-fangled torque converters for some applications. When I came back to Fuller in the summer of 1954 we were working on a new smaller version of the RoadRanger. Having learned about machine-tool operation at MIT, I spent the summer in the experimental workshop, making parts for the new RoadRanger.

While milling the slots in the main gears of the auxiliary gearbox that took the synchromesh discs, I didn't index them properly. Checking with my boss, we decided that we could salvage the pieces by cutting fresh slots in the remaining metal, leaving the earlier ones in place. Wouldn't you know it? My father showed up at the workshop to check the jobs in progress. He spotted the slotted gears.

'How come these parts have these extra slots?' he asked my chief.

'You'd better ask your son about that,' he replied.

In 1958 Fuller, which in the meantime had acquired some subsidiaries of its own, was bought by Cleveland's Eaton Corporation, a major global supplier to the motor industry. By 1963 my father had been promoted to Eaton's presidency and became chairman in 1967. He retired from that position in 1969 and remained a director until 1975. Lud died in 1978.

While a dyed-in-the wool member of the Gear Gashers Guild – and he had the tie clasp to prove it – Lud Ludvigsen was far more than a narrow technocrat. He was a trustee of Angola, Indiana's Tri-State University for 18 years, receiving an Honorary Doctorate from Tri-State, and chaired its Board of Trustees for five years. He was a director of the Simpson Paper Company of Seattle, Washington, and a former director of the Greater Cleveland Growth Association and the National City Bank of Cleveland.

As a youth, when his nickname was 'Spike', Lud was athletic and a strong swimmer. He became a passionate duck hunter, teaming up with like-minded friends to set up suitable blinds near Michigan's many waterways. Starting out with a Ford Model T he became interested in cars, owning two Auburns and a Lincoln Zephyr. Before and during the war he was a Buick man, later switching to Oldsmobiles and finally Lincolns.

Living not far from Lake Michigan, Lud Ludvigsen was drawn to yachting. Trading up from a 26 7-foot Chris-Craft to a 40-foot twin-screw cabin cruiser, he navigated Lakes Michigan, Superior and Huron in summer cruises with his family and friends. Finding inadequate local information on seamanship, he founded a Kalamazoo chapter of the Power Squadron, which taught the essentials of sound piloting and navigation.

Lud, whom my brother Eric and I always knew as 'Fa' in Scandinavian style, gave me good advice along the way. He encouraged my plan to study engineering at MIT, pointing out that engineering was a good basis for any career. He also urged me to study German in high school as it was 'the language of engineering'. This became hugely beneficial to my research into German auto marques. Lud had no objection when I veered away from engineering after two years to study industrial design at Pratt Institute in Brooklyn.

In the late 1960s Lud backed me when I headed a company importing auto parts and accessories. He was always supportive of my writing career, although he was frequently critical of the small type sizes used by *Automobile Quarterly*. When my first serious book was published in 1971, *Mercedes-Benz Sports and Racing Cars*, I dedicated it 'To Fa'. I owed him a lot.

FERDINAND ANTON ERNST PORSCHE

As Ferry and I chatted at a motor show, behind him was Porsche press and sports chief Manfred Jantke and behind me Horst Borghs, PR man at Ford and then Opel.

F erdinand Porsche's son was born in 1909. Nicknamed Ferry, he was immersed in automotive lore from his earliest days. 'I have, so to speak, come into the world with the automobile,' he once said. At the age of ten he was able to drive and at 16 he was behind the wheel of an experimental Mercedes.

Trained and apprenticed in every important discipline of the industry, Ferry Porsche became an employee of the Stuttgart office in 1931. There he was further tutored by Porsche stalwart Walter Boxan while he completed his first drawing – a Wanderer connecting rod. With a Wanderer, a car he test-drove as well as helped design, Ferry competed twice in 2,000-kilometre races over the open roads of Germany. In 1939 he took over the management of Porsche's Zuffenhausen office after his father was, made one of the directors of the new Volkswagen factory. After the war, Ferry was instrumental in the creation and production of the Porsche Type 356 sports car.

I first met Ferry Porsche when he and Huschke von Hanstein came to New York in 1957. Ferry was in the USA to accept a Franklin Institute award that recognised the role of his father in the creation of the VW Beetle. Porsche organised a reception for Ferry and Huschke in New York to which I, as technical editor of *Sports Cars Illustrated*, was asked along. Huschke gave me my first Porsche lapel pin, which I managed hold on to for many years.

I reflected on this first meeting in 1996 while I was serving as an honorary judge at the 50th-anniversary Porsche Parade at Hershey, Pennsylvania. On the same panel was actor and comedian Jerry Seinfeld. My colleagues at Bentley Publishing arranged for me to have some one-on-one time with Jerry, who is an enthusiastic owner, driver and admirer of Porsches. During our chat he said to me, in his no-nonsense way, 'You knew Ferry Porsche, didn't you? What was he like?'

Yes, I did know Ferry Porsche. He was of medium height with light-brown hair and a clear gaze. He spoke in a gentle tenor with a lilt that betrayed his Austrian origins. He preserved an Austrian awareness of the ridiculous, an appreciation that although things had at times been bad, they could always have been a lot worse. It was fascinating to discuss Porsche's affairs with a man who had driven the Auto Unions and shaken hands with Hitler.

Disappointments loomed large in the Ferry story. Like his colleagues, Ferry suffered from his demanding father's abruptness and unwillingness to praise. If it was meant as a way of hardening the young engineer, it failed. Ferry remained a man who got results by knowledgeable persuasion, not by command. He brought all of his unequalled experience and close observation to every decision, an attribute that could be frustrating to his colleagues but yielded great results in the long run.

Perhaps Ferry's deepest disappointment was his father's decision on the distribution of the Porsche patrimony at his death in 1951. The semi-feudal central-European custom was that the eldest son received the main inheritance, the house and the business, while token gifts were made to others. Ferry Porsche had every reason to expect that he would be similarly blessed. Instead, to his astonishment and dismay, Ferdinand Porsche divided ownership of his holdings equally between Ferry and his sister Louise without, said grandson Ferdinand Piëch, 'giving the slightest inkling as to whom he'd prefer to entrust the leading role in the clan.

'Apart from the fact that the daughter was five years older,' Piëch continued, 'she always seemed rather more mature, grown-up, stronger than her brother. At least in my view, she never lost a certain advantage and there is much evidence that my grandfather saw it the same way. My father absolutely wanted to bring my sister into the company's management,' Ferry acknowledged. 'It would have been more correct if my father had gone the way of the Rothschilds and said: "One bears the responsibility, the other one does it."'

Brother and sister found a Solomonic solution. They took joint ownership in their respective enterprises, while remaining separate in their management. Ferry ran the car and engineering company in Stuttgart while in Salzburg Louise headed the Austrian import company for VW and Porsche. 'Each sibling was ready to help the other,' said eldest grandson Ernst Piëch, 'but they remained separate.'

Little changed over the years in the high-tension relationship between brother and sister. Yet when Ferry was released from French detention in 1946, it was to his sister that he turned for long walks in the countryside to share his pent-up emotions, rather than his wife. 'One could sense that the relationship between the siblings Louise and Ferry was exceptional,' said Ferdinand Piëch. 'They loved and hated each other in the intense, violent manner that's customary between brother and sister. And naturally it fitted the picture that in high old age, in spite of all that separated them, they were again and again together.'

Forthright to a fault, Prof. Ferdinand Porsche had been constitutionally incapable of appreciating the subtle attributes that Ferry brought to business management. Ferry was conservative, to be sure. That very conservatism contributed to the remarkably subtle and at times glacial evolution of Porsche's cars from the 356 through to the 911 until 1972, when Ferry and his relations stepped back from the company's management. Without mentioning the controversial – to him – 924 and 928, Ferry said later that he wished he had stayed longer at the company's controls.

On 15 October 1973, when Ferry's departure from direct management was still fresh, I sat with him in his office in a villa on Stuttgart's Robert Bosch Strasse to discuss the company and its evolution. This was the first time that I, or anyone else, had heard of the 1.5-litre sports car that was designed before the war with the aim of creating the first Porsche-branded production model. They prepared it, he said, 'so we would have something to do after the war.

'It had a *five*-cylinder engine,' he told me with a smile. 'It's a very smooth, well-balanced engine,' he said, 'with nice firing intervals.' Such fives were in the news at the time, including a Mercedes-Benz diesel, so Ferry was proud of this much earlier application. Only when I went to the files to check on this hitherto-unknown design did I discover that Ferry had recalled the concept but not the actuality: in fact the Type 114 'F-Wagen' had a *V-10* engine. Fully designed in every detail, it could have been their post-war 'Porsche' but the design was far too elaborate for the straitened economic circumstances that prevailed.

Harking back to the creation of Porsche's Type 60, the Volkswagen, Ferry said that he was involved 'from the first pencil mark. But I was one of the youngest workers then – most of the others are no longer alive. Of course the Volkswagen was my father's achievement through and through, the culmination of his life's work, so to speak. I learned a great deal from him in those days. Through my position as liaison between design and the experimental side, I had a good deal of insight and influence, even in basic matters.

'Many of its features were undoubtedly new and ingenious for those days,' Ferry added, 'but my father had already built a forerunner, the air-cooled, rear-engined car for NSU. The test results we obtained from it had great influence on the later VW design. For instance we already understood the ways of a boxer engine and the difficulties it could present in mixture distribution. Items like cooling or the oil cooler were pre-tested. This all happened in 1932 when NSU's motorcycle business was not too good and they wanted to build an automobile.'

During the war, said Ferry Porsche, 'it was vital that the Volkswagen be constantly reviewed, improved and kept up to date to meet changing conditions. So, since we weren't allowed to design a synchromesh transmission or a hydraulic brake system for private use, we designed them for "military use" instead – as "improvements" to the Kübelwagen and the people's car.' In fact they used this ruse to try out a number of novelties for the VW including supercharging, turbocharging and several automatic transmissions.

In April of 1944, when the first bombs fell on the KdF-Wagen plant at Fallersleben, Ferdinand Porsche became highly agitated. The company's archives, he complained to his son after returning from Berlin, were stored in the attic of Werk I, where they were vulnerable to air attack. He insisted that they should be moved at once to the cellar, where they would be better protected.

The precaution of triplicating the original drawings had already been taken. One of the additional sets was stored in the Porsche villa and the other was at the Stuttgart residence of Ghislaine Kaes, Porsche's nephew and personal secretary. All were packed in special locked containers of sheet steel.

Dutifully, Ferry shifted the Zuffenhausen archive to the building's cellar. 'Eight days after we moved it,' Ferry recalled, 'during an attack a bomb came in diagonally from the west. It missed everything else but demolished the archive in the cellar.' It was becoming evident that at least some of the Porsche team would have to move.

The idea of a move from Stuttgart had already been discussed as early as May 1943. By the spring of 1944 it was becoming essential to the engineers' survival. Ferry Porsche took on the task of reconnoitring possible sites. Applying first to the authorities in Stuttgart, he was offered a property in Czechoslovakia. 'When I heard that,' said Ferry, 'I did my best to prevent it.' Though the senior Porsche was born in what was now Czech territory and both men had been Czech citizens after World War I, the idea was deeply unattractive. They didn't relish being abandoned there after the war among a populace who were less than thrilled about engineers who had helped the German war effort.

In wartime, the home base of the Porsche team remained at Stuttgart-Zuffenhausen – even though many other firms with important wartime missions had already been dispersed, either underground or to strategically less important regions. In fact Porsche had dispersed its machine tools, Ferry said: 'One third remained in Stuttgart, one third went to the flying school at Zell am See that we were allocated and a third went to Gmünd in Austria where we settled our engineers. My plan was that as long as we had one-third we could start again.'

Ferry described to me the way he moved a small engineering detachment from Gmünd back to Stuttgart in late 1949. They set up shop in the Porsche villa on Feuerbacherweg that his father had built when he became Daimler-Benz engineering chief in 1923. They used the spacious garage as a workshop – as it had been when the first VW prototypes were built – and the room usually occupied by the family cook, as their 'three-metre office'.

Although Porsche had built a small series of sports cars in Austria, it was not taken for granted that they would make cars in Germany, Ferry explained: 'In 1951 there were many discussions within the family about whether we should continue what we had started in Gmünd with the 356. I was always for it. After I pressed ahead there were no more arguments. In fact, arguments indeed continued about which part pays for what. If we pay for 50 per cent of engineering work on cars with car sales, for example, who is to say how the other 50 per cent was earned with consulting? You can divide up the amounts any way you want!'

When Porsche started producing cars in Germany, it rented the necessary space from coachbuilder Reutter because the US Army still needed their nearby Werk I as a motor pool. 'That was our greatest good fortune,' Ferry told me with a knowing smile. 'Other firms had buildings, tools and so forth but they didn't know what to do, which cars to make. They had overheads but no cash flow. We started with cash flow but no overheads!'

With his father still detained by the French, it was up to Ferry to seek a new engineering relationship with Volkswagen, where Heinz Nordhoff was in charge. 'I had known Nordhoff from meetings during wartime tests,' Ferry related. 'He was responsible for Opel Blitz trucks built in Brandenburg. We got together, drew a line under the past and agreed on a new license for the VW, a consulting contract, the import agency for Austria, favoured status on delivery of VW parts for building our own sports cars and joint use of the worldwide VW sales organisation. That was the basis for our fresh start.'

Earnings and royalties from that source soon built up a war chest. 'Since then the contract has been changed and extended at least four times,' Ferry said. 'But as I like to say, we have been married since 1934!'

A marriage of a different nature was proposed in 1954, Porsche told me: 'I was asked if I would go to Wolfsburg and take over VW's development there. I would have to give up the car business. I felt that they thought it would be easier and cheaper to tie me up that way than to take over the whole Porsche organisation.' Needless to say this did not happen. In fact Ferry devoted all his future efforts to warding off a closer and potentially stifling relationship with Volkswagen.

'When we started in Stuttgart with the 356,' Ferry recalled, 'we planned to make only 500 cars. All our plans and tools were made for that purpose. But the numbers kept growing so we built Werk II. It was ready in 1956. Then that same year, exactly on the 25th anniversary of our company, the Americans gave back our Werk I. If we'd known that would happen we might never have needed Werk II!' Of course both workshops were soon needed to meet demand.

This was typical Ferry, bemused by such coincidences and second-guessing past decisions. But he was fated to revisit the past because his philosophy was that: 'the decision is always a momentary thing according to the prevailing conditions. One must always remember that one makes decisions under the conditions that exist at the time. No man can see into the future.'

Speaking of decisions, Ferry Porsche explained to me the background of the relationship with Reutter. 'When we returned to Stuttgart, Reutter was making trolley car repairs there and general repairing in its other plants. Afterward they were 80 per cent occupied with work for Porsche. Father Reutter was killed by bombing here in Stuttgart and his son was killed in the war. There were eight heirs but none of them had any knowledge of the business so they hired a manager. When they had to invest more, as our production increased, the heirs didn't want to, so the manager advised them to sell the body plant.

'In a very difficult decision,' Ferry continued. 'we at Porsche bought the factory in 1963. It was *very* hard to get the necessary capital together when we had to give two-thirds of our profits to the Government. We had to make an investment which brought in nothing new. We laid millions on the table and nothing changed.' The only advantage was that the previous four per cent transfer tax on sales by Reutter to Porsche no longer applied.

While its sports-car production boomed, Porsche's contract with Volkswagen gave little satisfaction apart from project fees and royalties. 'After the war,' said Ferry, 'our first work for VW was to design a new car, keeping the existing engine. It had a completely integral structure and MacPherson-strut front suspension. But then the Beetle was selling so well they decided not to build it.

'We designed six or seven new cars for Volkswagen that were never produced. That's why I always thought that we should keep building cars,' Ferry told me. 'At least in one area we can show that we are always up to date, even if the others for whom we work don't produce what we have designed. If we weren't building cars, nobody would speak about us anymore.

'For the larger Type 3 they asked for styles from Porsche, Ghia and their own studio,' Ferry added. 'The board viewed all three and chose the Porsche design. But not to displease anyone and to avoid anyone crediting Porsche with the design, they mixed them all together! Ours had a lower belt line, lower lights – it was a lot prettier!

'Because the business went so well,' Ferry said, 'we could afford to go racing. But at first we approached it in the cheapest way!' This was a reference to the Gmünd-built coupes with their aluminium bodies and narrower low-drag greenhouses that they used for their first Le Mans effort in 1951.

'We found that with racing development we could improve the normal car,' Ferry added. 'For example the first 1,5-litre engines had Hirth roller-bearing crankshafts, mainly because that gave cleaner connecting-rod big ends that cleared the camshaft. One day Rabe came to me and said, "I have a connecting rod with a diagonal cut that will clear the camshaft." That allowed a change to plain bearings for the 1,5-litre four.'

When I spoke with Ferry, the issue of the Wankel rotary engine was still on the minds of all motor companies. Did this represent an investment that they had to make? In fact, on 2 March 1965, Porsche had taken a license to work with the Wankel on 'internal combustion engines from 50 to 1,000 hp for passenger cars (racing and rally vehicles).'

'I calculated that 65,000 engines were produced daily in the world for all purposes,' Porsche said. 'This represented an investment of many billions to make them. What advantages must an engine have, to replace those already being made?' The unspoken answer was that the newcomer's advantages would have to be far greater than the Wankel was able to provide. In fact Porsche did not progress the Wankel while its own Leopold Schmid developed a rotary engine that showed considerable potential.

Having successfully achieved the goal of combining car production with consulting engineering, Ferry Porsche could reflect on his company's success:

'The happiest thing for me when I go to Americais is to see what a good image we have on that great continent. That's a validation of what we have done. It shows that we've done things right.

'Others are making sports cars,' Porsche added, 'but no one makes a car like we do, made specially for the purpose, down to every last screw and bolt. Others in Italy do it but their cars cost twice as much as ours.' This summary of what makes Porsche Porsche was sustained well into the 21st century.

Each a titan in their own profession, Ferdinand Porsche's two children succeeded magnificently. Louise was the more dynamic and decisive, much like her father.

Executives

LOUISE HEDWIG ANNA WILHELMINE MARIE PORSCHE PIËCH

Louise Piëch, nee Porsche, was a towering personality in Austria. Though one of the biggest fish in that small pond, she sought little recognition beyond its borders. Unlike her brother Ferry Porsche, Louise never became a global icon. But the distribution organisation she ran outpaced the Porsche car company in sales and often in profitability. In its first 50 years it turned over some $25 billion, while selling and servicing two million cars. 'It was an oil well,' joked former VW chief Carl Hahn, adding that 'it produced not oil but gold.'

'At Porsche Salzburg', added Hahn, 'Louise was in every respect the commander in chief.' Indeed, added the VW veteran, 'She was a Maria Theresa for the 20th Century' – a reference to the only woman ever to rule the empire of the Habsburgs. While Maria Theresa was a formidable female in the 18th Century, Louise Piëch carved a phenomenal reputation in the second half of the 20th as the head of a company that imported Volkswagens, Porsches and Audis into Austria and ultimately commanded a wholesale and retail distribution empire that ranged far into East and West Europe.

The crucial turning point for Louise Piëch, was her 48th birthday on 29 August 1952. As that day dawned, she was the wife of Anton Piëch, lawyer and manager of their Austrian car-distribution company with its 71-strong staff, and the mother of four children: Ernst, 23; Louise, 20; Ferdinand, 15; and Hans-Michael, 10. Though home was the family residence at Zell am See, they had an apartment in Salzburg where their business was based. They also had a summer home on the Wörthersee, where Louise awaited Anton that Friday morning to join in her birthday celebrations.

Anton was late. The reason why was confirmed in a phone call from Klagenfurt. En route he had been struck down by a heart attack. 'Nowadays,' reflected his son Ernst, 'you wouldn't die of this. These days he'd undergo an operation and have a chance, but at that time it was impossible to save him. Nobody knew how to do it.' Less than a month short of his 58th birthday, Anton Piëch drew his last breath.

How was Louise to carry on? 'In reality,' Ernst Piëch reflected, 'everything my father did was more or less manipulated by my mother. *Very cleverly.* Everybody knows that. My father provided more or less a wall, a protective barrier, but what happened was determined by my mother. This was very good because when my father suddenly died, she was well informed on everything and she just took over and ran the company like nothing had happened! Everybody was a bit shocked that she did that, but she did.'

It was by no means taken for granted that Louise would seize the reins of the Porsche Konstruktionen GmbH, as the Austrian import company was named. Like the car company in Stuttgart, it was owned jointly by the two offspring of Ferdinand Porsche. With the death of Anton, who had managed it since 1950, were the skills available to carry on? The company had delivered its first 14 VW Beetles in Austria on 16 April 1949. Its sales in 1952 would be modest at 798 units. Who could tell if the business would amount to anything? Wouldn't it be best for Ferry and Louise to sell off the nascent Austrian company and concentrate on car building in Germany?

After intense discussions among the siblings and their advisors, they took the decision to carry on with Louise at the head of the company. If anyone in Salzburg had harboured the notion that she would simply be a figurehead, a 'Porsche' at the top of a Porsche company, they were deluded. She was the boss, make no mistake, and she was involved in every detail of the Salzburg operations. 'My mother was more effective at pushing things through than my uncle,' said Ferdinand Piëch, referring to Ferry Porsche, 'but nevertheless far removed from the caricature of an Iron Lady.'

'She had not only a gift for management,' added Carl Hahn, 'but also an artistic side and the corresponding ability to form links with the people she needed in the business world. For example, she had a good relationship with Josef Rust, secretary of state in Konrad Adenauer's office who was chairman of the Volkswagen supervisory board. She was also friends with Walter Haefner, who ran AMAG, the VW importer in Switzerland.'

Executives

Another important friend and ally was the all-powerful head of Volkswagen, Heinrich 'Heinz' Nordhoff. Said Ferdinand Piëch, 'When the Piëch branch of the clan was without a male head, so to speak, after my father's death, Nordhoff became an advising friend of Louise Piëch and felt himself in some sense to be a godfather of her children. From this private association, the marriage of my (eight years older) brother Ernst with Nordhoff's daughter Elisabeth finally evolved.'

Louise never remarried. In addition to her male friends in the business world 'she had a friend who was not official,' said her eldest son Ernst. 'I would say nobody in the family really accepted him. He was just a friend, who died relatively early.' For her part, Louise was vouchsafed a long life, passing away at Zell am See on February 10, 1999, at the age of 94. In his valedictory remarks, Ernst said that 'she always remained a Porsche, and together with her father Ferdinand Porsche developed a positive family spirit.'

Father and daughter enjoyed a very close relationship, recalls Ernst. 'She had a very, very good connection with my grandfather. This contact was so close that even without speaking to each other on the telephone they had the same thoughts. Grandfather always got in touch with her if something special was happening. They then discussed it, and it was done. The story within the family was that if grandfather and mother did not agree, nothing happened. This was very clear. She was always very, very well informed about what was going on in Stuttgart or at Steyr. She always tried to be the first to know what was happening. She was more or less the grey eminence in the family.'

Dynasty founder Ferdinand Porsche's respect for his daughter was reflected in the disposition of his estate. It was the semi-feudal central-European custom that the eldest son should receive the main inheritance, the house and the business, while token gifts were made to others. Ferry Porsche had every reason to expect that he'd be similarly endowed after his father's death on 30 January 1951. Instead, to his astonishment and dismay, Porsche divided ownership of his holdings between his two children.

Brother and sister took joint ownership in their respective enterprises, which however, remained separate in their management. This confidence was not misplaced where Louise was concerned. 'If anyone in the family had an overview of finance,' said Ernst Piëch, 'it was her. Hers was the more capitalistic philosophy. She tried to find the right accountant and then she made good decisions.'

Louise remained ever-faithful to her mission as staunch defender of the Porsche inheritance. 'In the ceremonies attendant upon her 90th birthday', said one observer, 'there was immense respect, but also a subtle sense was conveyed of the matriarchal power of a woman who had no need to try to be a woman's libber but ruled a family kingdom with an iron hand. Louise Piëch once said that to be a Porsche was not a pleasure but rather a responsibility.'

When not quite six, Louise became a media star in the summer of 1910 when her father and his colleagues at Austro Daimler – where he worked since 1908 – returned from their epic triumph in that year's Prince Heinrich competition. Sweeping the first three places with special Austro Daimlers against top-flight European opposition, they were the toast of Vienna. Memorable images of their celebrations included Louise with the winning car. In some she posed on the running board with the victor's colossal wreath, holding her own bouquet of flowers. In others she popped out of a hatch in the car's tail like Jill in a jack-in-the-box.

Before the war, Louise's father became general manager of Austro Daimler, accepting total responsibility for the works and its many products. Weekends saw Porsche setting out in his roadster for Hochwolkersdorf, where he had built a hut on his hunting land. He dubbed it the *Luisen-Hütte* after his wife and daughter. On Sunday, after mass, Porsche and his senior colleagues would meet at the factory to discuss their projects. Around one o'clock his wife and children would arrive to drag him away to Sunday dinner. His daughter was studying at Wiener Neustadt, where she graduated from the equivalent of high school in 1922.

In 1923, Louise's father moved to Stuttgart to head engineering for Daimler. Louise was keenly interested in her father's wide-ranging responsibilities there. A licensed driver since 1918, at the age of 14, she commanded the wheel with much of her father's take-no-prisoners aggression. In mid-decade she started taking part in competitions. In 1926, the year of the merger between Daimler and Benz, she joined company stars Rudolf Caracciola and Adolf Rosenberger in a rally. On one of the stages, a hill-climb section, she posted a better time than either of them. Ferry was convinced she triumphed because she had less respect for her engine's rev limit.

Executives

Then in June 1927, Louise piloted a Mercedes-Benz 8/38 – one of her father's designs – in a 2,700-kilometre competition organised by the German Automobile Club. She completed it without penalties, winning a silver trophy and plaque. Other women took part in the event, also successfully, but for Louise this was a notable personal triumph. It did not please her father, though. He felt that Mercedes customers should be scoring the successes, not members of his family. Porsche ended her competition career.

Louise continued to be a very fast driver, so much so that young Ferdinand Piëch crashed his Porsche when trying to beat her record from Salzburg to the Wörthersee. 'As drivers, my grandfather and my mother were very similar,' said Ernst Piëch, 'very aggressive, very uncomfortable for somebody who's sitting next to them. Always fighting with the car ahead, always wanting to be first. This was their style. Uncle Ferry was the complete opposite. He had a very, very gentle driving style but *fast*. He was using much less of the engine's energy than anybody else and much less brakes as well.'

Louise returned to Vienna to take up training in painting and watercolour. Her studies there led to a new relationship. Working in his father's law practice was Anton Piëch, ten years older and still a bachelor. Piëch's forebears were among those refugees from France's revolution who enriched other European nations in the 19th Century. His grandfather had been a lawyer in Brünn, now Brno in the Czech Republic, and his father Anton Paul Piëch followed in the profession, moving first to Wiener Neustadt and finally to Vienna.

Adding additional glamour was Anton's service as a pilot in the Great War, after which he joined his father's law practice. The two became an item. Louise Porsche and Anton Piëch married in Stuttgart's Saint Eberhard Church on 28 June 1928. The bride's father was seen to shed a tear as the pair set off on their honeymoon.

The new family settled in Vienna. There, Ernst was born in 1929, Louise in 1932, Ferdinand in 1937 and Hans-Michael in 1942. To house their growing brood the Piëchs built a home on a hill, the Küniglberg, in the Hietzing district southwest of Vienna's centre. It was at number 17 Serpentinenweg – a name that indicated the serpentine nature of the road climbing the hill. It has since been renamed the Hansi-Niese Weg. Near the expansive gardens of the Schönbrunn Palace, the hill's own greensward commanded magnificent views over the Austrian capital.

With his family settled in Vienna, Anton Piëch found considerable new responsibilities in Stuttgart, where Ferdinand Porsche decided to set up an independent engineering office in 1930. Anton took care of establishing it. When the company was restructured in 1937, Porsche showed his respect for his daughter and son-in-law by giving them 5 and 10 per cent of the shares respectively. The other 15 percent was held by Ferry while Porsche kept the 70 percent balance.

Although Anton maintained his Vienna law office, where his father was still active until his death in 1939, the demands of the new Porsche enterprise kept him on the road. He relied on Louise to keep the wheels turning on the Küniglberg. In this she was awesomely competent. 'Whenever anything at home needed repairing,' said Ferdinand Piëch, 'my mother always did it. She could even change a broken accelerator-pedal cable on the Beetle.' Fixing up his older brother's model railway, Ferdinand recalled, 'when I was stuck I asked my mother. Both technically and also in handicrafts she was right at home and knew her way around. She taught me earthing, current phases and all that.'

Planning for the long term, Anton acquired a nine-year lease on property near the factory where he hoped to build a new home for his family. But his commitment to the VW works confirmed a split that was developing between the marital partners. Louise and the children came to the factory only during the summer school holidays, where they lodged in the 'Porsche Hut', the cottage where Ferdinand Porsche lived and worked while the factory was being built. The banal countryside around the factory was no match for the dramatic peaks and lakes near their Zell am See property.

With conditions at home worsening during the war, the Piëch family decamped from Vienna to Zell am See in March 1943 to take up quarters in the three-storey chalet Ferdinand Porsche had built on land he'd acquired in 1939. Porsche invested much of his substantial earnings in property. 'This is a good investment,' he told his grandson Ernst Piëch, 'because land will always be there.'

The chalet was on the *Schuttgut* in Austria, a substantial property that had once been a copper-mining area. 'War is coming,' Porsche said. 'We need a farm.' He took the same precautions as he had at Wiener Neustadt during the Great War. At the end of 1943, Ferry's family also moved to Zell am See,

Executives

which was equidistant between Vienna and Stuttgart and south of Berchtes-gaden and Salzburg.

Ferdinand Porsche decamped to the *Schuttgut* in January 1945. That summer of '45 found Ferdinand, Anton and Ferry working the fields at the *Schuttgut*, hauling hay and repairing broken machinery. Survival was everything. Louise found herself facing a pistol brandished by an American soldier who demanded access to their excellent wine cellar. He was later hauled away by his colleagues in a distinctly inebriated state.

For these people of extraordinary skills and experience the outlook was bleak. 'If your father were a shoemaker,' one of the occupying British authorities told Louise, 'he would surely make shoes but he will never design automobiles again.' After a form of house arrest in France, Ferry was released in July 1946. Ferdinand Porsche and Anton Piëch were less fortu-nate. Accused by the French of having forced the abduction to Germany of both machinery and workers from Peugeot and Renault plants, they were bound over without trial.

Louise led the effort to free them. As one of the family members put it, 'She was the one out of prison.' She also coped with problems at home, one of which threatened to deny her engineers at Gmünd the means to continue their work. Exploiting post-war uncertainties, socialist-leaning Austria was eager to seize the assets of German-owned companies and nationalise them. The factories of big German enterprises like Siemens and AEG were falling into Austrian hands, as was Hermann Goering's big steel plant at Linz. All the machine tools and equipment that Porsche had installed at Gmünd could be confiscated as well.

'There was a major discussion among lawyers about this,' Ernst Piëch recalled, 'and no solution was in sight. Then my mother came up with a very simple idea. "I'm Austrian," she said, "and I already have a part ownership in the company. With that ownership I'll buy everything that's interesting in this company. That's it. I'll own this now." The lawyers transferred these assets to her and said to the Austrian government, "Okay, you can have the rest." What was left was just air, so nobody was interested in making it state-owned. Overnight we were Austrian.'

To Louise Piëch came one of the slender threads they were to follow toward their future. It was a letter from a young motorcycle racer named Karl Abarth, Vienna-born but now living in Merano in Italy's South Tyrol.

Married to the secretary of Anton Piëch, Abarth had escaped over the border to Yugoslavia in 1938 with Piëch's help. Now known as 'Carlo' in Italy, Abarth found it natural enough to write to Louise. He became the vital link between the engineers and wealthy Italian industrialist Piero Dusio, who commissioned them to design sports and Grand Prix cars.

Dusio and his associates were free to travel, unlike the Porsches, and with numerous contacts in France, offered the best hope yet for gaining the release of Ferdinand Porsche and Anton Piëch. Through old friends in the French racing world, including drivers Louis Chiron and Raymond Sommer as well as editor/official Charles Faroux, Dusio and Louise Piëch arranged to have one million francs – officially $8,380 at the time – turned over to the French authorities. This was bail amounting to a ransom.

As part of negotiations with Heinz Nordhoff at Wolfsburg, the Piëchs obtained the Austrian sales rights for Volkswagen. This would become a money-spinner, but in 1948 this was still in the future. In the meantime 1948 found the family's finances very tight. Only one bank, Salzburg's Spenglerbank, a small private firm, was willing to grant them credit against the VW import contract. 'With this decision,' said Ernst Piëch, 'we closed the engineering works at Gmünd and brought everything to Salzburg.'

Whether they would stay there was another matter. Vienna was viewed as Austria's trading epicentre, though it was on the nation's eastern border. 'It became a big discussion,' said Louise's eldest son, 'because many people in the company said it was impossible to do business without being in Vienna. Thinking about it, we realised that in Vienna we would be just one of the importers, while in Salzburg we'd be the *only* one. We'd be treated very well. In fact our arrangements there were so perfect that ten years later all the importers were in Salzburg! It was also strategically the right place, exactly in the centre of Austria.'

Louise Piëch led the expansion of her company's imports, which celebrated the 100,000th VW registered in Austria in 1961. She branched out to establish her own retail dealerships under the umbrella of Porsche-Inter Auto. Naturally enough, she also began importing Porsche cars as soon as they were produced in volume in Germany.

Louise's active stewardship had only one drawback, said son Ernst: 'The moment she took over I think she discovered that this was not just her job, it was her hobby. This was very inconvenient for all those for whom a job in the company was not a hobby. There were no official working hours; people were so involved in the company that they were sitting and working on Saturday and Sunday. This was sometimes a problem because most people don't accept that. They want their weekends.'

With her son Ferdinand Piëch in charge of engineering at Porsche in Stuttgart, Louise offered him every support. Porsche Konstruktionen had already exploited motor sports, pioneering Formula Vee racing in Austria. Now in 1970, it fielded a team of 917s in sports-car racing in parallel with the Gulf-backed team of John Wyer – to the latter's surprise and annoyance. They proudly bore the names 'Österreich 1' and 'Österreich 2' atop their windscreens. Serviced by the factory's mechanics, one of the 'Porsche Salzburg' cars won Le Mans in 1970.

When in 1971 Audi was added to her range, Louise reluctantly agreed with the then head of the VW Group, Kurt Lotz, that the German company would take a shareholding in its Austrian importer. Then a new VW chief, Toni Schmücker, involved his company in other Porsche-related ventures, selling back to it the design of the 924. In the midst of this, the plan for VW to buy a piece of Porsche Konstruktionen – already confirmed on paper – was abandoned. 'This was a masterpiece on the part of Louise Piëch,' said VW's Carl Hahn, 'to keep her company entirely in the family.'

Louise's success in this crucial negotiation was entirely characteristic of her management style, said Ernst Piëch: 'She had a very clear line. She knew exactly what she wanted. I would say the secret of her success was that when she had a goal she worked toward it so intensely that she achieved it. She worked so hard that she was able to realise her aims.'

Raising her youngsters without a man in the house, Louise veered between favouritism and subjugation. The child she most favoured for their high achievements would be honoured with the place on her right at dinner. Those who defied her, however, felt her wrath. When her son Ferdinand married at 22 she shunned him, deeply displeased. Later they were reconciled; she showed this by giving him the front and rear components of an Austro Daimler, which Ferdinand succeeded in putting together.

While some of her offspring felt that Louise's nurturing manner was divisive, pitting one child against another, others thought that her hermetic style, keeping them close in the environment of the *Schuttgut*, helped foster an intimacy that was to the benefit of the Piëch clan as a whole. 'She was always trying to keep the family together,' said Ernst Piëch. She showed this at the end of her life when she created a foundation for her children. In addition to its tax benefits, said Ernst, 'this was a very clever move on her part. We Piëchs have to stick together because we are all in this vehicle.'

In cooperation with Vienna's Technical University, of which she was an honorary senator, Louise established the Professor Ferdinand Porsche Prize to recognise inventors and innovations of long-term value to the automotive world. First given in 1977, it is endowed to the tune of 50,000 euros – some $61,000 – of prize money given jointly by the two Porsche companies. It is awarded biennially by a panel headed by members of the University. Among those who have received it are Jörg Bensinger, developer of the Audi quattro, and Porsche's Hans Mezger for his TAG Turbo Formula One engine.

Louise Piëch remained in fine fettle to the end of her long life. 'She was very sporty,' said son Ernst, 'swimming almost every day. She was a very good skier. When she was over 70 she had a skiing accident. She fell from a ski lift and down a hill with her skis behind her. Her Achilles tendon was so strong that the bone broke instead of the tendon. This is very rare!' At the age of 88 she had corneal implants to correct a cataract condition. 'Her paintings had been getting darker and darker,' said Ernst. 'After the operation she was shocked because everything was so bright.'

Louise maintained her speed behind the wheel as well. She was fortunate in having suitable cars. One of the first Porsche Turbo prototypes came her way, as did one of the first Audi quattros. The quickest machines from the family stable were always at her disposal. Memorably, Louise Piëch said, 'I have only ever driven my family's cars: first the cars of my father, then those of my brother and now those of my son.' Not many people could make that statement.

WERNER
BREITSCHWERDT

't is not the star that makes the difference but the fact that we build the best products. We must earn our star with each new car.'

This was the mantra that guided the actions of the steadily expanding teams reporting to Werner Breitschwerdt during his rise through the ranks of Daimler-Benz AG and his role as chairman of its management board from 1983 to 1987. During his tenure, the DBAG's global group sales rose by more than 60 per cent. Bolstered by new-model launches under his aegis, including the famous 'Baby Benz', net income in his last full year of 1986 rose by almost 80 per cent to 1.7 billion deutschmarks.

Born on 23 September 1927 in Stuttgart, Breitschwerdt was just old enough to be caught up in World War II at the age of 16. Returning from duty on the eastern front, he enrolled at the Stuttgart Technical University. After completing his general engineering studies he received his diploma in electrical engineering in 1952. Joining Daimler-Benz in 1953 as an apprentice engineer, Werner was soon put in charge of a team that developed one of the industry's first computer-aided design processes.

I first met Werner Breitschwerdt in the early 1960s, soon after he was promoted to head the office for design of production-car bodies. He and an experienced older colleague, Josef Müller, were touring the Detroit motor companies to assess the state of the art technology. One of their stops was at the General Motors Styling Staff, to which I was assigned as a press-relations representative. Having a reasonable grasp of German and some knowledge of Daimler-Benz, which I first visited in 1958, I was a good candidate to accompany them to their appointments.

Müller was short, bespectacled and a veteran of pre-war engineering at Daimler-Benz. He had worked on the company's rear-engined passenger cars, starting in 1933, and after the war pioneered radical small-car concepts that were never produced. Although the general perception was that

Although expert as an engineer, Werner Breitschwerdt surpassed that standard with his enthusiastic and knowledgeable leadership of Daimler-Benz from 1983 through 1987.

Executives

Mercedes-Benz had introduced the de Dion rear suspension with its 1937 Grand Prix cars, Müller told me that the system had actually been introduced in 1936 – completely concealed by the coachwork – and he sketched the layout for me.

Breitschwerdt was a slender, well-presented executive with a straight back and ready smile. I arranged to pick them up from their hotel and take them to dinner. My choice was the Pontchartrain Wine Cellar, which in addition to being Detroit's best restaurant, had a German-speaking maitre d'. They were astounded to find that my transport was a Citroën 2CV, my only four-passenger car and an extreme rarity in Detroit. As we buzzed and swayed down the city's broad avenues, the two Daimler-Benz engineers chortled with delight at this bizarre contrast with the long and lush machinery being produced by the Detroit auto makers.

After this memorable encounter I followed the activities of Werner Breitschwerdt with interest. Starting in 1960 he began a prolific patenting career, ultimately numbering well over 100 inventions. In 1963 he became a section head in the experimental department, then in 1965 took over car-body testing. In 1967 he was named director of the body-development department.

The last was Breitschwerdt's role when Rudolf Uhlenhaut's team started work on a Wankel-powered mid-engined sports car they called the C101. To replace its first crude bodywork, Breitschwerdt and his chief Karl Wilfert aimed for something more professional. 'Our objective,' said Wilfert, 'was a functional car with low aerodynamic drag. It was to be without lift and without movable flaps or spoilers.'

A simplified model of the car went into the Daimler-Benz wind tunnel at Sindelfingen at an early stage in the programme. Its internal air-flow requirements strongly influenced the body design. So did the front suspension, with its tall knuckle and coil/shock unit. It needed extra clearance over the front wheelhouses that forced the cowl line high and led the stylists toward a high belt line and a tapered wedge shape.

Inputs from the tunnel tests found their way back to the styling studio, where scale-model refinements were applied to a full-size clay model. By the end of January 1969, after only two months, the styling was completed.

In making the body, Breitschwerdt and Wilfert decided to explore a technique relatively new to Daimler-Benz: glass-fibre-reinforced resin, generally known as glass-fibre. It seemed well suited to the possible production of a small series of cars. The bodies were built by the Rastätter Waggonfabrik, a firm west of Stuttgart located near the big Daimler-Benz truck plant at Gaggenau. Ordinarily producers of glass-fibre truck bodies, they were asked to adapt their techniques to the needs of the C101.

On 15 July 1969, a C101 was ready to take to the road with its final body glued, riveted and screwed into place. The first complete car was taken to the veteran FKFS wind tunnel in Stuttgart to see how well its shape worked. Drag was satisfactorily low, with a coefficient of 0.335 and a frontal area of 17.9 square feet (1.665 m²). Stability was good too. At 155 mph, the C101 had a 66-pound downforce on the front wheels and a lift of only 22 pounds at the rear. The Sindelfingen stylists admirably achieved their design objective with nary a spoiler in sight.

Late in 1969 the C101 was renamed the C111 and revealed to the world with a three-rotor Wankel engine, followed by a four-rotor version in early 1970. Versions of the car were used to set speed records. Meanwhile Werner Breitschwerdt became deputy to Karl Wilfert and, at the beginning of 1974, his successor as head of body styling and engineering.

Breitschwerdt achieved a career goal on 21 March 1978 when he was elected a full member of the Daimler-Benz management board responsible for research and development. He succeeded Hans Scherenberg when the latter retired, stepping into his post in time to assist in a record-setting session on the circular track at Nardò in Italy on 30 April 1978. This was typical of Breitschwerdt, who was a hands-on engineer not content to be office-bound.

One of Breitschwerdt's first decisions concerned a hare-brained scheme of Uhlenhaut successor, Hans Liebold, to build a car to beat the fastest-ever officially-timed lap of a circuit: Mark Donohue's 221.027 mph at Talladega, Alabama in the 1,500-horsepower Porsche 917/30. The already existing C111-III was lapping Nardò only 18 mph slower. The record could be equalled, Liebold calculated, by the C111-III with only 100 more horsepower. But just slightly improving on Donohue's mark would not be very interesting. The objective was set instead to lapping Nardò at 400 km/h, close to 250 mph.

Would they do it? The key man in reaching and approving the decision was Werner Breitschwerdt, only weeks into his new board position. Convinced of the value of such an attempt, intrigued by the technical challenge, Breitschwerdt obtained board approval. A C111-IV would be built. While the advanced research department prepared a turbocharged V-8 developing 500 bhp, the body-design team refined the existing shape and created a self-stabilising system of flaps and spoilers. The result in May 1979 was spot-on with a one-lap speed of 250.918 mph [403.978 km/h] and a raft of world speed records up to 100 miles.

Also given the green light by Werner Breitschwerdt, was an official programme of world-championship rallying starting in 1979 with the 450SLC 5.0 coupe – later called the 500SLC. Overseen by Erich Waxenberger and supported by AMG, the effort scored impressive successes in 1979 before girding for a full-season entry in 1980. The new sports department housed in Waiblingen reported to Breitschwerdt and functioned as part of his R&D activity, which had an annual budget in the order of DM1.5 billion.

'We take part in rallies,' Breitschwerdt told *auto motor + sport*, 'because we think we should participate in sports again. It's not unlike the man in the street – he may take part in sports for a while, then stop for a bit, and then later decide it would be a good idea for him to be active in sports again. In our search for a new sporting activity, rallies seemed to us to be ideal: at these events we can demonstrate outstanding reliability with virtually standard automobiles. And we intend to take part with a commitment to victory.'

The 1980 season proved sobering for Mercedes-Benz, which ranked fourth in points at the end behind Fiat, Datsun and Ford after suffering seemingly random retirements. A one-two success in December's final Ivory Coast Rally was toasted at a special reception in Stuttgart. Team members and the press were greeted by Werner Breitschwerdt in a season-ending ceremony. None, however, was prepared for his announcement. The management committee, he said, had decided that Daimler-Benz would cease participation in rallies for the foreseeable future.

'We have decided to invest our available development capacity completely in research work to meet environmental demands, as a priority,' Werner Breitschwerdt said, 'and thus we are withdrawing from rallying.' The second Energy Crisis focused renewed attention on fuel economy throughout the global markets for Mercedes-Benz cars.

The R&D chief admitted that the firm's current cars were unsuited to European rallies, as the 1980 results demonstrated. Although Daimler-Benz would have liked to develop a special car for rallying, as other firms were doing, Breitschwerdt said that the development capacity for such a task was simply not available.

In fact Breitschwerdt's engineers were deeply involved in creating, virtually from scratch, a new small Mercedes-Benz production car. The first hand-built prototype ran in 1978. Its significance was recognised by its historic type number: W201. When it was introduced in November 1982 it revived the model number '190'.

This 'Baby Benz', as the Americans called it, underpinned the company's model offerings with a sophisticated four-door sedan that was a purebred Untertürkheim product. Design and development work initiated in 1970 yielded a new strut-type front suspension and a complex five-link rear suspension that Mercedes-Benz called a *Raumlenkerachse* or 'space-link suspension'. It introduced racing-car suspension technology to a family auto from the DBAG. Rightly enough, the 190 was viewed as the creation of Werner Breitschwerdt. The car that created the C-Class niche was to underpin Mercedes-Benz's market success in decades to come.

As of 1980 this new commitment was beeing followed with special interest by a new man at the top of the DBAG. The new chairman of the management committee was Gerhard Prinz. Formerly the board member for purchasing, Prinz assumed command of a company that now employed 180,000 worldwide and turned over DM30 billion annually.

In the Prinz era, Werner Breitschwerdt was not ready to alienate the DBAG from the world of sports. On 25 November 1981, Erich Waxenberger wrote to Werner Breitschwerdt, describing the SHS C6 sports-racer built by Peter Sauber's team to the new Group C rules, and asking for permission to test this interesting vehicle in the Daimler-Benz wind tunnel. In fact this car's aerodynamics had been created secretly by a small team of DBAG designers headed by Rüdiger Faul. In December the letter came back with Breitschwerdt's marginal note: 'Do it.'

Here was a small window of opportunity to learn enough about the aerodynamic needs of a Group C car to create a suitable shape and vehicle. An engine was also needed, one which the rules said had to be based on one from an FIA-homologated production car. Deciding on a direct approach, on 2 August 1982 Peter Sauber asked Werner Breitschwerdt whether the company had an appropriate engine for a Group C car. From there the R&D

head directed the enquiry to development chief Friedrich Van Winsen with the notation, 'See if we have anything suitable.'

Politically the selection of Van Winsen was an astute choice by Breitschwerdt. His passenger-car development group was deeply involved with current-car designing and testing and was unlikely to have the capacity for such a project. If Breitschwerdt could manage events so that development would take a positive view but, owing to lack of capacity, would commission research to carry out the work of building a racing engine, he would have a viable programme. But it was not yet possible. The discontinuation of motor sports was still too fresh. Nothing was found to be 'suitable'.

Behind the scenes the enthusiasts helped develop the design of a new BMW-powered Sauber C7, a model of which Rüdiger Faul tested in the new full-size wind tunnel at Sindelfingen. Emboldened, Faul applied directly for permission to test the full-size running C7 in the big Untertürkheim tunnel. Permission was granted by Werner Breitschwerdt, who was chafing under the ban on motor sports. 'You could speak to him one-on-one about racing,' said Faul, "under four eyes" as we say in Germany, but of course not in public. He had to be seen to uphold the ban.'

Fresh from Sauber's shops, the BMW-powered C7 was installed in the big tunnel where tests were started on 4 May 1983. Typical of a Sauber production, it was an immaculate, handsome and superbly-finished racing car. A telephone call to Breitschwerdt's office informed him that the tests were under way. 'In five minutes he was there with his entourage of five or six people,' Faul recalled. 'They stood around looking at it for three-quarters of an hour, losing my valuable tunnel time. But the car was beautiful. Breitschwerdt was charmed, impressed and excited by it.'

Faul decided to chance his arm. 'There's only one thing wrong with it,' he said.

'What's that?' asked Breitschwerdt.

'This engine,' pointing to the BMW.

'What should it have in it?'

'A Daimler engine,' Faul answered.

'Make proposals,' said the technical chief, no longer 'under four eyes'.

'Then off he went with his squadron,' Faul remembered. The car and the moment had provided the opportunity. Like Wilhelm Kissel in 1931 and 1932, who assured his board that Daimler-Benz was not in racing while he was making sure that Caracciola and Stuck had the help they needed, Werner Breitschwerdt had both seen and seized the chance to keep the flame alive in the 1980s with Sauber.

Although 'only' an aerodynamicist at Daimler-Benz and relatively new at the firm, Faul benefitted greatly from the work he had done on the C111-III and later projects. This gave him a network within the company, a network he now began to exploit. He took advantage of his full personal awareness that Breitschwerdt was firmly behind the building of engines for Sauber.

Again it was up to the development department to take the lead in making proposals. At this time Rudolf Hörnig was taking over passenger-car development from Van Winsen; their workload was formidable with both new cars and new engines in the early stages of proving and an ample supply of problems. Development was happy for the work to be assigned to research – which had been the objective all along.

The parties kept talking through the internal manoeuvring that was needed to initiate the building of a racing engine in a company that officially forbade racing participation. The fact that Rainer Schick, now the financial controller at passenger-car development, had been part of the 1954-55 racing effort, helped prise away the funds that research needed to do the work. 'Do good and speak not of it' became the motto of this 'car-crazy crew'.

The work done on the turbocharged V-8 for the closed-course record at Nardò became the springboard for the turbo V-8s that were quietly supplied to Sauber. Created in 1985, the Sauber C8 sports-racer began using the Stuttgart-built engines, which were carried over to the C9 introduced in 1987. The Mercedes-Benz involvement was openly declared for the 1988 season and in 1989 and 1990 the cars competed in the traditional silver livery, winning the Group C Championship in both seasons. And this all began when Werner Breitschwerdt allowed his enthusiastic engineers the scope to explore options for the DBAG in motor sports.

In 2007 I had the opportunity to renew my friendship with Breitschwerdt in his office at Untertürkheim. Our conversation roamed over many topics including the alliance with Chrysler that had just ended with the sale of the Chrysler shares to venture capital company Cerberus. I was interested in earlier contacts with other companies. I was to learn that quite a few had been discussed.

'Herr Prinz and I went to see Honda,' he disclosed. 'I remember that when we entered the Honda factory the Honda boss told us that they were all 21 years old there – the average age of their workers was 21½! He was very proud of that. I didn't say anything to him at the time but later I said to Prinz, "If his people are 21½ now, what on earth is he going to do in thirty years' time? They will all be 51 then!" If the company grows, that will be okay. He can just fill it up with young people. But what if the company does not grow? They'll all be 51! Of course the company *did* grow so he could bring in younger people.

'But at that time,' he added, ' the Honda people were much more interested in BMW because they wanted to develop the sporty aspect of their motorbikes and BMW was more geared towards the sporty side and we were geared towards comfort.

'We also talked to Subaru,' he added. 'I went for a drive with them and their top man on their test track. I was at the wheel and he was clinging on to the door handle because they had never driven that fast on the track! That was new for him! Anyway, they were closely liaised with someone else so we decided that it would be almost impossible to prise them away.'

The DBAG's overall aim at the time, Werner explained, was development of the Asian market. 'We did sell cars in Asia, but at that time our cars were much too expensive for most of the Asiatic markets. Why? Because industrial production was very underdeveloped in those countries so there was no upper class as such – or only a few people. And we only really sold to the upper class! I said at the time that if they develop their industries, the upper class will expand, there will be upper and middle classes. And then we can sell more and more of our cars there.

'But we certainly wanted a presence in that market,' he continued, 'not only with our cars but also our HGVs. At that time it was almost impossible to sell HGVs to those markets. It was possible to a certain degree in Ceylon because they needed the HGVs for transporting trees, so our very robust vehicles were in high demand. But otherwise it was very difficult.'

In search of a lighter delivery vehicle, the DBAG made a deal with Mitsubishi. 'I still have the fountain pen I used for signing that contract,' said Breitschwerdt. 'We wanted to produce their small van in Spain for the European market, together with Mitsubishi. The plan was that Mitsubishi would deliver their parts to Spain, where we would then assemble them and sell them on the European market. We did not have a vehicle in that bracket and it was quite in demand in Germany at that time.

'We tested the vehicle for safety and found that it was not as safe as we wanted it to be. So we increased the safety aspect, changed a few stylistic details and were quite willing to proceed with the project. Then Mitsubishi told us the prices of the parts, and they were so high that the vehicle would have been much too expensive for the European market! They wanted to make money out of us and therefore the whole thing fell apart. We signed the deal and found that it did not work and that was that!'

Toyota was the most compatible partner in some respects, Breitschwerdt explained: 'Herr Scherenberg and I had a conversation with Herr Toyota in the Park Hotel in Stuttgart. That must have been in 1975-76. We discussed whether there were any possibilities of working together – not taking over, just cooperation. Toyota themselves were very interested. They only had one old model in the top bracket and we had only top-of-the-range cars. That is why it was interesting for Toyota – they would not have had to develop their own, they could have just taken ours.

'However,' Werner added, 'we did not see any possibilities for the following reason: they really wanted to sell our top-of-the-range cars in their dealerships as Mercedes. That was what Herr Toyota wanted. We did not want to do that and we could not do it because we had our rep there, Herr Yanase. Yanase had worked very hard for us, there was no question about that. He always aimed for highest quality. When you visited his vehicle preparation centres, all the workers were walking around with white gloves. Yanase really handled it all very well.'

However, taking the long view, Breitschwerdt wanted the DBAG to have its own importer and distributor in Japan. 'Some people were quite cross with me at the time,' he recalled, 'but I said: "I know what I am doing." In Japan you can't cancel a contract just like that, otherwise your partner loses face and is more or less dead! Later, when I was chairman, I negotiated with Yanase for about three years. In those three years we worked out how we could take over the general importation. It took ages and required lots of preparation.

'I am sure you know what negotiations are like in Japan!' He added. 'I always had problems with my knees there. We spent hours sitting and drinking tea and hatching plans. Since I was usually the most senior person there

Executives

I always had the oldest geisha, since that is the most important one. At that time I was a relatively young man – relatively! – of around 55 and the geisha who looked after me was 82! She played the lute and poured rice wine for me. That's what we did for several years, so the whole thing would be possible without Yanase losing face.

'These were all normal business visits to find out about cooperation,' explained Breitschwerdt, ' and if it works out, that's good and if it doesn't, it's not the end of the world either. My pre-predecessor, Herr Zahn, got quite cross with us when we said that we wanted to build more than 600,000 vehicles. His opinion was that if you build fewer cars, you can set the prices! But of course things have changed. Today that would no longer be a viable option.'

The background of the relationship with Chrysler had roots in the past, Werner Breitschwerdt explained. 'I met Chrysler together with Dr Prinz in Stuttgart – I think it was 1984 – because we thought Chrysler would be a good fit. It was a relatively high-quality company as far as their technology was concerned. They imported some of our German engineers after the war and they are pretty good. However, the talks did not lead to anything at the time because we could see various problems.

'On the subject of DaimlerChrysler – or shall we say the merger with Chrysler, a share in Mitsubishi – as I mentioned earlier, that that was quite good! Because it is not bad to be able to say in this day and age that we have a premium brand, we have a brand in America which might not be premium but is still quite good, we have a brand in Asia, which is not bad either. Mitsubishi was not bad, Chrysler was not bad. That was quite good as far as our vision was concerned! I am only saying that the implementation was not brilliant.

Breitschwerdt continued: 'You have to be careful here: Mitsubishi had skeletons in the cupboard, which you cannot see if someone is being dishonest. That is quite difficult to handle, so in a way one should not be too judgmental. Regarding Chrysler, because it was a merger, not a takeover or a purchase, we could not have due diligence. When I merge, I do not have that right. I can have a guess at what they are worth but that has to be handled by someone else in order to find the right exchange ratio for the shareholders. As a company I cannot say, "Let me have a look at your books." So that was quite difficult at the time.

'But what we *did* see,' added Breitschwerdt, 'was Chrysler's programme! Here the gentlemen from Chrysler were rather clever: they convinced the Daimler board with the help of a racing car and fantastic SUVs. And that is where I think a mistake was made, because no one asked questions regarding the overall programme. After all, that would be continued for another 10 or 20 years. Insofar as we want to talk about mistakes at all, this is where I think a mistake was made.

'Bearing in mind that we could not see Mitsubishi's skeletons in the cupboard and that Chrysler's programme was not quite right, if you now implement the vision the right way it is a wonderful thing, I have absolutely no doubt about it. To be strong in America, to be strong in Asia, to be strong in Europe, all with their own production facilities and irrespective of currencies – when you bear all of that in mind the vision itself was good. It is only the implementation that is difficult.

'In the end,' said Breitschwerdt, 'you have to produce what the customers want. You have to be prepared for changes – that is the problem. Changes can happen any time. I used to say that it was very important that we produced the diesel and the petrol cars in the same factory and, if possible, on the same assembly line, although it is difficult, because legislation could kill off the diesel or the petrol car from one day to another! Therefore I suggested we put up with the disadvantages and produce both types on one line. Today of course we have separate petrol and diesel engine factories.'

In 1987 *Fortune* magazine assessed the stewardship of Werner Breitschwerdt as follows: 'Three major acquisitions over the past two years have given Daimler stakes in dozens of new businesses, transforming it into West Germany's largest conglomerate. The job of running the company has grown far more complicated – too complicated, Breitschwerdt's critics charge – for a simple fellow from Stuttgart to handle.

'Last summer,' *Fortune* continued, 'amid whispers of top-level dissension, the managing board carried out the first major reorganisation since the company was pieced back together at the end of World War II. Then, this spring, Breitschwerdt's arch-rival, Edzard Reuter, the forceful finance chief who led the acquisition drive, was named to the new post of deputy chairman. The arrangement left Breitschwerdt seemingly weakened and isolated.' Indeed, on 1 September 1987 Breitschwerdt stepped down and Reuter assumed command.

Executives

'Herr Reuter said he wanted to create a *"Technologiekonzern"* – a technology company,' Breitschwerdt recalled. 'This is not a bad idea – a *Technologiekonzern* is not a bad thing in our day and age. Adding AEG was an important factor. I have to say that that was a wise thing to do because all of us know – we all talk about it – that there are overcapacities in the car sector. And if there are overcapacities, then there are companies left over, aren't there? So that would have been quite the right thing to do. However, what was wrong was the implementation!

'It was not implemented strictly enough,' he added. 'Strategy and visionary thinking – that is not a problem, but implementation is! That requires a lot of rigour and that was something Herr Reuter did not really have.'

Fortune summed up Werner Breitschwerdt as follows: 'What Breitschwerdt may lack in elegance he makes up for with hard work and a quality that Germans call *Pfiff*, the equivalent of street smarts. Breitschwerdt's manner and appearance make him an easy target for detractors. He looks as if he would be more comfortable dressed in the blue worker's overalls worn on Daimler's production line than in the off-the-rack suits that seem a mite too large for his wiry frame. He regrets that he never acquired the formal training that gives most German chief executives their polished veneer.'

Indeed, in Reuter the great Daimler concern acquired a chief who had dreams but lacked the impulse to implement them fully, instead building elaborate corporate headquarters near the airport – far from the factories that made the money – that soon acquired the nickname 'bullshit castle'.

This was a far cry from the practical rigour spiced with enthusiasm that Werner Breitschwerdt brought to his responsibilities. 'Top management should create the motivation that gets more ideas out of the organisation than the company can use,' he said. It was advice he continued to deliver as a member of the Daimler-Benz supervisory board until 1993. In 2009 Werner Breitschwerdt was elected to the European Automotive Hall of Fame. All those who ever worked for him applauded.

ROBERT ANTON LUTZ

I call this picture 'His Master's Voice' as I listen to Bob Lutz expatiating on some topic during a picnic at his home while we were both Ford of Europe executives.

O ctober of 1963 found me moving from Detroit to New York to take up my new post as press officer of the General Motors Overseas Operations Division (GMOO). There I met Robert Anton 'Bob' Lutz. Tall, good-looking and outgoing, Lutz arrived at GMOO only a month before me, and was two years older. I learned that he and his brother Mark were born in Zurich, Switzerland, scions of a family whose head was vice chairman of Credit Suisse bank.

Young Lutz was Americanised by a spell in New York in the 1940s, becoming an American citizen in 1943 and returning to Switzerland in 1947

Executives

to attend school in Lausanne. He continued his schooling abroad at the University of Berkeley, gaining degrees in production management and marketing. Meanwhile he was flying jets with the Marine Corps on active duty from 1954 to 1959, then on reserve with the 4th Marine Aircraft Wing until 1965. Bob aggregated 1,500 flight hours.

This was the multilingual character who worked in forward planning at GMOO during an interesting period when GM was launching all-new small cars in Germany (the Kadett) and in Britain (the Viva). His first posting abroad was with Opel at Rüsselsheim, on the fringe of Frankfurt, in the marketing department. I paid Bob a visit there in 1967 on my first trip to Europe after leaving GMOO.

Lutz arrived at Opel in time to influence the creation of the Opel GT, which appeared as a concept car at the 1965 Frankfurt Show. This was precedent-breaking, for European producers rarely showed new cars that were not production-ready. Its styling was overseen by American chief designer Clare MacKichan, showing the rakish lines of a mini-Corvette but without that car's often over-egged decoration. It was a shock for other makers because Opel was not associated with sports cars.

As the GT moved toward production a key issue was the position of its engine. With parts of the Kadett chassis being used, it was easiest to leave the four-cylinder engine in the same position as that in the production car. Bob Lutz argued that this would impair the handling, which mandated a more rearward engine position to give the more balanced weight distribution that a sports car should have. Chief engineer Hans Mersheimer and his staff stoutly defended the less costly solution of the original Kadett location.

To resolve this impasse, two test cars were built, one with the four's forward position and the other with the engine moved rearward. Both were taken to the ultimate arbiter, the Nürburgring, to be evaluated by racing drivers Hans Herrmann and Eberhard Mahle. Neither was informed about the difference in engine position. Of the two drivers, Herrmann was the most analytic, saying that the car with the forward engine position had more sluggish handling, tended to roll more and had more understeer. With the other car, which had more agreeable and neutral handling, he achieved faster lap times. It felt more like a sports car, he said, more sensitive in response and better balanced. The rearward engine location won the day.

Meanwhile, events that would affect Bob Lutz's future were maturing in deepest Bavaria at the headquarters of auto maker BMW. Since 1960 its chief and guiding spirit had been Paul G. Hahnemann. From unpromising clay – the factory was on the brink of becoming Daimler-Benz Plant 14 – the hard-driving Hahnemann had moulded a lively and competitive organisation that took advantage of niches that opened with the collapse of Bremen's Borgward. In fact, the executive came to be nicknamed 'Niche-Paul' [Nischen-Paule] for his shrewd positioning of new models in profitable gaps in the market.

Pitching lively and louche Bavaria against staid and satisfied Baden-Württemberg, Hahnemann provided an option for Germans who did not want to be seen driving Mercedes-Benzes. 'The Mercedes-Benz owner rides with a chauffeur beside him,' he told me. 'The BMW owner drives with a beautiful woman beside him.' As a way of dramatically contrasting the personalities of the two marques, this could not be surpassed.

By the beginning of the 1970s BMW was trading successfully on this fresh new reputation. At that time it received a new chief, 42-year-old Dr. Eberhard von Kuenheim, who had impressed Herbert Quandt in his various positions with the Quandt Group. With its 75 per cent shareholding, dating from the time it rescued BMW from oblivion, the Quandt interests conducted internal audits that suggested that in spite of its evident success, the Hahnemann reign was not without its faults.

Von Kuenheim's position gave him total authority. Although a member of the supervisory board, he was also chairman and CEO of the management board. But he now lacked a board member for sales and marketing. Purring into action, Germany's well-oiled head-hunting organisations identified a man who had shown merit in such tasks in GM's European companies. He had the languages and – even better – he was enthusiastic about motorcycles. At the end of 1971 Lutz became a BMW executive vice president and the board member responsible for global sales and marketing.

'Leaving GM was an easy decision,' Lutz related in his book *Icons and Idiots*. 'I was hired away at roughly ten times the annual salary I had at GM, which was admittedly derisory. I would live in the Munich suburbs with a generous social allowance, two company BMWs, a full-time driver and a reasonable number of motorcycles. And I was to report to the CEO of a small but prestigious and fast-growing independent auto company, not

Executives

to some CEO of a subsidiary that reported to a subsidiary, which reported to a regional manager, who reported to the vice president of GM Overseas Operations, who had several more reporting layers separating him from the CEO of GM.'

Lutz found an overflowing inbox. The Quandt audits had revealed 'massive corruption', with all the ill-gotten gains ending with Hahnemann. Some of it required the collusion of the equally crooked ad agency, which engaged in fictitious billing, a hard-to-spot crime wherein the agency bills the client for media buys that were never purchased. The resulting millions were split between Hahnemann and the agency.

'And on it went,' Lutz continued: 'improper kickbacks from foreign distributors in exchange for larger vehicle allocations, "special arrangements" with certain dealers – any and all commonly found corrupt practices that an unethical head of a large sales and marketing department could engage in.' In any case Bob intended to install BMW subsidiaries in national markets world-wide, replacing private enterprises like Max Hoffman's. He wrote that he 'had von Kuenheim's full support as I battled bribes, threats on my life, offers of Mediterranean yacht cruises with a crew of nubile and guaranteed available females. In about two years we got it done, thus vastly improving the profitability of BMW.'

Although BMW's press department was instructed to avoid favouring particular board members, Germany's enthusiastic press could not get enough of the 'two-metre man', as they nicknamed Lutz, and his exploits on cars and motorcycles alike. This exposure rankled at the top of the new four-cylinder BMW headquarters. 'I was approaching the last year of my initial three-year contract,' Lutz mused, 'and was doubtful that it would be renewed. Moreover, I was doubtful that I wanted to spend another three years in such an uncollegial environment, especially with hopes for significant growth seemingly stymied.

'Adding to my uncertainty,' Bob continued, 'was the fact that the Ford Motor Company was actively recruiting me to be head of Ford of Germany which, despite the CEO title, was a lesser job than what I currently had. Ford of Germany was a badly underperforming sales company in the broader context of the centrally managed UK-based Ford of Europe. But the decision, when I finally made it, was surprisingly easy.'

The job at Ford in Cologne was what Germans call a *Schleudersitz* – an ejection seat. Three men had filled it in the first four years of the 1970s. Sales and market shares were languishing. Fighting the good fight with Britain-bound Ford of Europe, Lutz convinced them to give him scope to deviate from 'business as usual'. He and his team gave their Fords more opulent standard equipment that raised their perceived value. Radically, he broke ranks with his rivals by extending Ford's warranty from six months to a year.

The impact was electric. Ford was now a progressive and more popular vendor of automobiles, gaining share in a rising market. 'These results,' Lutz said, 'were sufficient to get me promoted to vice president, Truck Operations, in Ford of Europe. It was an area of the vehicle business I had no previous experience with or cared little about but I soon learned to love it. Unlike the passenger-car sector, where brand image drives most of the purchasing consideration, the medium and heavy truck business is ruled by logic and cost of ownership.'

Now on the Ford fast track, Bob Lutz moved from trucks to the presidency of Ford of Europe, an operatings job, and then to its chairmanship in 1979, a policy position. Chapters of the subsequent Bob Lutz story are well known: joining Chrysler after seeing little prospect of meaningful advancement at Ford, CEO of battery maker Exide, re-joining GM in 2001 and remaining through 2010. Less celebrated, however, are two automotive ventures that struggled to reach take-off velocity.

The first of these initiatives was brought to Lutz while he was still at Chrysler by entrepreneur Larry Black and Briggs Cunningham III, son of the man of the same name whose Florida factory built the Cunningham road and racing cars of 1951-1956. The two visitors intrigued Lutz with their aim of reviving the Cunningham marque, which in its heyday had used Chrysler V-8 engines. As the owner of one of the 27 C-3 road cars produced by Cunningham, Bob was interested.

Lutz's interest survived the merger of Daimler and Chrysler and continued while he was CEO of Exide. He easily grasped the concept of Black and the younger Cunningham – a former racer himself – of a 'virtual car company' that would outsource its parts manufacture and assembly while retaining the design, sales and intellectual property. Lutz and Cunningham shook hands on the initiative with each investing one million dollars in shares in the Cunningham Motor Company. Also supporting the project were loans to a similar value from Switzerland's Credit Suisse.

Their goal of selling 600 C-7 Cunninghams annually at a price of $250,000 each was unveiled at the 2001 Detroit Auto Show when the wraps came off a full-sized model of the auto in question, styled by independent Detroit designer Stewart Reed. By the following August, Lutz had left Exide and was working at General Motors, which obliged him by investing an additional $2 million in his dream car. GM also took steps toward designing a bespoke 12-cylinder engine for the C-7.

At the C-7's Detroit debut I discussed the Cunningham project with Bob and his project chief executive Jack McCormack. I was active as a car-industry consultant at the time and hoped to get some business from this new initiative. I heard nothing more from them while they made contact with some two dozen suppliers and laid plans for an offering of shares to raise the $85 million needed to launch production of the Cunningham coupe and a sister cabriolet from the pen of Stewart Reed.

In mid-2002, Credit Suisse served notice that it was requiring repayment of its million-dollar loans. This was an unwelcome surprise to Briggs Cunningham III, who assumed the loan would be rolled over at maturity. Obliged to sell his Cunningham shares at a loss to meet the demand, Briggs filed suit in September, saying that Lutz was scheming to gain full control of the company. He sought recompense. Bob Lutz denied culpability, saying through a spokesman that to avoid any conflict with his new role at GM, he was solely an investor in the Cunningham company and not involved it its management.

The upshot was that the lawsuit ended any hope of raising the money needed to build Cunninghams. At least $4 million had vanished with nothing to show for it save a large metallic-grey model car, one that in retrospect was not particularly exciting to look at.

Robert Lutz returned to the exotic-car world in 2013 with the display at the Detroit Auto Show of the VL Automotive Destino. This was based on a product of another exotic-car venturer, Henrik Fisker, who had successfully launched an upmarket four-door hybrid road cruiser, the Fisker Karma, only to have his battery supplier go bankrupt. In partnership with venturer Gilbert Villarreal, Lutz interceded to buy a handful of Karmas and fit them with Corvette ZR1 drive trains. Presto – the VL Destino.

With Fisker folding his interests into those of Lutz and Villarreal, in 2016 the company became VLF Automotive. It moved into the building in Auburn

Hills, Michigan, that was once used to build Chrysler's first Prowlers and Vipers. Indeed their newest model, the Force 1 V-10, is essentially the abandoned (in 2017) Viper with a new set of extremely elaborate clothes, as extroverted as the Cunningham was conservative. The V-8-powered Destino is still on their agenda, as are modified Ford Mustangs.

'Force 1,' said Lutz, 'is another dramatic example of what we are going to do at VLF Automotive by combining proven world-class platforms and components with elegant designs to produce stunning bespoke luxury sports vehicles.' Meanwhile in semi-retirement, Robert Lutz as an author mines his experiences with his previous employers and as a speaker indulges in outrageous speculation that pleases his clients and makes headlines. These anecdotes from the colourful career of the 'two-metre man' were never far off the mark.

GIANNI AND UMBERTO AGNELLI

*Gianni, right, and Umberto Agnelli were at home in the Turin industrial
environment where they were pictured. I was closer to the younger man
who was of my generation.*

'**D**o you remember what happened that time we landed here
a few years back?' asked my wife Annette as our British
Airways flight touched the concrete at Catania, an airport
on the east coast of Sicily. 'It caused quite a stir as I recall.'
We had gone into the then-modest terminal and were waiting for our bags
when a man broke free from a sinister-looking group and walked toward us,
smiling. It was the urbane figure of Umberto Agnelli, the 13-years-younger
brother of Gianni Agnelli, chief of the Fiat empire.

As Agnelli's swarthy minders looked on in astonishment and some trepi-
dation, and to the amazement of other travellers, to whom the Agnellis were

at the right hand of God, Umberto engaged us in casual conversation. He was in Sicily for a conference while we were en route to our holiday in Taormina.

Umberto was darker and more slender than his older brother and blessed or cursed with large brown eyes that might all too often betray his emotions. Youngest of seven siblings, Umberto lived in the shadow of his silver-haired oldest brother, he of the boldly Roman profile. But I always had a soft spot for Umberto, mainly because we were about the same age.

Although I had met him in the past as a journalist, my first serious contact with Umberto was during my years as an executive vice president of Fiat Motors of North America at the end of the 1970s. He and his brother took a close interest in our struggles in the troublesome American market. Umberto paid several visits to Montvale, New Jersey, where our headquarters of handsome design measured up to the egos of visitors from the headquarters in Turin. My empire included relations with dealers, customers, the press, government and legal affairs, so there was much to discuss.

In the early 1980s when I was a vice president with Ford of Europe, my contacts with the top floor at Fiat's headquarters at 10 Via Marconi in Turin were facilitated by my long friendship with Rudy Mailander. A former photojournalist and PR man at Daimler-Benz, Rudy was now the main point of contact between the Agnellis and all international governmental and business bodies. He carried on in this capacity with Umberto after his brother Gianni died.

Later, when I was running a London management-consulting company, I saw that Umberto had effectively taken over at Fiat Auto after Gianni's death and would thus be an important business target for me. Though Rudy had since retired from Fiat, I asked if he wouldn't mind setting up a meeting for me with his former chief. Somewhat to my surprise Mailander demurred. It turned out that before my friend's retirement there had been talk of arranging an ongoing consulting relationship with Fiat that would have been to his considerable benefit. Umberto, however, scotched the idea.

This didn't surprise me, since I had been treated in much the same manner by Walter Hayes and Bob Lutz when I left Ford of Europe. But it did not make me eager to do business with Umberto. I last saw him at the Turin Salon in 2004, making the rounds in the company of Giorgetto Giugiaro.

Only weeks later he died suddenly of lung cancer at the age of 69. He was the last Agnelli to lead the company.

Gianni would have been both surprised and pleased by the way his younger brother dealt with Fiat's problems after his death in March 2002. Umberto had often acted like the ultimate pragmatist, swayed by the demands of the day. At times he seemed poised to jettison the autos unit if it seemed likely to pull down the rest of the Agnelli empire. In contrast Gianni more consistently supported autos, the business founded by his grandfather of the same name that provided the foundation of the family's wealth.

In the 1970s Umberto Agnelli had been active at the top of Fiat as managing director to his brother's chairmanship. This was the era of the Group's diversification, giving it a broader base. Umberto flirted with politics in 1976, achieving election to the Senate, but found the atmosphere frosty in Rome and soon returned to Turin to resume his managing directorship.

These were the poisonous and dangerous years of the Red Brigades in Italy, when it was a courageous act to be a prominent industrialist. I vividly remember the precautions taken when we were on the town with senior Fiat man Rudy Mailander. In 1980 Umberto stepped down in favour of hard man Cesare Romiti. In the next ten days Fiat's shares rose almost ten percent – a harsh verdict on the younger Agnelli's stewardship.

After Gianni's death, Umberto more than made up for these vacillating years with his staunch backing of both Fiat Auto and his no-nonsense choice as the Group's chief executive, Giuseppe Morchio. The younger Agnelli deserved credit for persuading his family to stump up 250 million euros to bolster their company's capitalisation. 'He impressed me with his deep love of Fiat,' said Morchio of Umberto on his demise, 'the sense of duty, of responsibility and the spirit of service. I will miss him a lot.'

I had several opportunities to admire the poise and skill of Gianni Agnelli in my capacity as a journalist in the 1970s. He gave an impressive press briefing to the SAE in Detroit before making a keynote speech. His press conferences before Turin Salons were the stuff of legends. He was a shrewd observer of the automotive scene throughout the world, a role he had accepted as inevitable when he shook off his youthful playboy persona and began to get to grips with Fiat.

Gianni Agnelli also visited us in Montvale. I remember well a meeting with him in my boss's office to go over some current matters during his stop with us. Although immaculately suited, he was oddly booted in what looked like Hushpuppies, a style he adopted after his feet were injured in an auto crash. As usual he wore his wristwatch on the outside of his shirt cuff, a distinctive style that he originated and that was also adopted by my friend Rudy Mailander.

When we launched the Fiat Ritmo in America, named the Strada for US and UK consumption, we pulled out all the stops with a dealer meeting in Las Vegas. As a major coup for us, Gianni Agnelli agreed to attend and address the crowd. One way or another I had made my bones in a quiet manner with Agnelli, who referred to me in discussions with Fiat insiders as 'that young American'. One of the attractions of a post with Fiat in Turin – which I was offered but turned down – would have been the chance to get closer to this most remarkable man.

Both brothers had sons who were seen as potential future leaders of Fiat. Born in 1954, Gianni's son Edoardo was considered but he went well off the rails, finally ending a troubled life himself in 2000. Thereafter Umberto's son Giovanni Alberto was in the frame but tragically died of cancer in 1997 aged only 33. Immediately the mantle fell on the eldest son of Agnelli sister Margherita, John Elkann, who was named to the Fiat board at the age of 22. He now chairs both Fiat and the Agnellis' private investment group.

In 2005 I closed the loop with the Agnelli clan when my book *Ferrari by Mailander* was published. This featured Ferrari photography from 1950 to 1955 taken by my friend Rodolfo Mailander. Thanks to his daughters Monica and Carolina, we were able to arrange an exhibition of my curation of his Ferrari images in the Pinacoteca Giovanni e Marella Agnelli, a magnificent gallery at the top of the redeveloped Lingotto factory in the heart of Turin. For the opening, Ferrari enthusiasts parked their gorgeous cars on the rooftop test track outside the Pinacoteca's doors.

The Agnelli clan was represented at the opening by Lapo Elkann, John's brother, who was director of Fiat marketing at the time. A man of taste and imagination, in this respect he reminded me of Oddone Camerana, who oversaw Fiat's presentation to the world in my days with Fiat in New Jersey. Although he went astray soon thereafter, Lapo cleaned up his act to become the initiator of design and marketing schemes of benefit to Abarth and Ferrari as well as consumer goods through several companies.

Executives

Always at the fringes of the Agnellis was Luca Cordero di Montezemolo. Like Gianni Agnelli, he is dubbed '*Avvocato*' by his staff, by virtue of having studied law. As head of Fiat's public relations at the end of the 1970s he was the counterpart in Turin of my activities in America. Luca is supernaturally bright, incredibly focused at all times and he can talk for Italy. When he held court at motor shows, not only the press but also the Fiat or Ferrari people would be on the edge of their seats to hear what he had to say.

In 1991 Gianni Agnelli selected Luca as chairman and CEO of Ferrari, where he led a renewal of both the Formula One team and its road-car products. As the boss of hyper-successful Ferrari he had charisma to spare. Before he arrived, Ferraris were sexy toys but not serious cars. Luca made Ferraris even more sexy, if anything, and at the same time raised their quality enough to allow them to be driven every day. In 2014 he stepped aside in favour of Sergio Marchionne, who subsequently took Ferrari's ownership public.

During crucial years in the post-Agnelli period, Cordero di Montezemolo loyally held the fort at Fiat. On behalf of the Agnellis he headed non-auto companies in the Group, which prepared him well to guide such businesses as well as public initiatives, such as Rome's bid for the 2014 summer Olympics. The charismatic Luca's blend of talents will always be in demand.

Although here the picture of geniality in his office, Abarth was a stern task-master. His path to success was a demand for perfection in his designers, builders and drivers.

Executives

CARLO ABARTH

When I was in Italy in 1958, I attended the Turin Salon and, with photographer Jesse Alexander, visited Carlo Abarth's workshop on Via Trecate to see what the Austro-Italian conjuror of power was up to. We were welcomed by the tweed-jacketed Abarth and his sidekick engineer Renzo Avidano, who took us through the details of his latest engines and cars.

With its clusters of consonants, 'Abarth' wasn't mellifluous to the Italian ear. It was a gift from Abarth's Austrian father, who with his wife from Merano, welcomed their son Karl into the world in Vienna on 15 November 1908.

Apprenticing with coachbuilder Castagna in Italy, the swarthy youngster was soon besotted with motorcycling. Working with cycle shops in Vienna, he also began racing. Into the 1930s he was a successful competitor and triple champion who made a name for himself in Austrian circles.

Showing his mechanical flair, Karl Abarth designed a special racing side car fitted with its own steering-wheel control to adjust its angle to the motorcycle. With this he cleaned up in his category. He also used his special rig in 1934 to beat the time of the famed Orient Express over 853 miles from Vienna to the Belgian coast at Ostend.

Around the same time, Abarth married Maria, a legal secretary. In Vienna she worked for Anton Piëch, lawyer son-in-law of car-engineering legend Ferdinand Porsche. Anton was deeply involved in all aspects of Porsche's business, including his creation of the future Volkswagen car and factory. 'He was always in contact with us,' Piëch's son Ernst said of Abarth, 'but because he was Jewish he had to leave Austria. He went to Yugoslavia with Maria. There he was said to be a mechanic for Tito's partisans.'

At war's end Abarth went to his mother's home town of Merano, now part of Italy. He divorced Maria and married a strong-willed Italian lady who became an important asset to his business activities. 'I'll live the second phase of my adventurous existence as an Italian,' he declared, signing his name as 'Carlo'. Abarth's Italian became serviceable, if guttural.

In 1946 Abarth was living in Merano in Italy's South Tyrol. Considering his options, he wrote a letter to Ferry Porsche's sister, Louise Piëch, informing her of his whereabouts and availability and enquiring about the Porsche's team's activities. This small gesture yielded big consequences.

A regular correspondence developed between Abarth and Ferry Porsche. Released from confinement by the French in July 1946, Ferry was in Gmünd, Austria, with a cadre of engineers and mechanics but barred from travelling outside his immediate district. Drawn into the correspondence was another Austrian living near Merano, engineer Rudolf Hruska. From 1939 through 1941, Hruska had served as a co-ordinator of the Volkswagen project, providing liaison between the Porsche engineering team in Stuttgart and the VW production staff in Fallersleben.

Early in 1945 Rudolf Hruska travelled to Brescia to follow up an inquiry from truck maker OM, which wanted to make transmission parts for experimental vehicles. When he tried to return to Austria in April, however, he found such a journey impossible in the chaos of the last weeks of the war. Hruska went instead to stay with friends at Lagundo near Bolzano, from which he made contact with Carlo Abarth.

In the meantime, Hruska liaised independently with Porsche chief engineer Karl Rabe and the Porsche cadre at Gmünd. Constrained in his travel as he was for the time being, Ferry Porsche suggested that the two Viennese might want to act as agents in Italy for the designs and abilities of the marooned Porsche group. Porsche cast many such seeds. In this instance they fell on fertile soil.

Carlo Abarth put more than one message in a bottle on the turbulent postwar waters. His postcard addressed simply to 'Tazio Nuvolari, Mantova' was rewarded one day by the arrival on Abarth's doorstep of the great racing driver himself. Nuvolari also knew Hruska, the two having met in 1938 when Nuvolari was driving for the Auto Union team. Nuvolari was eager to find some way to start designing and building a new Grand Prix car, for the pre-war Maseratis then available were in less than pristine condition.

Why not arrange for the Porsche staff to create a new racing car? This was the suggestion of Abarth and Hruska, which Nuvolari thought an excellent idea. Hruska wrote to Gmünd and, in a letter of 9 September 1946, received Porsche's assent that such an effort was feasible. 'Of course to be in time for the next racing season, work should start now,' said Ferry. 'Assuming the approval of the Allied military occupation government, one might begin immediately with the design. According to our estimate, the design work will cost 30,000 Austrian schillings per month.'

This was good news to the Austrians and to Nuvolari. Porsche could do the job. But where was the money to come from? The financial link in the chain was Corrado Millanta, a well-known German-speaking photojournalist. Nuvolari phoned Millanta with the news from Porsche. Impressed and intrigued, Millanta took Nuvolari and the two Viennese to Milan to see Count Giovanni 'Johnny' Lurani, a genial driver-editor with a wide circle of friends. Their conversations lasted late into the September evening and revolved around one man in particular, Piero Dusio.

They all knew Dusio, who was making a big splash in post-war Italian motor circles with his Cisitalia company and cars. Nuvolari was among the leading drivers who had just started racing the D46 single-seater that autumn of 1946. So convinced were they that Dusio was their man, that during the meeting in Milan, Johnny Lurani, speaking for the Porsche representatives, phoned Dusio in Turin.

Taking up the role of agitator and facilitator, Corrado Millanta secured confirmation from Gmünd that he and the two exiled Austrians could legally represent Porsche Konstruktionen in Italy. The idea of a Porsche-designed car appealed greatly to Dusio's passion for the avant-garde. He authorised Millanta to open discussions with Gmünd.

After further correspondence, Abarth and Hruska journeyed north to Kitzbühel, the ski resort in the Austrian Alps, to begin discussions on an agreement between Cisitalia and Porsche. Meeting on 7 December with Ferry Porsche, Louise Piëch, Karl Rabe and Hans Kern, they reviewed what Porsche had to offer and how it could best be presented to the Italians.

On 9 December Hruska wrote to Nuvolari: 'Today I wish to inform you that the Grand Prix car and sports car are to be manufactured in Italy. This information is currently only for you personally.' This marked an agreement in principle with Cisitalia to pursue both those projects: the Type 360 Grand Prix car and a sports car, the Type 370. Karl Rabe immediately began design work, both being entered into the Porsche job list on 11 December 1946.

Cisitalia made a down payment of 30 million lire to Porsche Konstruktionen to secure licences on all the patents involved in the contracted projects. The funds were remitted in three currencies as 10 million lire, $11,000 and

900,000 schillings. Of the latter, Ferry and his sister received 400,000 with the balance, 500,000 schillings, going to the company itself. Through old friends in the French racing world, Dusio and Louise Piëch arranged to have one million francs – officially $8,380 at the time – turned over to the French authorities to free Ferdinand Porsche and Anton Piëch from detention in Dijon.

Agog over Dusio's ambitious effort, describing his four-wheel-driven Grand Prix car with a supercharged flat-12 engine behind the driver, Italian journals naturally featured it heavily. With Rudolf Hruska not shy about characterising his role, some credited him as the 'chief engineer' of the project. Carlo Abarth too was mentioned on the periphery. Later, however, in his writings, Corrado Millanta would be scathing about the Austrians' arrogation of involvement with Porsche, pointing out accurately that they 'never had anything to do with the basic operation of the famous project office.' They simply profited from being in the right place at the right time.

A subtly different perspective came from Mario Simoni's portrayal of this interval in the chequered history of Cisitalia. 'The main decisions were taken separately by the "German" technicians,' he wrote, 'and then developed on the road or in the workshop under the direct control of Abarth, who at the end of 1947 became the Cisitalia sports director, a sort of "number two" of the company, reporting only to Piero Dusio.

'Abarth was respected but perhaps not loved too greatly within Cisitalia,' Simoni added. 'To many at the time, his habit of speaking to his interlocutors in German was debatable, excluding as it did the Italians from the conversation. Arguable as well was his habit of wearing white gloves in the workshop, even if in reality this behaviour was due to what was said to be a skin allergy.

'The ideas that led to the birth of the highly successful Cisitalia Type 204' continued Simoni, 'are almost certainly the result of Abarth's intuitions, but he surely would not have been able to materialise them without the ability of Rudolf Hruska, Luciano Scholz and other Cisitalia technicians.' A new interpretation of the 1.1-litre Fiat-based Type 202 Cisitalia, the 204 had a Porsche-influenced torsion-bar front suspension, the first five sets of which were made at Gmünd and brought to Turin in early 1948.

'Altogether about ten of the Type 204 were produced,' said Mario Simoni. 'Many of these were purchased in 1949 by Abarth, thanks to capital pro-

Executives

vided by his partners, the Scagliarini father and son, together with the liquidation of Cisitalia and the six million lire that constituted his 20 per cent commission from the 30 million lire paid by Dusio to Porsche with the signing of the initial design agreement.'

Thus assuming the mantle of the Italian arm of the failing Cisitalia – Piero Dusio having decamped to Argentina – the new Carlo Abarth Team rose as an activity of the new-born Carlo Abarth & C. established on 31 March 1949 in Bologna and transplanted to Turin in 1951. They competed initially with the D46 single-seater and the 204 spyder, now dubbed 240A. Carlo used his astrological sign, the scorpion, as the company and product logo.

By the time I visited Carlo Abarth in 1958, he had experimented with various combinations of Fiat and other raw material to produce a variety of sporting autos. His breakthrough came with the introduction in 1955 of the rear-engined Fiat 600, which proved to be amenable to greatly enhanced performance. With more power and soon with light aluminium coupe body-work, he was producing what I described in my article about his company as 'Tiny Tornadoes from Turin'.

It was always a treat to visit Abarth because something exciting and interesting was bound to be happening, be it a new twin-cam engine on the dyno, a record-breaker under construction or a new sports-racer being completed. The small quarters were always in perfect order. 'If there's anything he hates,' driver Hans Herrmann said of Carlo Abarth, 'it's dawdling, disorder and dirt. The factory halls are almost as clean as a pharmacy. Materials, tools and cars have their designated places. He takes care that his cars go to the start sparkling.'

Abarth exploited another money-spinner found at Cisitalia. Giovanni Savonuzzi had created a novel exhaust silencer. Impressed by the effectiveness of the silencer on an American pistol, Savonuzzi dismantled it and found a fine netting of wire mesh surrounding the barrel. Designing a straight-through muffler on similar lines, the engineer achieved much improved performance. Patented in a variety of configurations, the silencers became Carlo Abarth's cash cows. Crackle-finished with chrome tips, they sold all over the world and especially well in America, where they introduced the Abarth name. Even Ferrari fitted Abarth mufflers as standard equipment.

Abarth had another source of funding for his racing adventures that was little appreciated at the time. He negotiated a pact with Fiat that delivered a

bonus for every racing success achieved by cars based on the Turin company's components. Accounting for the name 'Fiat-Abarth' given to Abarth's
products, Fiat paid the benefit for all successes including those of private
clients. This accounted for the close ties between Fiat and Abarth.

Carlo flirted with Simca and Alfa Romeo to keep Fiat on its toes but
always came back to the Turin mother company. One such instance was the
launch in February 1962 of the Abarth Simca 1300, the creation of which
benefitted from the activity of Rudolf Hruska as a consultant to France's
Simca. Based on Simca's new 1000 model, it was Abarth's first rear-engined
car with an engine bigger than 1,000 cc.

Now for racing, the new model needed to be homologated by the FIA
as having been produced in 100 units within a twelve-month period. Klaus
Steinmetz, an Abarth engineer, explained to me how homologation was
achieved:

'We needed to show at least 30 – and we only had four. Avidano took
them to Paris and parked them near the hotels of the FIA delegates. Then
he moved two of them near the FIA offices where they were meeting. When
he met with them, Avidano said, "We have sold ten to Spain, 20 to Germany and, oh, 20 in France." The officials agreed with this, one of them
saying, "Yes, I've seen three this morning." They say that they will pay us a
visit.

'In Turin we show them around the factory with components strategically
placed. Then we go to the body builder where they see some thirty in various stages of construction. They said, "Fine, now let's go see the rest at your
plant." We said, "Sure, but it's now a quarter to twelve so there's not enough
time. Let's have lunch." While we're eating lunch all the bodies and parts are
moved to the Abarth assembly hall.

'Around 4:00 they all return to view this activity. "Fine," they say, "let's
weigh some now." We say we don't have enough trade plates to weigh more
than four, so they go out to be weighed and return. "Yes, we'd like to weigh
ten of them," they insist. So we take them back, switch the plates around and
weigh the same four again.

'But the yellow one has a dent in the front fender, made when it was first
weighed. We try to block a view of it but one of them sees it and says in
French, "That has a dent. Didn't that other yellow one have a dent?" Meanwhile I go back with a big hammer and put dents in the fenders of all the

other yellow ones. I also use a torch to warm the cylinder head of one of them.

'"We had a guy who messed up the bodies of all the yellow cars on the line," I explain. "Besides, this one was just driven back…it's still warm!" We got our homologation.'

Soon Abarths were part of the American racing scene. Franklin Delano Roosevelt, Jr., a striking dead ringer for his father, imported them in addition to Fiats. *Sports Illustrated* ad salesman John Norwood ran Roosevelt's racing team and drove the cars as well. Rampaging on American circuits, the red coupes soon made Abarth a household name in the races of the Sports Car Club of America (SCCA).

Moving up to a twin-cam one-litre engine, the coupes began outrunning their Fiat 600 underpinnings. Assigned one by Briggs Cunningham for the three-hour race at Sebring in 1962, Bruce McLaren found that they 'would have benefitted from some attention to the handling, braking and steering. It seemed that at every corner you were in danger of landing on your head! There were several of them racing and on nearly every corner you would come upon one spinning crazily, either on its wheels or roof.' Nevertheless McLaren outfumbled Walt Hansgen in a sister Abarth to win the three-hour race.

Carlo Abarth and his trusted lieutenant Renzo Avidano improved their cars and built more adventurous machinery, competing well in classes up to two litres. Attempts at Formula One and Two and a big V-12 to fight the Porsches and Ferraris were a reach too far, however, for Abarth and his team. Their high costs contributed to the company's acquisition by Fiat on 31 July 1971. Abarth continued to manage it as CEO for a period. Later he moved back to Vienna, where he died in 1979 just short of his 71st birthday.

I next visited Abarth in 1978 when I was an executive vice president of Fiat Motors of North America. My reason was that the fabled premises were now the headquarters of the Fiat Rally Team, which competed with versions of the 131 saloon and the 124 sports car. We were negotiating to obtain cars and servicing for a Fiat challenge in the rally programme of the SCCA. I discussed this with Cesare Fiorio, formerly the moving spirit of the Lancia rally and racing effort and then doing the same for Fiat. It was heartening to find the former Abarth premises buzzing with purposeful activity.

I have a table that tots up more than 3,600 Abarth class and overall victories through 1966. A claim by owner Fiat that Abarth successes total more than 7,000 does not seem improbable. That tally has been growing with Abarth again in gear. Fiat is using the Abarth name actively for special sporting models: a good idea. All it needs to do to complete the argument is to shine more light on the remarkable man who created the company and its sparkling reputation. There are more motor-sporting heroes in Italy than Enzo Ferrari.

DESIGNERS

The artwork behind him was no pretense because Giugiaro was an artist who turned his talents to car design to earn the money he needed to fund his study of painting.

GIORGETTO GIUGIARO

For the historic 50th Turin Salon in early November of 1968, Italy's coachbuilders were out in full force. Vignale had the latest Maserati Indy, a rebodied Matra and a Ferrari 'station wagon' commissioned by Luigi Chinetti. Bertone showed the Alfa-based Carabo that was the season's star so far, while Ghia wheeled out three studies on Maserati and Serenissima chassis. Pininfarina exerted a full-court press with seven cars, all painted 'pearl or hand-cream white', including a Ferrari P6 study and a wedge-styled Alfa Romeo Type 33 roadster.

Could any newcomer prevail against competition like this? Surprisingly one did. On the Bizzarrini stand was a Chevy-powered mid-engined machine called 'Manta' in a striking jade green. A rebodied racing car, it shocked and amazed with its one-box design fronted by a windscreen sloped at 15 degrees from the horizontal. Its driver sat centrally with a passenger on each side. 'It really looked like a projectile,' said Giotto Bizzarrini, who provided its chassis.

The outrageous yet handsome Manta marked the official debut of Giorgetto Giugiaro and his new Ital Design company. If it was his aim to stake out a prominent position as a designer to be reckoned with, the 28-year-old succeeded in spades. 'The strongest rival to Pininfarina and Bertone for the Carrozzeria sweepstakes,' said *Road & Track*, 'was undoubtedly the Bizzarrini Manta.' The influential magazine put the Manta on its March 1969 cover, fronting a major feature by Griff Borgeson on Giugiaro that declared that 'as an individual he dominates his art as perhaps no one has before.'

Was this impressive newcomer a one-car wonder? Giugiaro swiftly proved that he had more strings to his bow. On the Alfa Romeo 33 chassis in 1969 he showed his Iguana coupe with the scaly features that inspired its name. A major *tour de force* in 1970 was his Tapiro on Porsche's 914/6 platform, a masterly wedge-shaped exercise with transparent gull-wing access to both cockpit and engine compartment. A production car in 1971 with all the glamour of a concept car was Giugiaro's 1971 Bora, the first mid-engined Maserati for the road.

An ultimate expression of Giorgetto Giugiaro's inventiveness was his Maserati Boomerang of 1972. Sloped at an excruciating 13 degrees from horizontal, its windscreen was, said one commentator, 'bordering on the very limits of feasibility.' Built on a mid-engined chassis, the Boomerang took viewers to 'the world of unbridled fantasy where Giugiaro treats us to a treasury of his visual ideas. The entire composition thrives on trapezoids and alternating dihedrals.' Almost as extreme was Giugiaro's 1972 design for the Lotus Esprit, which ultimately reached production.

With this stunning series of spectacular sports and concept cars, Giugiaro and his Ital Design earned a prominent place among the Italian coachbuilders whose imaginative and influential designs were the envy of the world. For those in the know, however, since the beginning of the 1960s Giorgetto Giugiaro had been a man to reckon with as a designer and innovator. His precocity had been hidden, however, behind the famous names of *carrozzerie* who were happy to use his designs without giving him credit.

Giorgetto was born on August 7, 1938, as one of three children of Mario and Maria Giugiaro. His was the third generation of a family of painters who specialised in large-scale frescos in churches, palazzos and public buildings. His birthplace was the town of Garessio with a population of 6,000, some 60 miles south-west of Turin in the Maritime Alps near the coast. At the age of 12 he began studying painting at Turin's Accademia di Belle Arti. Under multi-talented Professor Eugenio Colmo he added illustration and fashion design to his artistic portfolio.

Nicknamed 'Golia' or 'Goliath', the protean Colmo made no small impression on the young Giugiaro: 'He was really a "maestro", an artist who was so deeply convinced I could become a good artist that he persuaded my parents to let me leave home to enter his school of fine arts. I remember enjoying the design of all sorts of items for hours every day. But I learned more than just fine arts: he taught us how to live and how to think about broad aspects of life. He was also a sort of philosopher, as an artist needs to be.

'I wanted to be a painter and so did my family.' Giugiaro continued, 'They encouraged me to study and paint.' But practicality entered the picture. 'One day my professor said to me: being an artist is hard, you starve. Use your talent for drawing in other disciplines.' The opportunity to do just that arose when Giugiaro found himself short of funds to continue his education.

In 1955, an exhibition of academic work included some of the student's satirical caricatures of automobiles. A nephew of Giugiaro's professor was Dante Giacosa, who was nearing the end of a great career as Fiat's chief engineer. Seeing the drawings at the professor's suggestion, Giacosa discerned potential and recommended the young man to Fiat's advanced-design group, which made him an offer. 'I decided to take the job at Fiat to have a steady salary,' Giugiaro told me. He had just turned 17 when he joined Fiat in September of 1955.

'There I discovered the world of creativity,' Giorgetto Giugiaro said of his stay at Fiat, where the imaginative and experienced Luigi Fabio Rapi was in charge of special-vehicle design. 'But I still dreamed about becoming a painter,' Giugiaro admitted. The Fiat job was just a way for him to earn the funds he needed to continue his education. At the Mirafiori headquarters he gained the skills of vehicle rendering and presentation while polishing his technical drawing ability.

Tall and well-built, young Giugiaro was a keen skier and winner of several amateur competitions. Looking forward to the 1959 winter season, he had his eye on a new pair of skis but lacked the discretionary funds. He conceived the idea of moonlighting for a coachbuilder by selling a design he had in mind. Through a friend he was introduced to Nuccio Bertone at 1959's Turin Salon. 'For me he was a creative Olympian,' Giugiaro recalled, 'a superhuman being, and I approached him with great timidity and circumspection.'

Assessing the well-presented young man on his stand during the show's press day, Bertone asked him to sketch what he had in mind. His design looked promising, said the acknowledged master. 'Please do something more concrete,' he asked. At the end of the Salon, Giugiaro returned with two fully worked-out versions of his idea. 'Both were met with suspicion,' related engineer D. O. Cozzi. 'Bertone refused to believe that Giugiaro alone had done the work. Giorgetto was angered and offended and, typically, he asked for an assignment. After two weekends in the Bertone studios he presented his first complete car: the Alfa 2600 coupe.'

Not slow to recognise talent, Bertone offered the young man a job. He had a vacancy, Franco Scaglione having left to set up on his own. 'In the beginning,' Giugiaro said, 'there were just the two of us in the design office: Bertone and me.' In fact the first official design in the Giugiaro canon is stated to be the British Gordon GT, which came to market as the plastic-bodied Chevy-powered Gordon-Keeble. His profile drawing of it is dated December 31, 1959. However its lines were close kin to those of the Alfa Romeo 2000/2600 Sprint, first shown at Turin late in 1960.

The Bertone years were crucial in the evolution of the young designer. 'If I had not known Mr Bertone – without the experience and type of opportunity I had at his firm – I would never have become the car designer I am today,' Giugiaro told Giancarlo Perini in 1974. 'He understood me and gave me the confidence and freedom which enabled me to design cars. I hope I gave his company many good designs in return.'

A pivotal concept car for both Bertone and Giugiaro was the Corvair Testudo – for 'tortoise' – introduced at Geneva in 1963. Unlike the elegant but sober designs of Tom Tjaarda for Pininfarina on the rear-engined Corvair platform, Giugiaro's creation was an ultra-low coupe with a sleek, carapace-like body and a canopy-cum-doors that hinged up and forward. Nuccio Bertone personally drove it from Turin to Geneva for the Salon.

For Giorgetto Giugiaro the Testudo was a landmark creation. 'When I entered the field of cars there was already a form, a discussion, a language about cars,' he told me in 1974. 'A car had two parts: one part was the side view and the other part was the plan view. In the Testudo I broke down these two parts. This was my first attempt to avoid having two separate parts but rather to have one part blending into the other.

'I wanted to express to myself that I was able to do something, that I was able to give something of myself, from my mind alone,' Giugiaro added, 'that I was no longer following a chain, following other ideas. With the Testudo I proved to myself that I was able to break with the past and begin with something coming from my own imagination. I believe it was a radically new kind of car, a new concept. In my opinion it seemed to provide a new source for car designs. That was a car with which I really felt I contributed to car designing.'

The creation of the Testudo was one of the miracles of speed so characteristic of the Turin *carrozzerie*. 'I started working on the Testudo on the third of January,' Giugiaro said, 'and on the third of March the car was driven from Turin to Geneva for the show.' Bizarrely, as related by Chuck Jordan, at the very same time GM's designers were working on the Monza GT, also Corvair-based, with a similar lifting canopy.

If the Testudo – called 'dynamic but awkward' by *Road & Track* – made its impact by dramatic exaggeration, another Giugiaro concept car of this era had an appeal that was more subtle but no less profound. This was the Alfa Romeo Giulia 1600 Canguro, built on the TZ's tubular space frame. Although looking nothing like a kangaroo, said Griff Borgeson, 'it appears to be on the verge of catapulting forward even in repose, hence the name.'

Conceived as a more attractive and wind-cheating body for Alfa's Giulia Tubolare TZ, yet also offering interior habitability, the Canguro was sublimely, subtly curved and proportioned in a manner that rejected 'three-view' conventions. Never realised in production by Alfa Romeo, one of its deeply regretted lost opportunities, the Canguro remains a touchstone of excellence for enthusiasts of the four-leaf clover – which was artfully incorporated in its vents behind the side windows.

By now industry insiders were well aware of the talent that lay behind Bertone's creations. An attractive offer was made by Ford's Cologne operation. 'Ford offered me the best salary,' said Giugiaro, 'but I would have had to move to Germany. I preferred to stay in Turin and build cars as we have the best of everything here.' Turin was also closer to the skiing the designer enjoyed.

Giugiaro joined Turin's Carrozzeria Ghia instead. This seemed promising but soon after his arrival in November of 1965, the company was bought by American interests that put émigré Argentinean Alejandro de Tomaso in charge. The most important results of the new alliance were visible at the 1966 Turin Salon in a magnificent new sports Maserati, the Ghibli, and an impressive mid-engined de Tomaso model, the backbone-chassis Mangusta.

The schism with Bertone was creatively traumatic, said Giorgetto Giugiaro: 'When I left Bertone I was obliged to leave behind everything that I had contributed. All the shapes I had created at Bertone had to be left behind.' This demanded of him a huge intellectual investment in a new design language. Though sublimely spectacular and destined to be one of the most-admired Maseratis, the Ghibli was the more conventional of the two.

'The Ghibli was made for a customer,' said the designer, 'and I wasn't sure that Maserati could understand what I wanted to say with its design so I was obliged to change it slightly – but not too much.' Nevertheless when he left Ghia he again had regrets over what he'd had to leave behind: 'When I did the Maserati Ghibli it cost me a lot to leave that idea. The habit of being forced to abandon a design that you like forces you to give up being a romantic.'

In contrast to the Ghibli, said Giugiaro, 'I did the Mangusta for myself, as a way of expressing my ideas.' At a time when mid-engined sports cars for the road were much in the news, the Ford-powered Mangusta made headlines. Using a design he had originally conceived for a Bizzarrini chassis, Giugiaro created a hunched-down, sleek-lined bullet of a car that bespoke its substantial power. Its interior was little more than a sketch, a flat dash with gauges, but its exterior was sublime. By dipping its door line and sloping its screen, the Mangusta showed Giugiaro's first effort to guide the eye up and over the shape instead of along the belt line.

When quizzed early in his career about his favourite designs, Giorgetto Giugiaro never failed to mention the Ghibli and Mangusta. 'There simply is no "best" car,' he said. 'Many of them are good with respect to their functions. But several I am quite fond of are the Ghibli and the Mangusta.' The effort needed to evolve a new design language for them had left its mark.

During his brief but turbulent and productive sojourn at Ghia, Giorgetto Giugiaro began to consider his future. 'At Ghia I could work quietly without trouble,' he related. 'But I wasn't working the whole day for Ghia. So I could look around and find other work. I started a separate activity, a business, together with two other people. Aldo Mantovani had great knowledge of all technical matters and the creation of engineering drawings, while Luciano Bosio knew methods and infrastructure. My aim was to create not only design ideas for someone else to realise but also everything that would be necessary to realise that idea.'

Giugiaro and his partners in Ital Design – for that was the business – rejected the traditional concept of a *carrozzeria* in the style of Pininfarina and Bertone, who were not only designing cars but also producing them. 'I felt that the idea of a normal *carrozzeria* was already old,' he told me. 'I wanted to bring something new. The meaning of a *carrozzeria* is to become an industry and produce cars, but I didn't want to produce cars. I wanted to produce ideas. My concept is to leave production to the big industries.' His company's main brush with manufacturing came when it helped BMW

Designers

get its M1 – a Giugiaro design – into production at Baur in Germany when the original contractor, Lamborghini, was unable to build it. A few concept cars like the 1991 Nazca and 1993 Aztec Barchetta have been built in small numbers.

The understanding of manufacturing of Giugiaro and his Ital Design partners was comprehensively tested from mid-1967 when they were commissioned by Alfa Romeo to take care of body design and engineering for an all-new car to be built in an all-new factory at Pomigliano d'Arco near Naples. This was the birth of the Alfasud, which was unveiled at the 1971 Turin Salon.

Both the car and its factory were the creation of the peripatetic Viennese engineer Rudolf Hruska. He was the author of the Alfasud's flat-four water-cooled engine driving the front wheels and its coil-sprung suspension. Giugiaro first met Hruska in 1960 when the engineer, based in Milan but working in Turin while advising Simca in France, was assisting Bertone in the design of a pretty coupe body for Simca's 1000 model that came to market in 1962.

A man of experience and determination who had helped plan the Volkswagen factory before the war and worked with Cisitalia after it, Rudy Hruska was a tough taskmaster. 'I never succeeded in persuading him to accept some of my proposals which contrasted with some of his ideas,' Giugiaro said of Hruska. Nevertheless he had great respect for the Austrian. 'He gave me the technical understanding and feeling for the car, such things as practicality and functions,' the designer explained in 1974. 'Hruska is one of the best product engineers I have ever met.'

The work of Giorgetto and his Ital Design team with Rudy Hruska and Alfa Romeo was vital to Giugiaro's next major step in the motor industry. It came about in an interesting way, said the designer: 'Kurt Lotz, who was president of the Volkswagen Group, came to the Turin Show in 1969. He walked around studying all the cars and taking note of the ones he liked best. Then he asked an important specialist journalist there to tell him about the designers of those cars. All the cars Mr Lotz appreciated happened to be my designs. After answering his questions, the journalist introduced me to Mr Lotz. A few weeks later I started working for Volkswagen.'

At first, opportunities in Wolfsburg seemed limited. Under Lotz, the Beetle's designated successor was a mid-engined small car being developed and styled by the Porsche office in Stuttgart. However, this was peremptorily terminated by Rudolf Leiding, who took over from Lotz in 1971. The experienced Leiding launched work instead on a completely new generation of cars. Giugiaro would be their stylist.

The designer looked back on this period as one of exceptional accomplishment. 'I worked very well to my complete satisfaction with VW,' he said, 'even if the schedule was very short. Normally doing a new car takes three years and I had to do this in three months! The Volkswagen Golf, Passat, Scirocco – all three.'

For the Golf, Giugiaro employed a technique that he first essayed on his Mangusta. He eliminated the traditional belt line, the upper surface of the car's main body along which the eye tends to travel. By doing this he aimed to have the eye moving in a different manner: 'I tried to have the eye follow the shape up over the windscreen instead of being broken as it had to travel back along the belt line,' he explained to me. In this, the Golf's downsloping hood and stiff screen cooperated.

When asked which of his designs entered production much as he presented them, Giorgetto Giugiaro credited 'the first VW Golf and Scirocco, as well the Audi 80, the Fiat Panda, Uno, Punto and Grande Punto, the Lancia Delta, the Alfa Brera and 159 and the Lexus GS300.' Perhaps not thinking it important enough, he didn't mention the Yugo Florida, which at its introduction in 1987, he considered a notably successful realisation of his design.

These jobs and later projects meant expansion for Ital Design. Initially in Turin offices, the company moved in April of 1974 to bespoke premises in the city's Moncalieri district. There it continued the long series of design successes that added lustre to its name. At the beginning of 2007, Giugiaro and his son Fabrizio acquired all the outstanding shares in Ital Design, making it entirely a family property. Through Lamborghini, a daughter company of Audi, the Volkswagen Group acquired 90-per cent ownership of Ital Design in May of 2010, amply securing its founder's retirement.

In 1999, when his career was in full swing with mainstream styling work for Seat, Fiat, Hyundai, Alfa Romeo, Daewoo and others, Giorgetto Giugiaro was named Designer of the 20th Century by a panel of 120 international experts. Each year his company astounded motor-show goers with imaginative and provocative prototypes. An offshoot organisation, Giugiaro Design, was designing products from yachts to pots and pasta.

Giorgetto Giugiaro's astonishingly broad and deep contributions to design derive from the intellectual investment in design that he made over a career spanning more than half a century. A reader of philosophy, Giugiaro has given deep thought to the underlying principles of his profession. To this he brings his invaluable experience gained in working with auto makers in all parts of the world save America – with the notable exception of the DeLorean DMC-12.

This doesn't mean that his clients are undemanding, quite the contrary. They expect short-order miracles from this renowned designer. 'Many think that perhaps I am a magician,' Giugiaro reflected during our talk. 'It's not that I arrive one morning and say, "Okay, I have an idea." I have to work for ideas! People say that I'm a lucky man because I arrive with an idea, that I wake up with an idea! In fact I feel like a worker, a builder. I put bricks in a wall, one upon the other, to build something. But people think that I do it all in one go. A magician! Mandrake!'

This portrait successfully captures the geniality of Albrecht Goertz,
a quality that suited him well for success in industrial design as a protégé
of Raymond Loewy.

ALBRECHT GOERTZ

O pening my copy of the 1951 Enlarged Super Edition of Dan Post's *Original Blue Book of Custom Restyling* I find three photos of a rakish coupe based on the post-war Studebaker. It had a teeny-tiny cab and an ultra-low bonnet beneath which was one of the Granatelli brothers' hot-rodded Mercury V-8s. Standing next to it in one photo is a tall fellow with swept-back hair wearing a tee-shirt, a moustache and a big smile. This was none other than Albrecht Graf von Schlitz gen. von Goertz und Freiherr von Wrisberg.

Inheriting titles that included both Count and Baron, Albrecht Goertz was born on 12 January 1914 into one of Germany's noble families. Their properties were in Lower Saxony between Hanover and Göttingen at the village of Brunkensen, set in an idyllic valley. The family's scions would be expected to maintain its traditions. However, Albrecht was the second son with few prospects of inheriting its stewardship. In 1936, at the age of 22, Goertz decided to seek his fortune in America.

'I did all kinds of odd jobs,' he said. 'In 1939, the beginning of the hot-rod era, I rented a small body shop – a corrugated metal shack on Rodeo Drive in Beverly Hills – and modified Fords.' One of his creations based on a 1940 Mercury was a low, handsome coupe with suicide doors, clearly influenced by Jean Bugatti's pre-war designs. Adopting this as his personal car, he named it the 'Paragon'.

Albrecht Goertz had no time to enjoy his creation before being drafted into America's army. After V-J Day he was mustered out with little more to his name than the Paragon. Exemplifying the theme of his autobiography, *You've Got to Be Lucky*, Goertz was driving this spectacular machine in New York one day when he was spotted by Raymond Loewy. Sensing a diamond in the rough, the famed industrial designer sent Albrecht to Brooklyn's Pratt Institute to learn the rudiments of formal design before granting him an apprenticeship at the South Bend, Indiana, styling offices of Studebaker, which were the responsibilities of Loewy.

'This was possibly the best education into design that one could get,' Goertz said later. After helping with Studebaker's 1950 spinner-nose facelift, he left South Bend to set up his own industrial-design office in New York. There the tee-shirt-wearer took full advantage of his exposure to the stylish Loewy. He metamorphosed into a suave and affable European who lost no time in making contacts in New York's motoring circles. One of his calling cards was a series of sketches of car-design proposals for *Motorsport* magazine.

Another émigré who had made a home in New York was BMW importer Max Hoffman. The two met at the city's automobile show in the spring of 1954. Hoffman had just returned from a visit to Munich where he was disappointed by design proposals for a sports car on the V-8-powered Type 502 chassis. Showing photos of it to Goertz and explaining the situation, Hoffman suggested, 'Why don't you make some sketches?'

Ten days or so after sending a portfolio of drawings to BMW, Albrecht Goertz received a telegram asking whether he could come over to discuss the project. Flying to Munich, he reached an agreement with the Bavarian company on a design assignment for two cars. In November of 1954 he started work on them both at BMW and in his New York studio. One, the 503, was a 2+2 model on an unaltered 502 chassis. The other, the 507, was a pure two-seater sports car on a new chassis shortened by 14 inches to a 97.6-inch wheelbase.

What Goertz called his 'breakthrough' came at the Frankfurt Show in September of 1955 when the two new BMWs were shown. The 507 in particular has stood the test of time as one of the most stunningly beautiful cars ever created. In his eyes the design had a particular cachet, he said: 'I think I was the only guy able to change the BMW front without anybody saying a word.' He did change it but sympathetically, with the 'kidneys' split horizontally instead of vertically.

In the late 1950s another German company was considering an important new model. Considering that owners of its Type 356 might welcome a larger car with similar attributes, Porsche began work on a full four-seat model with new coil-spring suspension and a longer wheelbase. For such an important project, Ferry Porsche considered getting help from outside to complement the work of his veteran engineer-designer Erwin Komenda.

Impressed by Albrecht Goertz's rakish styling of the BMW 507, Ferry commissioned the German-American designer to work at Zuffenhausen on a new look for the budding Type 695. This was a rare privilege for an outsider and a big opportunity for Goertz, which he seized with both hands.

Working with the traditional Volkswagen 94.5-inch wheelbase, Goertz produced a fastback design in 1957 with generous glazing, including a wraparound rear window, that would have ample room for four passengers. Featuring quad headlamps and sextuple tail lamps, it was completed as a full-size model in the Porsche studio with the modelling help of Heinrich Klie, who had founded the model shop when he arrived at Porsche in 1951. One version also had conventional headlamps.

'In the course of conversation,' Goertz related, 'Dr Porsche told me he had a son who was studying at the Hochschule for Design at Ulm. Lacking faith in the formal training offered by design schools, which is usually overweighted to the theoretical – I prefer reality to theory – I suggested that the boy, Ferdinand "Butzi" Porsche, leave school and work with me on this project at the Porsche studio, which was part of the factory. Butzi did not return to Ulm and that was probably my biggest contribution to Porsche.'

As for his design proposal, Albrecht Goertz was doomed to disappointment. 'I well recall its presentation to Dr Porsche's sister, Frau Piëch,' he related. 'Dr Porsche walked around the model several times, talked to his sister, then came to me and said, "This is a very beautiful car, but it is a Goertz, not a Porsche." It was a priceless lesson for me. It is easy to design a car for oneself but much more difficult to design one specifically for others.'

In fact, having paid Albrecht Goertz for his work, the thrifty Porsche company did pay some attention to his ideas. With Heinrich Klie, another full-size model was developed in the new-model programme that used elements of the Goertz proposals under the designer's direction, moderating the more extreme elements of his original design. Most significantly, the Goertz proposal reduced the substantial sheet-metal overhang of the wheelhouses, a major Komenda trademark, by bringing the periphery of the automobile much closer to the outer surfaces of its wheels. In this manner the Goertz design's more modern flanks had an influence on the future Type 911.

In 1961 Albrecht Goertz became one of the first occidental designers to take up the challenge of Japan. After five visits, Nissan assigned him a consulting contract. Working with their designers he created the handsome Sylvia coupe of 1965 and a fastback sports car that failed to reach production. After no little controversy, Nissan later grudgingly granted that 'the personnel who designed [the 240Z] were influenced by your fine work for Nissan and had the benefit of your designs.'

In 1970 Turin Salon visitors saw two special-bodied Porsche 914/6s. While one version of the mid-engined Porsche was principally a show car to publicise the ability of its designer, the other was a serious proposal for a new shape for the 914, created with the encouragement if not the express authorisation and support of Porsche. This was a design produced by Albrecht Goertz.

On his Stuttgart visits, New York-based Goertz kept in touch with Butzi Porsche, who had taken responsibility for styling. On one occasion, the Count said, 'Butzi asked me if I would be interested in designing and developing a prototype outside of Porsche. I was delighted at the chance to do something with cars again and asked if Porsche could in some way support me in such a project. They gave me two 914/6 cars to work with and told me that when the job was done they would take care of registering one of them for my personal use.

'I developed some sketches of a design I felt would be feasible and built a one-fifth-scale clay model,' Goertz related. 'I found a small body builder in Turin, Eurostyle, that had built the Miura for Lamborghini. Though somewhat irresponsible, they were very reasonable in price and I commissioned them to build a prototype. It is ridiculous to go from a scale model to a prototype. Without a full-scale model to work from, Eurostyle could do no more than a side elevation drawing. It was chancy but I had a time/financial problem and went ahead, hoping for the best.'

This time Goertz's interpretation was more faithful to the Porsche tradition. It had a diving nose which recalled the rakish profile of the 904. Sheer and straight, its flanks were broken only by a raised surface that curved up and around the rear-wheel opening and then merged with the rear deck. The original quarter and side windows were used, along with most of the interior. Behind them small rectangular windows and air scoops were positioned on each side.

Albrecht Goertz's 914/6 had several unusual design touches. One was the use of circular black caps above the tops of its front-wheel suspension struts so a low hood line could be achieved. The other was a roof line that ran straight back to a squared-off rear end, into which the rear window was

Designers

deeply recessed. Above the window was a clever movable spoiler integrated with the roof, providing on a road car one of the techniques Porsche had been trying on its racers. Vision toward the rear quarters was through sets of louvres.

With its forged five-spoke Fuchs wheels the Goertz Porsche matched in appearance the individualistic and functional qualities of the 914 chassis. 'I was about 70 per cent satisfied with the way my car came out,' said the Count. 'The press was mixed – some favourable, some not.' Porsche did review the Goertz prototype; indeed its final detailing and road-readying took place in its Zuffenhausen workshops. It arrived on the scene too late, however, to be seriously considered for use on the 914. Although its styling was strongly polarising, the 914 was destined never to be given a facelift, let alone a completely new body.

'Model 914 was dead,' reflected the designer. 'You can't win 'em all. I wound up with the Porsche prototype I had designed and used it whenever I was in Europe. Finally in 1990 I donated the car to the Deutsche Automuseum, which is sponsored by Mercedes and Porsche and housed in Schloss Langenburg.'

In New York in the 1950s and 1960s I enjoyed my frequent contacts with the well-informed designer. He was engagingly persistent in his attempts to arrange, through me, a design-consulting relationship with the people in our GM Overseas Operations who had product responsibilities, but that never came to fruition. Meanwhile he was busy with his work for companies that eventually numbered 62; creating boats, cameras, furniture, jewellery, sportswear, pens, clocks, irons and lighters, to name only a few of the products of the versatile industrial designer.

In 1990, at the age of 76, Albrecht Goertz upped stakes and transplanted his design business to the family estate at Brunkesen. Rightly enough he continued to be feted throughout the world not only for his creativity but also for his effervescent personality. While at the resort city of Kitzbuehl on 27 October 2006 Goertz passed away. The world of cars lost one of its most engaging and colourful individuals.

LARRY KIYOSHI SHINODA

An example of the resourcefulness and ingenuity of Larry Shinoda was the miniature wind tunnel that he built to test the aerodynamics of the slot cars that were a passion.

I just missed Larry Shinoda at General Motors Styling Staff in the summer of 1956. I left in September when Larry arrived. When I returned to GM in 1961 in my new role as the public relations man assigned to Styling, I soon made the acquaintance of this remarkable Japanese-American, born in California in 1930. Given guidance by GM Styling chief Bill Mitchell, I found Larry and his colleagues in the cellar, working in an anonymous space repurposed from what was known as a 'hammer room' under the lobby where they could create radical new cars in complete secrecy.

Round-faced with oriental features, Shinoda spoke with a deep rumble, eliding his remarks with a hasty delivery that gave the impression that he was communicating important secrets. Larry was known for his forthrightness, as he admitted: 'I have always said what I thought. If a design stinks, I say so. I'm also not known for great flexibility. I used to have a sign above one of my styling areas that read "If you don't like it, obviously you have bad taste." Little things like that contribute to your reputation.' In spite of – or because of – his truculent style, senior figures in the car-design world were willing to trust Larry with their design needs.

At General Motors, Larry Kiyoshi Shinoda was effectively Bill Mitchell's personal designer, the man through whom his dreams and desires came to life in three dimensions. This came about in a serendipitous way as Larry described to Wayne Ellwood:

'GM puts all its new designers through a six-month orientation, mostly to learn the corporate game. I was given a clean sheet in just three weeks. During those three weeks my designs attracted the attention of Chevrolet, so I was assigned to that studio and started work on the 1959 Chevy. I then moved to the Pontiac studio where I worked on a few of the 1960-61 wide-track cars and even a concept for a 700-horsepower two-seater sports-type car, based on the Tempest.

'I got lucky with my next studio change. I think it mostly came about as a result of a drag race on the way home from work. It was 1958 and Bill Mitchell had replaced Harley Earl as head of Styling at GM. I basically smoked him in a stop-light tournament. I was in my 1955 Ford, which was really more like a full-fledged NASCAR racer, when he rolled up beside me in this red Pontiac.

'I didn't see him again for a couple of weeks but then he showed up in the studio and asked if my car had a supercharger. I told him it had only two four-barrel carburettors but he knew that there had to be more to the story than that. So he asked me to bring it in to the GM Styling garage so they could look at it. GM was very eager to keep abreast of the competition. It wasn't long after that he recruited me to assist with special styling projects.'

The first major project of this description resulted from an abandoned racing effort. For long-distance racing in 1957 Chevrolet built a pure competition car, the Corvette SS, designed by émigré Russian engineer Zora Arkus-Duntov. Untested as it was, the space-framed racer showed promise before failing in its first effort at Sebring. Although Chevrolet cancelled the project, the racing car and a cruder test vehicle that had shown impressive speed at Sebring had survived. The latter caught the eye of Bill Mitchell.

The newly minted Styling chief saw in the test SS the makings of a car he could mould to his own purposes. He persuaded Chevrolet chief Ed Cole to sell it to him personally for a token $500 as the basis of a racing-car project of his own. Mitchell had the idea of bodying it on the lines of a promising styling study that had been developed in the Research Studio. The test-SS chassis went to his secret studio where he had installed Larry Shinoda and studio engineer Tony Lapine. Ed Wayne was in charge of the studio while the crucial full-size modelling was done by Tony Baltzar, Chester 'Chet' Angeloni and Doug Cross.

This was the story of the creation of the Sting Ray sports-racing car that impressed me at Bridgehampton and led to my rehiring by General Motors. Although dictated by Bill Mitchell, the design was implemented by Shinoda and the rest of the team. Its concept was radically new with a low, wide grille and sharp-edged body cross-section with prominent bulges for clearance above its wheels. The body's flat upper surface and undercurving nose and tail represented a serious attempt to create an inverted wing profile that would generate downforce.

Although he used GM resources to revive the abandoned racer, Bill Mitchell had to finance the racing activities of the Sting Ray – as he aptly named the rebodied SS – from his own pocketbook. Although this had expanded with his elevation to a GM vice-presidency, its size was by no means unlimited. He took advantage of free tyres from Goodyear and negotiated a deal with the tax man that allowed him to write off some of his outgoings.

'Bill tapped a lot of sources inside GM for technical and engineering support,' Shinoda related, 'including Zora's group. This was one of our first efforts at using aerodynamic forces. Chuck Pohlmann and I did most of the final design in the "hammer room" after the basics had been set out in his Research Studio.' Although its engine output was not a match for its rivals, the developed Sting Ray was a capable racer that won the SCCA's Class C Modified Championship.

When it came time to put a body on the new Corvette chassis created by Zora Arkus-Duntov for the 1963 model year, the Sting Ray's shape was the obvious choice. It was, said Shinoda, 'the direct inspiration for the 1963 Corvette. Mitchell had most of the ideas clear in his mind. He had sketched out some lines which reflected the theme he was trying to achieve. Chuck Pohlmann had a hand in the first version. Then I was called back from an assignment in the Body Development Studio and put in the secret studio to work on the 1963 Corvette. As lead designer it was my job to take the concept and manage the project through to finished design.

'The ideas we generated,' Larry added, 'were turned into real-world form in the Chevrolet Studio headed by Clare MacKichan and Irvin Rybicki. This was an exciting time for me. It was the first car for which I had total responsibility. However I worked only on the exterior. Other stylists did the interior, including Don Schwarz, George Angersbach, Sue Vanderbilt, Frank Ileinin and John Shettler. I was very pleased with the car. There were some trim items I could have done without but overall the production car was very close to the original theme. I'm quite proud of it.'

Looking back it's surprising to realise that the second-generation Corvette, Bill and Larry's Sting Ray, lived for only five model years in both coupe and convertible form. And it's fifth model year, 1967, was regarded as a stopgap because the new 1968 Corvette was late to market. Nevertheless their total production was 117,964 units. This was the coming of age of the Corvette, which during these years added disc brakes and a 7.0-litre V-8 to its arsenal.

Avant-garde in both looks and performance, the 1963-67 Corvette Sting Ray marked Larry Shinoda as a designer to be reckoned with. The swathes of sketches that he produced during the car's gestation testify clearly to his commanding role in its creation under Bill Mitchell's direction. Shinoda had a unique and distinctive presentation style. In addition to rendering the car or specific area with Prismacolor on a black or grey background, Larry drew the longitudinal and lateral section lines on the car's surface, thus to make crystal clear the forms he was recommending. This gave his work a technical precision that was uniquely compelling.

Meanwhile, Shinoda, Lapine and the 'hammer room' team pressed ahead with new projects, including the Corvair-based Monza GT and SS – cars that I helped publicise – Duntov's four-wheel-drive CERV II and sportsracers made by Chevrolet's Research and Development Department. Among them were outright racers, the GS-IIa and IIb. Shinoda remarked that 'the Chaparral 2C and 2D built by Jim Hall carry a lot of the lines of the GS-IIb that we did.'

In fact Larry and his studio colleagues did design work for Chevy R&D and the Chaparral team that was not directly authorised by Styling Staff. A major contribution by Shinoda was the design of the 'basket-weave' wheels that appeared on several R&D concept cars and then on the Chaparral sports-racers. Efficient in its lightness, strength and ventilation, the design was later taken up and widely sold by Germany's BBS.

Larry Shinoda also took full advantage of the craze for slot-car racing that was sweeping America in the 1960s. Made carefully to scale, his slot cars faithfully replicated the real thing. Larry built experimental slot cars to explore the aerodynamic downforce that was being applied at the time, especially by the Chaparral whose high wings were jointly patented by Chaparral creator Jim Hall and GM engineers. Shinoda even designed and built a mini wind tunnel to test his theories.

With the production Corvette Sting Ray well on its way, said Larry, 'I was put in charge of Chevrolet Studio 3 in the warehouse on the south side of 12 Mile Road. John Schinella was my assistant and we had two other designers, Allen Young and Dennis Wright, who did a lot of the work. This is where we worked on a number of show cars.' One of them was Mitchell's Mako Shark II, a stunning concept car that inspired the shape of the third-generation Corvette that made its tardy appearance in 1968. This rakish design endured in successive facelifts through 1982.

That a third-generation Corvette was in the works soon after the paint dried on the 1963 Sting Rays was a manifestation of the tremendous energy that Bill Mitchell brought to the evolution of his favourite GM model. 'For the 1968 model,' Shinoda related, 'we produced a winning concept in competition with Henry Haga's Chevrolet Studio 2. The job of turning it into the final street car was then turned over to Haga's studio.'

Based on the 1963 chassis, the sensational new Corvette was a winner with Chevy's dealers snapping up the year's production well in advance. From 1969 the new cars carried the 'Stingray' name instead of 'Sting Ray' as used on their production predecessors. But Larry Shinoda, the man who had done so much to create it, was no longer at General Motors.

It hadn't been that easy for Larry to get a job at GM Styling in the first place. He won the credentials he needed the hard way. When he was in his teens, his Japanese-American family was interned at Manzanar, a central-California camp, from 1942 to 1944. A humiliating experience for a U.S. citizen, this left an indelible impression on Shinoda: 'The barracks were unfinished when we moved in and the roofs had no tar paper, so we slept with towels over our heads, which were dirty by the time we awoke in the morning.' Working in the camp as a part-time cook, to occupy his spare time he designed and built furniture out of orange crates.

'I grew up sketching,' Shinoda recalled. 'My favourite subjects were the trucks, greenhouses and flowers of my family's wholesale flower business. The first time I actually got paid for drawing was for doing the program covers for the Russetta Timing Association.

'I never really gave much thought to being an auto stylist,' Larry admitted. 'After two years at Pasadena City College with an art major and a wartime tour of Korea, I attended the Art Center School of Design in Pasadena, source of many Detroit stylists.' There he was told that he didn't have to attend classes, that handing in the assignments was enough. This backfired, however, with the result that Shinoda was asked to leave.

Meanwhile Larry was deeply into the hot-rod culture that was sweeping California. His 1929 Ford roadster used a hopped-up Mercury V-8 to clock 114 mph in the standing quarter-mile in 1949. In 1953 he was at the Bonneville Salt Flats with a Chrysler-powered roadster that set a new Class D record with a two-way average of 166 mph. His drawings were chiefly of racing cars when Ford Styling's recruiters came to California to interview candidates for their studios in Dearborn, Michigan.

'To Larry's way of thinking,' wrote Mike Anonick, 'Ford would be getting the better part of the deal. Shinoda would have to leave sunny California and his cheap room and board for cold, expensive Detroit. Shinoda wanted Ford to pay the expenses of the trip for him and his race car to Motown for a six-month trial. If things worked out, fine. If not, he was heading back to L.A. Shinoda recalled saying, "You guys need me more than I need you." Despite the young man's outrageous demands – or maybe because of them – the Ford people were impressed by Shinoda. They agreed to give him a try and Larry Shinoda was on his way.'

Ford only lasted a year, with Larry contributing to the design of a spectacular Mercury Turnpike Cruiser concept car before moving to Studebaker-Packard for 1956. 'I was working on the 1957 Clipper for Packard,' he related, 'when the die shop requested payment in advance before converting the models to dies. The handwriting was on the wall. In early April the word came down that there was no programme. We were still employed so they would still send us our pay cheque every second Tuesday but there wasn't much to do.

'I had been hanging around Indianapolis a lot,' Larry said, 'so I took off for there. At Indianapolis I picked up with the John Zink Special team. This was a very competitive Offy-powered car built by A. J. Watson. I designed the bodywork and paint for the car. It was driven to victory by Pat Flaherty that year, 1956, reflecting – I hope – not only the efforts of the whole team but some of my contributions. After that, everything was oriented to developing my portfolio to apply for work at GM. It was largely focused on my work at Indy.

'I had quite a bit of trouble trying to get an interview at GM,' Shinoda recollected. 'The Personnel Director at GM Styling let me sit outside his office for three days without recognising my request to have my portfolio reviewed. After that I wrote to Jules Andrade, because the Personnel Director had told me that Jules had reviewed my portfolio and said it was no good. Jules, of course, had never seen it. I knew that. It had never been out of my sight in the Personnel Director's office area. Anyway, Jules asked me back for another interview.

'When I came in and opened the portfolio,' Larry added, 'the first car on top was the Indy car. So Andrade went and got Mr Earl. In about twenty minutes Mr Earl came in and opened up the portfolio and saw the Indy car. He flipped a few pages through to the Packard stuff and then back to the Indy stuff. He asked how much it would take to get me to come to work for them. I added about $200 to the number I had thought up. Earl added another $200 and that was that.' Shinoda joined GM at the same time as another refugee from Studebaker-Packard, John Z. DeLorean.

The activities of Oklahoma combustion-equipment producer and racing-car entrant John 'Jack' Zink helped connect Shinoda with a highly placed GM executive. This was Semon 'Bunkie' Knudsen, then in charge of the Pontiac Division which he was busily reviving; DeLorean had landed there. 'I met him before I even joined GM,' Larry remembered. 'In 1956 Pontiac was running at Daytona and I was there working with the John Zink team. Mr Knudsen was heading up Pontiac and took an active role in the division's racing efforts. He asked me for my opinion about aerodynamics of various body styles. I gave it and apparently he liked it. After I joined GM we worked together on a number of projects. I had a very deep respect for the man and I guess he liked my design work.'

Shinoda's connection with Knudsen had consequences when the executive, whose father had been GM's president, jumped ship to the presidency of the Ford Motor Company in February 1968. Feeling jaded at GM, Larry was weighing up an offer to join Toyota's new California styling studio when he received an offer from Knudsen to join him in Dearborn. Thus Larry returned to the company that had first employed him in the auto industry. He described the transition as 'Rough. I was supposed to start two weeks after Mr Knudsen but it took him two months to get me in. Ford Styling didn't exactly welcome me back.

'He created the new job of Director, Special Projects Design Office for me. I was in charge of all high-performance production and limited-production vehicles. There was a lot happening at Ford behind the scenes – really messy. Lee Iacocca was not thrilled by Mr Knudsen's arrival in the job that he wanted. Everybody walked around with a big "I" or "K" on their back.

'The primary project I was recruited to work on at Ford had been a possible two-seater sports car to compete with Corvette. We were competing internally with de Tomaso in Italy for final design and production. Called the Mach 2C, my design lost and the de Tomaso design won.' Here politics certainly played its part because Lee Iacocca was a friend of Alejandro de Tomaso, an Argentinian working in Italy. The defeat of an ally of Knudsen was a political victory inside Ford for Iacocca.

Larry was in Turin, Italy, in September of 1969 working on the preparation of de Tomaso's Pantera for production when the news reached him that Knudsen had been peremptorily fired by Henry Ford II. 'Things just didn't work out,' Ford told reporters. Told that Knudsen's firing didn't affect his position, Shinoda completed his Turin mission: 'I returned to the U.S. from Italy on a Friday. On the following Monday I was fired. They wouldn't even let me go into the studio to bid farewell to the stylists I'd worked with. Firing me gave them great pleasure, I guess.

'The firing from Ford was a blow,' Larry admitted. 'I got some job offers but Mr Knudsen wanted me to join him in a new venture. After some market study we decided a recreational vehicle was the way to go. We were joined by a top GM engineer, Jim Musser, and together we formed Rectrans in February of 1970.

In early 1971 we had our Discoverer 25 on the road. We were in business for a little over a year when White Motor Corporation appointed Mr Knudsen as chairman of its board. Rectrans was absorbed by White.'

While Shinoda was at Rectrans I was a freelance writer, the capacity in which I visited their factory at Brighton, Michigan. Ironically this was a former Ford facility where Larry's sports car design for that company would have been produced. He and Knudsen hired me to research and write descriptive texts about their vehicles and their design. When truck-maker White hired Knudsen and absorbed Rectrans, said Shinoda, 'politics being what they are, I went with him.' Engineer Jim Musser, with whom Larry had worked since they were both designing for Chevrolet R&D, made the same transition.

I visited Larry Shinoda in White's Research and Design Center in Farmington, Michigan, where he was the company's vice president in charge of design. 'We're busy revamping White's lines of trucks, farm equipment, tractors, combines, implements and lawn-garden products, industrial and construction equipment including that of our Euclid Division,' he told me. He was now the creative master of some of the world's biggest vehicles, which needed epic amounts of modelling clay for their design.

In 1976, at the age of 46, Larry left White to establish Shinoda Design Associates Inc. in Detroit. This allowed him to work for a kaleidoscope of companies on a wide range of design assignments. After moving to England in 1980 I had less contact with Shinoda, who was working on a range of products from vast motor homes to what he called 'a two-seater moped with weather protection' named 'Gashopper'.

Only after Shinoda's death of kidney-related heart failure in 1997 did I learn of my friend's last battle. Self-confident and combative as he was, Larry was less than thrilled in 1992 when the newly introduced 1993 Jeep Grand Cherokee showed clear signs of the design he had presented in 1985 in competition with Alain Clenet and Giorgetto Giugiaro. At that time he was well aware that in spite of calling his design 'terrible, brutal' and ordering destruction of his clay model, officials of Jeep builder American Motors (AMC) had stripped his studio of his full-scale model's drawings and design templates.

Soon thereafter Shinoda learned from colleagues working at AMC that a vehicle code-named 'XJC' was being designed in its studio on the lines he had established. Adding injury to insult, Larry pointed out that his compensation for the work was $177,000 less than he felt he was owed.

With the instruction of attorneys, negotiations began with Chrysler, the owner of AMC since 1987. After five years of parleying, a settlement was reached just in time to satisfy Shinoda before his untimely death at the age of 67. True to his principles, Larry Shinoda left the stage as emphatically as he had arrived.

PETER PFEIFFER

Peter Pfeiffer confirmed the prominence of the Star in the styling of Mercedes-Benz vehicles for the 21st century while introducing more modern design techniques.

'When a customer stands in front of a Mercedes-Benz he should think: I want that car.' This was the philosophy of Peter Pfeiffer, who headed the design of Daimler products from 1999 to 2008. In this post he was the successor of Italian-born Bruno Sacco, who had held the same position from 1977. Remarkably, Pfeiffer's career at the helm of Mercedes-Benz design was in close synchronicity with the existence of the merged company DaimlerChrysler from its creation in 1998 to its dissolution in 2007. Thus I considered his insights on these dramatic years to be of special interest.

Born in August 1943 in Dallwitz in the Sudetenland, Pfeiffer grew up in Franconia and lives his life according to Prussian punctuality and the

Prussian motto: 'Be more than you seem to be'. Expelled as they were from the Sudetenland at the end of World War II, his family settled in Germany's Franconian region in the small town of Schönbrunn near Staffelstein. After completing lower secondary school, Pfeiffer followed his father's vocation by training to become a porcelain modeller at the firm of Alboth & Kaiser in Staffelstein. Thereafter, he attended the Technical College for Porcelain Design in Selb, also in Franconia.

Although he was well-schooled in this demanding discipline, young Pfeiffer discovered a new world during a study trip to the Ford factory at Cologne. There he met Wesley Dahlberg, who under design chief Uwe Bahnsen had designed the third-generation Ford 17M Taunus. Contrasting greatly with its 'baroque' predecessor, this dramatically improved model won the friendly nickname 'Bath Tub' for its smooth and harmonious lines.

Dahlberg, a Swede who had been sent to Ford in Cologne to help build up its styling studio, contributed to a design revolution at the Ford subsidiary with this new mid-range Taunus that enjoyed record sales in its cycle from 1960 to 1964. Showing initiative, Pfeiffer asked Dahlberg whether a work placement was possible. As a test, the youngster was asked to model a wing. He performed this so well that Pfeiffer was hired by Ford – although this was not the future envisioned by the lad's father.

In 1967, after five years in Cologne, Pfeiffer received a call that ultimately led to a change in location. His older colleague Josef Gallitzendörfer, also a Franconian with a career in porcelain similar to Pfeiffer's, had moved from Cologne to the Stuttgart suburb of Sindelfingen to work for Daimler-Benz AG in its expanding styling department. Pfeiffer resisted the Swabian entice-ments for a year, but after contemplating the stature of the Mercedes-Benz marque and its history, at the age of 25 he decided to make the move – one that would be his last.

His possession of both design and modelling skills suited the profound transformation that was underway at Sindelfingen; a change from elaborately crafted wooden models to clay models. These could be made more quickly and of course were more adaptable to improvements. The use of clay, and later Plasticine, was accelerated by Gallitzendörfer and his close collaborator Pfeiffer.

Pfeiffer also had a role in the implementation of the next revolution in design, from clay model to computer model based on computer-aided design

(CAD). CAD greatly influenced the design process by reducing the time required for assessment and by enhancing the opportunity for creativity.

By the end of the 20th century, CAD allowed digital models submitted by many designers at remote studios to be assessed in a room packed with state-of-the-art computer processing technology referred to as the Computer Aided Virtual Environment (CAVE). The CAVE supercomputer was able to create full-size images of selected designs, using its five projectors to show such detail that designers could inspect every inch of every surface rendered.

An example was the development of a new exterior design for the SL series that commenced on 27 January 1996. Ten designers in Germany, California and Japan submitted hundreds of sketches that formed the basis for twelve quarter-scale models that were digitised for computer manipulation. Design of the sporting car code-named R230 progressed through two different formats. From the dozen scale models, the next stage was selection of four designs to be created as full-scale models. This allowed the final choice to be made.

Although the patent for the R230 design listed both Bruno Sacco and Pfeiffer, the latter was primarily responsible for the concept. Thus it was fitting that he presided at its introduction, having succeeded Sacco in 1999. Despite its larger size, the new SL harmoniously married elegance with brand identity and sportiness. Its launch in 2001 attracted euphoric acclaim, with commentators rating the car as the most beautiful Mercedes-Benz for some time. Its production ended in 2011 with 169,434 produced.

Closely associated with Pfeiffer's stewardship of the Mercedes-Benz idiom was the 2004 introduction of the CLS Class on the E-Class platform. This was the strikingly rakish 'coupe' configuration which, startling at first, soon won not only enthusiastic acceptance but also widespread emulation. Pfeiffer shared its design patent with Murat Günak and Hans-Dieter Futschik.

In a patent application of June 2000, Pfeiffer was the sole inventor of a wonderful miniature sports car that was fated never to reach production. It was striking for its big wheels on a short wheelbase, sculptured nose and grille as well as an industrially designed interior that broke with all traditions.

In 2007, I met with Pfeiffer to discuss the DaimlerChrysler era and the relationship of his team and their speciality with their counterparts at Chrysler in Auburn Hills, Michigan.

Karl: I am trying to understand what exactly went on with Chrysler and Daimler. When you went to Auburn Hills, was it primarily to look at styling in the different studios? Do you recall your first impressions of their styling? Was it interesting to see what they did differently in Auburn Hills?

Pfeiffer: I already knew Tom Gale, Trevor Creed and John Herlitz, who became Tom Gale's successor. I had known these people on a personal level for a long time. We used to meet at Pebble Beach for the Concours d'Elegance and we frequently met at motor shows, when the subject Mercedes/Chrysler wasn't even under discussion. When the merger finally came, we had no problems getting to know each other. It was very easy for me to say, 'Let's go to Detroit and pay them a visit.' And that is obviously what we did.

We were always welcomed there in an open and friendly way, which really is one of the Americans' big assets – the fact that they are always very open and friendly. We are a bit more reserved over here. We are not quite that demonstrative. It takes us longer before we open up as they do. It was very exciting to find out what they were thinking and planning.

Of course the design processes at Chrysler differed from what we do. We build our models a lot more meticulously and include more design steps – but on the other hand, Chrysler build theirs a lot quicker than us. Both approaches have advantages and disadvantages. It was interesting to find out how fast they are and how that is possible and why we are doing it the way we do. Aspects like that are closely connected to questions like 'What sort of quality do we want and how long do we want it to last?' In my opinion this is a matter of company philosophy and ours is a 'successor philosophy'.

What I mean by this is that we have had an S Class for many generations, an SL for many generations and an E Class for many generations. If we then have a C Class, that too will have its successor. When we build an M Class, again there will be a successor. This is definitely different at Chrysler or generally with the Americans. They prefer to jump from one point to another! I once jokingly called this their 'gold digger mentality'. They find a nugget, look at it, say 'wow!' Then they go somewhere else to look for another one, whereas we would continue digging. We however, would try to find an entire gold mine!

Designers

Karl: After the meetings and the exchange of views, did you in any way change your own methods? Did you adopt anything from the Chrysler design process?

Pfeiffer: We obviously examined our various design steps and asked ourselves whether they were really all necessary or whether we could possibly speed one or two of them up or drop them completely. And Chrysler looked at our models and asked themselves how they could improve their own global appeal and create a safer basis for decision-making. You see, the models we build here are in no way different from the real cars. Chrysler have never done that and are still not doing it – not the way we build a complete mockup out of man-made material on the basis of the clay model.

Design processes are to a large extent also dependent on your workforce and on their skills. Chrysler for example build all their 1:1 scale models in clay. We have a different process: we use digital data and then build the model straightaway in our milling plant. So our design processes differ. It wouldn't make any sense at all if we now decided to work with clay models as well, because our workforce might not have the required know-how. We have different skills.

We have an enormous milling plant and Chrysler does not, so we have been using this way of data processing for many, many years. We just say that this is good and this is not good so let's change the data and make another model. Some things are obviously done by hand, especially the finer aspects, but we do use the milling plant a lot. We can no longer imagine what it would be like to work without data models and milling machines.

We would need twice as many staff if we wanted to make simple models by hand. From time to time we might build a model by hand but for factors like symmetry etc. we only use the milling machines. We no longer have people moving templates from the left side to the right. The milling machines are very good and have cost a lot of money so it's only right that we use them as much as possible.

Karl: What differences did you notice in the leadership's interest in styling – Daimler's top people and Chrysler's top people. Was there a noticeable difference?

Pfeiffer: I think I would answer that with 'yes and no'. To some extent this also depends on the personal commitments, interests and opportunities of the different directors. It comes as no surprise that someone like Dr Dieter Zetsche is, on a personal level, much more interested in design than his predecessors.

I really cannot remember any board that was indifferent to this aspect. They all put a lot of effort into design. It's just that sometimes you get someone who has a deep personal interest in the subject and of course that makes a difference.

You can certainly say that for Chrysler, design plays a much more important role than for Mercedes. My impression is that for Chrysler, the design is and has always been one of the deciding buying factors. When you look at the 300 model for example, that is primarily purchased because it looks the way it looks. Even in previous years Chrysler was primarily concerned with the look and appearance of their cars.

Similarly at Mercedes, design was and still is an important aspect – and it is actually becoming more and more important – but it is only important for us in the way it is connected with the technical side. Mercedes does not exclusively define itself through its design. Mercedes also stands for innovation, high quality, safety. All these must be very closely interlinked. A Mercedes that defines itself exclusively through its design is no longer an authentic Mercedes. Design is only one vital feature – all the others must be just as strong. Only then will you get an authentic Mercedes that is able to continue our long tradition and deliver what our customers expect.

Karl: You have explained the importance of continuity in design. However, development brings more freedom to enhance the technical side. You don't always need a different exterior design and then the required technology. Those two aspects can be developed side by side.

Pfeiffer: You are right – innovative technology and design have to be linked right from the start. What happens is a certain give and take: new innovative technology and engineering also offer an opportunity for new and innovative design. The two factors must forever be closely linked. It is typical of Mercedes that it does *not* only concentrate on quality. You can compare it to decathletes: they can only win if they are more or less equally good at ten different disciplines. There will be some disciplines where they excel but that must never mean that other disciplines will be neglected, otherwise they will never win the overall competition!

The same applies to Mercedes. We have decided for example that we will not try to be sportier than certain other manufacturers. However, we do want to have more comfortable cars than others. So this is a decathlon where we have to ask ourselves: where do we put the main emphasis at Mercedes? This of course does not mean that we want to be unsporty! By no means! But we are not trying to outdo others in this area. It is not what we represent.

Twenty years ago, design did not rank very highly on the Mercedes list of priorities. Today it plays a much bigger role. A CLS is a car that is not only bought because it is a Mercedes but also because of its attractive styling. So there has definitely been a shift. That model is bought not only because it is safe and because the quality is good. People buy it because they see it and simply want to have it!

ANATOLE LAPINE

Pictured in his General Motors years, Lapine, left, sat with Corvette guru Zora Arkus-Duntov. Tony's studio did design work both officially and unofficially for Duntov.

I met Tony Lapine when we both worked for GM Styling in 1956. He was known as 'Lapping' in those days, a usage which echoed more clearly in American ears. Tony was an appealing figure on first acquaintance, always cheerful with a wry outlook on life and dead keen on automobiles. When I returned to Detroit in 1961, I found him, his wife and first offspring living atop a Detroit carriage house that perfectly suited his passion for cars.

Anatole Carl Lapine was born in Riga, Latvia, on 23 May 1930. At the age of eleven, his family was forced to leave Latvia by the German forces thrusting along the coast and into Russia. Then in 1944 the Soviet counter-attack forced them out of Poznan in western Poland. Their next home was in Hamburg, where young Anatole was able to get a workshop apprenticeship with a Daimler-Benz subsidiary.

Equipped with working papers, Anatole – was ready for the United States. 'The opportunity presented itself to migrate to the United States for the entire family. The Lutheran World Federation found a sponsor in Nebraska, so we went to live in Lincoln, Nebraska, and paid back our debts to the organisation that sponsored us.'

Young Lapine soon discovered, to his dismay, 'that any mechanic needed his own tools just to work at a gas station. That's something German mechanics don't know because tools are furnished wherever you work.' Finding Lincoln the coldest place in the world, Tony 'got a job with the Burlington Railroad, greasing locomotives until I had enough cash to buy a decent suit, get on a Greyhound bus and go to Detroit.' The Motor City beckoned.

In those days both GM Styling Staff and GM Research were housed on different floors of what was called the Research Building, adjacent to the General Motors headquarters in downtown Detroit. Entering the impressive multi-storey structure, Tony asked for GM Research. 'I took the wrong entrance and wound up at Styling on the 10th floor. Harley Earl ruled the roost at General Motors Styling and I got to see him more or less by mistake, I guess. It was beautifully refreshing. Americans will give you a chance even if you are some strange-looking bird.

'Since I had drafting and engineering drawing ability from being an apprentice,' Lapine continued, 'they asked if I would like to work in the body development department. Hell of a nice place to start at GM for somebody who wanted to spread out a little. They were very lenient. They gave me enough rope to hang myself. I didn't. About four months later I got a whopping raise and I knew I was on my way. I could buy some decent clothes and pay my rent'.

'I carried a full daytime load in night school as well,' Tony added, 'got fairly good marks and that managed to keep me out of the Army and the Korean conflict. I wasn't particularly keen, having escaped the Second World War in one piece. There was plenty of overtime and an awful lot of work. You learned to position components like pedals and people. After time spent in the drafting room I wound up at Oldsmobile when they came looking for studio personnel. I did pretty much the same thing there too – seating arrangements and all that. I stayed in body development for two or three years.'

This was long enough for Tony Lapine to join the northbound exodus from downtown Detroit to the sparkling new GM Technical Center in Warren, Michigan, where he was soon added to the small team that was carrying out bespoke design for Bill Mitchell, the design director under Harley Earl. As a packaging and layout expert he was a perfect partner for designer Larry Shinoda. After the launch of the Corvair in late 1959, Tony related, 'Bill Mitchell thought it would be neat if we had a two-seater Corvair.' The Porsche 904 – one of which GM bought with the help of Lapine – was an inspiration for what became the Corvair Monza GT.

'I think it was not a bad looking car,' Tony opined. 'Bill Mitchell showed the clay model to Chevy chief Bunkie Knudsen and those two agreed it was a very exciting little car. We envisioned that it should be a mid-engined Corvair coupe. Bunkie Knudsen asked Frank Winchell of Chevy R&D to bring over some men. Ten of them came into the studio in lab coats and they looked the model over. About three days later they already had something you could recognise as a chassis with wheels and engine and stuff. It was a very quick-moving group. A week later the chassis was being tested on the GM track. Then the body was made, everything got combined and the car was shown at Elkhart Lake in 1962.'

Tony Lapine joined the SCCA to do some racing. 'I had an XK120M Jaguar which I managed to flip on a half-mile dirt oval. I just mangled it. The first time out – and this is the worst thing that can happen to a person – I won my first race and the second week was pretty good, too. But the fourth time out I took a chicane flat out and flipped over the hay bales. And the down payment was not even covered. Three more years to pay and all I had was a heap.'

Lapine moved on to a Porsche 1600N Speedster with which he and his wife toured Europe in 1957. Developing his skills, Lapine also competed in VWs, Alfas and Volvos. In 1959, Bill Mitchell trusted Tony to co-drive his racing Sting Ray at Elkhart Lake. When I returned to Detroit, Tony was driving a Porsche 356A plain-bearing Carrera coupe. He specified a black car with black interior, a rare combination that had the Porsche salesmen questioning his choice.

In 1957, Lapine recalled, 'We were getting into the Corvette SS era and Bill Mitchell was even hotter than Earl on cars like that. Bill would come down and tell a bunch of us what he had in mind, so it was a sunny, beautiful time – like working on the king's new clothes. Bill obviously thought a couple of us were the kind who might do a sports car the right way for him, so we tried to do our own thing and still please him. I think it came out a pretty nice cocktail.' Here he referred to the one-off 1959 Sting Ray sports-racing car based on the Corvette SS chassis.

In the meantime one of GM's star studio chiefs, Clare MacKichan, had been sent to Rüsselsheim to build up the strength of Opel's styling activity. To improve involvement with engineering – which looked down on styling – he had the idea of building a concept sports car. This became the handsome Opel GT, for which the engineers did the chassis and styling the chiselled body shape.

Bill Mitchell decided to bolster MacKichan's engineering assets, as Lapine recalled: 'One day Bill Mitchell says, "Hey kid" – I was 40 by that time – "Hey kid, why don't you go over there too and help Mac MacKichan?" It was less a question than a command. 'It wasn't so much that I spoke the language,' Lapine said. 'A lot of people around the styling centre spoke it and some were German nationals, whereas I was Russian-born. I think Bill just figured Opel needed a new kind of car to replace its retirement-car image, something a young European chemical engineer with a blonde wife could picture himself owning.

'Since Mac was in need of a research studio,' Tony recalled, 'I immediately went to work and formed a group which got active on making Opels appear and act a lot more sporty. MacKichan had shown the prototype Opel GT at the 1965 Frankfurt auto show but that car had no chance of getting into production because it derived few of its assemblies from production cars. Bob Lutz and I scratched our heads and finally decided to borrow most of the hardware needed for the underbody from the Opel Kadett. Second-generation Kadetts were winning rallies and Bunkie Knudsen gave the okay to produce the GT.'

I recall an incident from the press days that precede the opening of the Frankfurt show. One of the journalists headed over to the Porsche stand with his hot news. 'You won't believe it,' he said, 'but there's a sports car on the Opel stand.'

'You must be crazy,' he was told. 'That's impossible. Opel doesn't build sports cars!' For Germany's car builders, the idea of challenging the established order was unthinkable.

'Another Opel at that time, the Rekord, was not doing all that well,' Lapine recalled. 'It was competing in the marketplace against BMW sedans, Fords and Fiats. My idea was to do a Rekord that could get out on the race track and beat the 911. It was all a question of power-to-weight ratios and how much rubber you could make available to get that power to the ground. It worked. Our Black Widow beat Group 5 BMW sedans and a fair number of 911S drivers, too.'

With their Rekord painted black with classic oval Opel emblems on its flanks, the Lapine outfit tweaked the paddock establishment by plunking a 'TAXI' sign on its roof. Their Rekord staggered German racers late into the 1968 season. Driven by headstrong Erich Bitter, it breezed past an ex-Penske Camaro at Zolder and outraced the Group 5 BMWs and Porsche 911s at Hockenheim. Called the 'Wonder-Opel' by the press, it gave fair warning that Opel had ideas above its station. It was exactly the mocking of the status quo that Tony Lapine relished.

On a visit to Opel, Tony Lapine took me into his 'secret' styling workshop that was able to design, engineer, build and test advanced sports and racing cars. It was a real 'skunk works' with stylists and engineers working arm in arm next to the shop floor, much like the Chevrolet R&D unit that had built the Monza GT chassis so quickly. They built single-seaters and sports cars using Opel hardware with space frames and monocoques, front- and mid-engined, testing model body shapes in wind tunnels and trying out bare chassis on the track. One of their aims – sadly not realised – was to create an Opel that could be built in enough numbers to create a one-make racing class.

'When Chuck Jordan became head of Opel styling,' Lapine related, 'he figured it would be a good idea if we had friends in the German automobile industry, like the relationship between Bill Mitchell and Rudi Uhlenhaut – which was very good for both GM and DB. Talking about whom to invite, I said I could help out with Dr Porsche. Ferry was delighted to get the invitation because they were deep into the problem of building their Weissach proving ground and Opel's facility at Dudenhofen hadn't been open long.

'Ralph Mason, head of Opel at the time, said, "Bring them right over. Families too." It was a typically American gesture, no complications. The Porsches arrived in two Pontiac station wagons. Butzi had one and so did Ferdinand Piëch. They both came with Dr Porsche and, I think, Peter Porsche. They toured the proving ground and our styling and engineering facilities. And they saw our harmony between engineering and styling. Porsche always realised that styling could be very much engineering-oriented. That side was very dear to Dr Porsche's heart. The next logical thing was to ask me if I would perhaps come down and talk to Dr Ferry. I said yes.'

This led to an invitation to join Porsche, which happened in the autumn of 1969. Lapine brought to Zuffenhausen both a flair for the unconventional and some of the talented young stylists he had come to know at GM and Opel, including future stars Dick Söderberg and Wolfgang Möbius. In fact he recruited some modellers too, with the result that he received a firm 'cease and desist' phone call from Chuck Jordan.

Officially Tony Lapine's first post at Porsche was under studio chief Ferdinand 'Butzi' Porsche, the idea being that he would move up when the oldest Porsche son retired in a few years. 'Butzi had a beautiful studio going with enough modellers and designers. I worked for Butzi at first, but he left after about a year to start his own firm. At the beginning he was my boss and the deputy of his dad. When Dr Porsche hired Professor Fuhrmann to direct the company, the family ceased to actively influence matters at Porsche.'

In Tony Lapine's baggage was as deep an appreciation of and affection for the Porsche traditions as any man in the company. When the centenary of Ferdinand Porsche's birth was celebrated in 1975, the blond, bearded Lapine drove his Porsche to the Professor's birthplace in Maffersdorf, now Vratislavice in the Czech Republic, and brought back to Stuttgart a container of soil from that historic site. Now that is real Porsche enthusiasm.

'When I was invited to the Porsche residence near Salzburg,' Tony recalled, 'it was like a dream, like a Christian going to Bethlehem. They were all there – the Porsches, the Piëchs, Ferry's sister Louise. He wouldn't make any big decision without first talking to Louise.'

Lapine also brought a highly personal style to Porsche's design activities. 'He didn't like tourists,' a colleague recalled. Company officials who sauntered into the studios without invitation were sternly told to clear out and to come back to see completed proposals when they were ready. For liaison with the technical departments he relied on his highly competent and powerful studio engineers – a cadre that he was the first design chief to recruit. From engineering, design chief Wolfgang Eyb would come in to negotiate the tough points with Tony and his team. From time to time company head Ernst Fuhrmann and later Peter Schutz would visit with Ferry Porsche to see new concepts.

Tony Lapine had two watchwords for his men. One was, 'If the engineers come in and they like it, you have to start again.' The other was, 'If marketing comes in and says something, ignore it.' The drawing-board designers were kept on their toes by the studio's chief modeller, Peter Reisinger, another refugee from Opel. An acerbic and observant Austrian, Reisinger 'would make a sarcastic remark that would lead to a change in the shape,' a designer recalled. 'A big part of the team, he would tell the guys what to do.'

Creative stress was a characteristic of Porsche design under Lapine, recalled Stephen Ferrada: 'His style was to set designers against each other, a classic way of keeping the upper hand. This raised the tension in the studio. Lapine would not remain neutral. He would get angry over a design he didn't like, swearing about it. The successful design was praised highly. One day champagne, the next day the complete opposite – tears and shouting.'

'Lapine was charisma personified,' said designer Dawson Sellar. 'He could be charming and infuriating. We had many disagreements but there was always mutual respect. He did little hands-on design work, spending nearly all his time in his office working on his project cars – much to the incredulity and bemusement of the rest of the company, including Dr Fuhrmann. He always said he had such a brilliant team it was best to leave them alone to get on with it, only stepping out into the studio to resolve disputes.'

On one of my visits to Weissach, Tony took me into his office's small side studio in which – of all things – stood an MG TC. But what a TC! It had new aluminium body panels, a reinforced frame and an A-bracket locating its front axle. Its drive train was a two-litre twin-cam Fiat with five-speed gearbox driving an Alfa Romeo rear axle. Its pedals and titanium steering rack were recycled 917 parts. The mighty MG was a typical Lapine snook cocked at the establishment, built to outrage.

Similar motivation lay behind Lapine's acquisition of a Chevrolet-powered sprint car built by Wally Meskowski. Titivated with a new nosepiece and bespoke livery, the sprinter was just the thing to upset the purists at the

Nürburgring's August vintage race meetings, where Lapine would blow off their expensive British and Italian classic machinery. Later, Tony acquired and raced a Mark 1 Lola, Eric Broadley's classic design.

Designer Ferrada noted Tony Lapine's affinity with Austrian engineer Ernst Fuhrmann, who ran the company during most of the 1970s. 'He was close to Fuhrmann,' Ferrada related. 'We would visit his office for celebrations, birthdays and the like.' Fuhrmann in turn appreciated Lapine's eagerness to make advancements and adventurous excursions. 'I prefer people who want to run ahead,' he told me, 'and whom I only have to guide and control.' Lapine was an obvious example.

'When I first arrived, the 914 had just been introduced,' Lapine recalled. 'To be honest, that was the only Porsche I never really loved. People back at Opel even thought its shape was some sort of really ingenious prototype camouflage until they saw the finished car at the Frankfurt Show. But the 914 was a good three-seater so, quite naturally, there was much thought about another mid-engined car with more cylinders and three seats, with perhaps tremendous horsepower like the Professor would have loved.

'At the same time Porsche was very busy on a sedan for VW with its engine under the rear seat.' This was the EA1966 project to create a definitive replacement for the Beetle. 'Our first job,' said Tony, 'was to make a higher seat position look good. We came up with some graphic proposals for this sedan, under real time pressure. It was a very important job because it would help decide which pieces we might get for our new small Porsche to go with a powerful model.

'We were active in keeping the 911 alive,' Lapine stated. 'That decision was forced upon Fuhrmann when Volkswagen decided in 1971 not to build the EA1966 that Porsche had designed for it. From that car we planned to take all the pieces to make the 911's replacement. That went up in smoke. In order to get distance between that and the new car we had to have another five or six years of 911 building. So the 911 began to get raced seriously again. The Turbo was introduced and paint jobs had to be done and whale tails, wheels, wheel arches and bumpers had to be designed.

'More people came by and felt sorry for us having to deface the 911 with bumpers,' Lapine related. 'The 911 had a very dainty little bumper, a pretty thing. But we knew what was coming with the American safety requirements. Later more people were telling us that the new ones look so much better. So maybe we did a good job there. Then we had a handful of 914 modifications to do, on a small slate.

'In the meantime, the 924 and 928 were in progress,' Tony added. 'The so-called soft line of our 928 was done because it would live longer than the folded-paper school of design. The cardinal difference at Porsche, the thing which makes us unique, is that we have to do a car for a minimum of 15 years ahead. And also because of Porsche tradition.' This was a reference to the work of Erwin Komenda, who created the Porsche look that has guided many later designers.

'The soft line is more entertaining because it is a more complex way of handling surfaces,' Lapine explained. 'After a buyer has owned a "soft" car for maybe three years they will discover some corner or play of light they haven't seen before. And they'll think, "Son of a gun, now I know why I liked the car." The line's trickier to handle, of course, and it takes a little longer to iron out a surface until it undulates and flows into another surface.'

Although in his General Motors years he worked under the mercurial Bill Mitchell, who had no compunctions about adding 'visual gimmicks' where he felt they were needed, with only a nod toward their possible functionality, Tony Lapine as editor of Wolfgang Möbius's work was entirely comfortable with taking a diametrically opposite approach with the 928.

'I could not go up to Dr Porsche or Professor Fuhrmann and talk "designer lingo" to them like at GM Styling,' said Lapine. 'There should be a dominance of logic. You'd better come up with very sound, well-founded arguments. Especially at Porsche where there are 43 designers surrounded by 2,000 engineers.' Making ultimate judgements, he added, 'You had a living legend presiding at a meeting. If you wanted to know what a Porsche was all about, you could ask the source.'

Porsche's engineers were delighted with the look of the 928, recalled Stephen Ferrada, then a Weissach designer. In its very simplicity, its lack of visual pretension, it highlighted the $80 million investment that the engineers had made in its technology. To put it another way, the 928's engineering was not upstaged by its styling.

'This was also the time of the 917,' the designer added. 'I got here almost the same day those 25 917s were being photographed in a row during homologation. Traditionally we can do anything as long as we don't goof up what the racing people delivered to us. Some body configuration is decided upon based on past successes, and then we get a whack at it, which can be a very uncomfortable situation in the sense that you can't practice. It's sort of like starting a revolution – you have to do it right the first time.

'But we do get into the wind-tunnel side of things,' he added. 'It's not just graphics. We work on spoilers and wings, all the things that make it faster and prettier – but never worse. We do graphics too, of course, because Count Rossi likes to see his colours in some fresh, new fashion. We still manage to surprise him every time.

'The Pink Pig came from us too,' Tony said with some pride. 'Everybody participated in the short 917 of 1971: engineering, our bunch and the Paris wind-tunnel people who had a pipeline to the man who says what is legal at Le Mans. Ours had the lowest drag and the most downforce, plus the car looked spectacular. But it seemed maybe more judicious to use the French shape and let us paint it for them.

'The year before, we had that psychedelic green and purple car, so every-body wanted to see what we would do next. Maybe we went a little too far, since some people thought it wasn't quite "Porsche," although the French had a good laugh and a lot of pictures were taken. Have you ever seen a pig doing 200 mph down Mulsanne Straight?' With the passage of time, the Pink Pig has become a respected classic among Porsche's racing cars.

Late in the 1970s, when the initial work on the 924 and 928 was complete, Butzi Porsche might have wondered why business fell off for his new Porsche Design studio at Zell am See. When phone calls were put through to the Porsche styling office by people who thought they were reaching Butzi's Austrian operation, Tony Lapine would say, 'Yes, this is it!' If any business was going, Lapine wanted it to make use of his spare capacity. Major contracts with Airbus and Linde forklifts resulted.

Tony Lapine carried on through the Peter Schutz years of the 1980s, restyling the 911 one more time and advancing the art of the front-engined Porsches. He worked at the Stuttgart company from 1969 until the autumn of 1988, when he gave way to Harm Lagaay. 'Nothing has changed,' his boss told him at the time, 'except you don't come to work.' One couldn't ask for a better arrangement.

Lapine retired to the German spa city of Baden Baden, where I inter-viewed my friend one last time in 1999. He died on 2 May 2012. He had a great life of his own definition.

An MIT-trained engineer and a great car enthusiast, Stefan Habsburg contributed substantially to the design of the spectacular Firebird III whose model sat before him.

Designers

STEFAN HABSBURG

With the passing of Stefan Habsburg in November of 1998 the motor industry lost one of its most creative and productive participants and – equally important – one of its most charismatic personalities. Habsburg's deep personal knowledge of cars and their design came through clearly in the talks and presentations he gave in his role as director of educational relations at GM's Design Staff, his final responsibility after a lifelong career at GM, before his retirement in 1987.

Born on 15 August 1932 in Mödling, Lower Austria, Stefan was the eldest child of Archduke Anton of Austria and his beautiful wife Princess Ileana, the youngest daughter of King Ferdinand I of Romania and a great granddaughter of Britain's Queen Victoria. As a member of the House of Habsburg, the youngster was an Archduke and Prince of Tuscany by birth. Although baptised as Stefan von Habsburg-Lothringen, he adopted the simpler 'Stefan Habsburg' in his personal and professional life.

Stefan spent the early years of his childhood in Castle Sonnberg, Austria, which his father acquired in 1934. In the far north-east of modern Austria, the castle gained a landing field thanks to Anton's passion for aviation. In 1942, with Sonnberg functioning as a military hospital, Stefan moved with his parents and four sisters and brother to Romania.

At the beginning of 1948, Stefan's first cousin, Michael of Romania, was given five days to pack and leave the country, lest he and his family face trials and execution. Forced to abdicate and expelled by the Communist regime late in 1947, the family left the country.

'Any item of value was considered state property,' wrote Stefan of this crisis. 'Bank accounts were frozen and telephones disconnected. Mama had some jewellery in a simple drawer in her room. When there was a moment of inattention from the guards, she wrapped a beautiful diamond tiara in a nightgown and I helped her sneak it into a suitcase that had already been inspected.

'We travelled to Switzerland and then Argentina,' added Stefan. 'Three years later Mama and her children arrived the USA while Papa returned to

Austria. Eventually they divorced. Mama sold her tiara in New York to buy a house in Newton, Massachusetts and clothing for her children. She bought furniture at a used furniture store and pots and pans at the local 5 and 10 cent store. She also bought a cookbook. She had to find a way to clothe, feed and educate six growing children and realised that she had to start earning an income.

'She began to give lectures about her experiences. She started writing a book which would be called *I Live Again* and two years later one called *Hospital of the Queen's Heart*. She managed to place each of us children in boarding schools so that travelling to her lectures was possible. As each of her children grew, Mama felt less and less pressure to support them and more and more the need to return to some form of community service.

'The year 1959 must have been terrible for her,' Habsburg related. 'Her oldest daughter Minola was pregnant and traveling with her husband Rusch to South America. The airliner missed the runway in Rio and all aboard were killed. Her oldest son, yours truly, suffered a nearly fatal attack of viral encephalitis and emerged from it with serious brain damage. For six months Mama let me, my wife Jerrine and our three little children stay with her in Newton. After we returned to Detroit, Mama sold her house and moved to France where her bishop had sent her as a postulant to the Orthodox mon-astery at Bussy-en-Othe. She became a fully professed Orthodox nun, her name becoming Mother Alexandra. She was eventually sent to America by her bishop to help start an Orthodox monastery for women.'

This extraordinary woman, with energy beyond her years, lived until 1991, leaving the living Monastery that she brought into being with the total commitment that characterised her life. She put Stefan through Malvern Preparatory School in Pennsylvania and saw him matriculate in mechanical engineering at Boston's MIT. At a dance he met tall and gorgeous Mary Jerrine Soper, a student at the Massachusetts School of Art. They married in 1954 and ultimately had five children. 'We didn't really plan it,' Stefan told me, 'but we wanted to see what the next one would be like.'

In 1954, Habsburg began his final year at MIT, initially living in the Num-ber 6 Club, the name of the MIT branch of fraternity Delta Psi. I arrived at Number 6 in the autumn of 1952, also studying mechanical engineering. Encouraged by Stefan, in my second year I took a course in Creative Engi-neering created by Prof. John Arnold, that he had greatly enjoyed. I too

Designers

found it stimulating, so much so that at Arnold's recommendation I left MIT to study Industrial Design at Brooklyn, New York's Pratt Institute.

At Number 6, Stefan and I hit it off from the start, sharing an enthusiasm for automobiles and industrial design. Tall, bespectacled and deep-voiced, with a thick head of dark hair, he was a serious presence with a sharp sense of humour. Still courting Jerrie, as she was known, he had a Morris Minor, then a VW Beetle and later a Mercedes-Benz 180 saloon; the company's first modern unit-body automobile. I took advantage of Stefan's Spanish to get Juan Manuel Fangio's autograph when the great driver came to Thompson Raceway to demonstrate a new Maserati sportsracer.

Joining General Motors in 1955, MIT graduate Stefan Habsburg was one of a cadre of engineers whom Harley Earl was then hiring to strengthen the technical capabilities of his Styling Staff. For Habsburg, this was a personal mission, as he later wrote: 'Although my degree is in engineering, I have been accepted into employment as a designer. I believe in the importance of good aesthetic design and functional validity being combined in the initial thinking to make a really novel and functionally valid product. Having read article after article in both foreign and American journals, that the stylists in America don't know a thing about engineering, and the engineers have limited imagination in making the stylists' excesses into high-quality running vehicles, I hope to participate in changing that by going to work as a designer rather than an engineer.'

In the Research Studio headed by brilliant Firebird I designer Robert McLean, one of his first projects was the never-built XP-53 intended to be Le Sabre II, a front-drive prototype with a toroidal CVT and a rear wing that also acted as an air brake. A project on which he and I worked on together in the summer of 1956, this was a warm-up exercise for the important efforts in which Habsburg played a major role: the creation of the turbine-powered Firebird II and Firebird III concept cars. As assistant chief designer of the Research Studio he contributed to many of their design elements including the principles of their automatic lane-following systems, a technology that only now is incorporated in some automobiles.

Habsburg was engaged in some of the first serious aerodynamic studies conducted at Styling Staff, including early efforts to develop aerodynamic downforce. A key contribution by Stefan was the vehicle architecture, with wide-spaced frame rails, that led to Pontiac's adoption of the 'Wide-Track' look as mentioned by Chuck Jordan. This transformed the fortunes of the Division. Pontiac promoted it well but Habsburg's was the concept that created the look.

As mentioned earlier, a serious setback to Stefan Habsburg's career that almost cost him his life was his contraction of viral encephalitis in 1959. I visited him in hospital soon after he was out of the illness's mortal phase. He seemed the same jovial Stefan of old as we settled down to talk. But after a quarter-hour he began to repeat the same questions as before: where was I living, what was I doing – matters we had already discussed. He remembered me from the past as well as his wife Jerrie, although he didn't recall their marriage or children.

Habsburg had lost four to five years of recent memory. Nor was his current short-term memory up to scratch. He affixed a prominent pennant to the radio aerial of his Corvair so he could find it in the parking lot. A road map on the sun visor helped Stefan find his way to work and home again. He often had to endure the poking and prying of neural-system experts because, they told him, it was extremely unusual for a person to recover from the virus that felled him.

Although his loss of retentive memory in no way degraded Stefan's spirit and creativity, it introduced severe practical problems in his daily life. Typically he overcame this with the help of his friends and family to earn a Masters Degree in Business from Wayne State University in 1972. He made a case to GM Design that his contributions would be enhanced by an assistant who could backstop him but this practical suggestion was not implemented.

Habsburg continued to make important contributions to the work of GM Design. 'I worked on the very first computer graphics terminal in General Motors,' he recalled, 'which was in the basement at GM Research.' He became active in GM Design's pioneering ergonomics studies as well. His transition to educational relations came, he said, 'because I started giving lectures at colleges on the Firebird III.'

Design Staff was the right environment for Stefan Habsburg: 'I've always liked to draw and sketch and I love cars,' he said. 'I wanted to work in this building, not where they make engines and transmissions.' His stimulating influence came to be felt throughout GM and the many institutions that nurtured its best people.

Designers

To illustrate the Habsburg state of mind, I am appending here his own story of an unusual adventure that he called 'Project VW'. It took place more than ten years after his battle with the virus.

Ken Pickering returned to us in 1968, a year of change. A bright young man who started at Styling Staff as an engineer then left on a company-sponsored MBA programme, Ken worked several years successfully in Pontiac Division's advance planning department. Bill Mitchell put him in charge of a small engineering planning activity. I made a point of going to his office to welcome him and offer my services.

Ken was cheerful and friendly and told me that he appreciated my offer to help. He promised to involve me at the first opportunity, after he got his immediate office work in order. He knew my 'Creative Attitude' work. I looked forward to the possibility of making some kind of contribution to the 'real' world.

In October of 1968 the first opportunity came. Ken invited me to participate in a 'think session'. Design chief Bill Mitchell, who hated Volkswagens with a passion, had asked Ken to come up with an explanation of how something as 'dumb looking' as that 1936-design 'Beetle' could have such a sales success in America. He also wanted some idea of what direction VW might take in the coming years. He felt that the Beetle looked 'like a frog that swallowed a box.' Could Ken provide some insight into what foreign competition might do in the future? As usual I made a quick courtesy visit to our resident engineering guru, Peter Kyropoulos, to tell him of the invitation. He smiled and said 'Go to it, young man!'

Ken and three other people from his department formed a task force to look into the problem. We studied the recent marketing figures, ran some quick local surveys and held regular meetings to review what we had found. Then came the part I especially enjoyed: venturing speculation about the future. I was put in charge of that aspect. I decided to approach the problem by imagining myself in the role of heading an advanced research design studio at VW, preparing a car for the American and world market.

My associates liked what I had to say so much that they decided to use my approach in the presentation of our work to Mitchell, which took place in late November. We knew that Mitchell had a very short fuse so it was virtually impossible to get him to sit still for more than ten minutes for any presentation, yet we felt that we had more to say than that.

Ken told Mitchell that he was ready to present his findings but he added a couple of special requests. First of all he requested an hour and a half of his time. Second, he wanted to have Mitchell completely alone without his usual retinue of assistants, executives, department heads and staff men. To meet these two rather stringent conditions we were willing to set our presentation to whatever date he chose.

Mitchell got a kick out of our conditions and we scheduled a date and time of day. We told him that we wanted to 'take him away' from the usual pressures of the building and had, therefore, prepared to present our report in Design's auditorium conference room. Mitchell's chauffeur drove him to the auditorium.

When he arrived, alone as promised, Ken welcomed him at the door and accompanied him into the auditorium. There, sitting like a little mushroom in a vast meadow on the huge grey and circular auditorium floor, stood a bright white VW Beetle illuminated by a single overhead spotlight. Ken guided Mitchell past the car – which represented the antithesis of every idea of design Mitchell stood for – and into a small wood-panelled executive conference room.

Three of us were sitting at one side of the table with nameplates in front of us. We stood for his entry. A nameplate was located prominently where we wanted Mitchell to sit. When he sat down, we did as well. There was a big blue and white GM insignia on the front of the lectern. Ken introduced the session by reminding Mitchell that some months ago he had asked for some facts on where VW gets its market appeal. 'To do this adequately,' Ken continued, 'we thought it would be best if you could put yourself in the role of VW management looking at America. Rather than take the American view, we thought it would be interesting to look at the problem as though you were a director of VW to whom we are reporting. Would that be acceptable to you?'

Mitchell responded, 'Sure, why not, that's not what I expected...but go ahead.' Ken flipped over the big GM insignia on the lectern. Under it there was an equally clear circle with the VW trademark. He reached over to Mitchell's nameplate and flipped it to show in elegant German script 'Herr Wilhelm Mitchell'. Each of us flipped our plates and also revealed German-ic-looking writing with VW insignias. Bill loved the charade. He broke into a big grin and settled down to some serious listening.

Designers

There was no question that we had his attention! Ken now proceeded to introduce the roles that each of us would play and outlined our general findings. The VW buyers were often repeat owners. They had higher incomes than many of the GM mid-size car buyers. They tended to be well educated and had small families by choice. One of us, Bob Bierley, explained that we had found that the VW was perceived not so much as a car (i.e. a status symbol) but more as an appliance. One of the most interesting findings was that among the actual buyers, no GM products were even considered as substitutes. Only other foreign cars of similar characteristics (reliable, efficient, with good resale value) were mentioned as alternate choices.

Ken then introduced me as director of design research to talk about the next generation of product. I continued along the parameters defined by Bob. I forecasted a small, efficient car powered by an overhead-valve – possibly overhead-cam – gasoline or diesel engine. I stated that the engine would be small and placed between the front wheels – a drastic change from the current product. I recommended that we include a low cost air-conditioner as standard equipment and above all make sure that the car had superior serviceability.

To hold the American market 'we' needed to maintain top-notch dealer service with adequate spare parts and expert repairs. I also showed some material samples which displayed high-durability finishes, rustproof construction and integrally coloured elastomeric bumpers. I ended my talk by saying 'We intend to build the best quality, most reliable, transportation appliance in the world and continue to expand our markets on all the continents of this earth!'

Mitchell listened to us without interruption for the entire hour and a half. He was clearly very pleased. He was relaxed and talked to us for quite a while. He told us that we had opened his eyes to several facts and ideas. He was so pleased with both the content and the way we presented it that he wanted us to put on precisely the same act for his two top executives Irv Rybicki and Clare MacKichan. He said he wished Jordan could also hear it and that we should have our materials ready for Chuck Jordan's next trip to the US.

We did the presentation for Rybicki and MacKichan a few days later. Their reaction was one of similar enthusiasm. There was little doubt that we had not only caught our management's attention but had also made them see a totally new picture in a rapidly changing world. As asked, we also presented the same material to Chuck Jordan when he returned from Europe in January.

For me personally, this was another benchmark of achievement. I had actually made a product presentation directly to the Design vice president. I had in fact told him and his two top executives what I thought the 'world car' should be like. [KEL note: It was remarkably like the VW Golf which would be introduced some five years in the future.]

When I headed home for my usual extended Christmas vacation with my family I felt, for the first time, that I had actually accomplished something along the lines of what I had followed at the beginning of my career, in what seemed like a lifetime ago: I had managed to contribute some fresh thought to the automobile business. Although I was far from being in the mainstream of design activity, neither was I buried in the basement of GM Research trying to structure a computer program in a language whose essential words I could not recall. I had presented some of my thinking to the top management level of Design Staff and it had been well received.

ENGINEERS

Silver-haired Alex von Falkenhausen showed one of his BMW engines to a visiting group of American journalists including Bob Fendell, left, and the author behind him.

Engineers

ALEX VON FALKENHAUSEN

How much influence can one man have on the character of an automobile company? If it's a small one, like Lotus, a Colin Chapman can make a difference. Or a Ferrari at Ferrari. But a big car producer like BMW? In this case the answer is that one man could and did have a profound effect on the company and the cars that it still produces. BMW's 'Engine Pope' Alex von Falkenhausen had the genius and foresight to give BMW's managers the engines they didn't know they wanted and needed.

Von Falkenhausen faced his first big test as a creator of engines for BMW at the end of the 1950s. The company's most popular cars were small rear-engined models, descendants of the Isetta bubble car, with two-cylinder air-cooled engines derived from the company's motorcycles. BMW's directors wanted to upgrade them with water-cooled fours but they were wary of going too large because they feared that would put them in conflict with other German car makers. 'The directors wanted a 1,300 cc,' von Falkenhausen recalled. 'Others like Borgward and Opel had 1,500s so it took much work and persuasion to get them to accept a 1,500.'

The size of the new engine was one thing but its design was another. 'Then many cars had pushrods and three-bearing crankshafts,' the engineer recalled, 'but I knew we must have something more. Alfa Romeo had already made many five-bearing engines with two overhead camshafts, so I fought for a BMW 1500 that had an overhead camshaft and five bearings for the crankshaft. We made the block very, very stiff.'

When BMW decided to build an all-new front-engined sedan at the beginning of the 1960s, its executives were still thinking small. As far as they were concerned 1,500 cc was the upper limit for their new sedan. Von Falkenhausen could see into the future, however. 'I thought we needed to have a good two-litre to ensure a good market for the car,' he reasoned.

'So first they agreed to build a 1,500 and I designed it so it could easily be made an 1,800 and then, with a new casting technique, a two-litre. It was only a year before they wanted a 1,600, then another year before asking for an 1,800.'

His ability to anticipate the future was a talent that Alex von Falkenhausen regularly exercised. He was accustomed to having board members approach him with their engine requirements for a future model, one for years ahead, only to be informed, 'It's ready now.' This, said the engineer, was the result of his ability 'to have an idea about what'll be needed a few years down the road.'

Famously, von Falkenhausen's four became the heart of the 'New Class' of BMWs introduced in 1962, the car on which the company's modern fortunes are founded. It was the first BMW power unit in production to have its vee-inclined valves offset longitudinally, instead of directly across from each other, so they could be opened by straight rocker arms from a single central camshaft. This contributed a rugged and durable valve gear that tolerated high revs.

Alex von Falkenhausen's choice of five main bearings and a counter-weighted crankshaft for his four was another decision that he defended in order to secure his engine's future. He knew these would not only set BMW apart from its rivals but also produce an engine that could be used in racing as well as on the road. 'I thought the block was good for 200, even 300 horsepower,' he told Chris Willows, 'but I never thought it would take 1,000 horsepower!' That's just what it did take – 1,200 horsepower in fact – in the turbocharged engine that powered Nelson Piquet's Formula One Brabham to the world driver's title in 1983.

Thinking ahead as usual, Alex von Falkenhausen extrapolated his four into an in-line six in 1968. By then its combustion chamber was exploiting its offset valves with a new 'triple-hemi-swirl' combustion chamber that was the work of von Falkenhausen's colleague Karl Rech. The cost-saving modularity achieved between four and six was a goal toward which Rech had also striven.

Creation of the six, said von Falkenhausen, was 'the most satisfying' of his achievements at BMW. 'This six was smoother than any other and still is,' he said in 1990. He was understandably proud of an anecdote that came back from a meeting between the directors of Daimler-Benz and BMW. 'You have a good car but we have a better car,' the Daimler men said. 'The only thing you do better is the engine.' The modest engineer admitted: 'From this moment on I was very popular.'

Alex von Falkenhausen's drive to keep BMW at the forefront of engine design was the result of his intensely competitive character. His competitiveness was the backbone that allowed him to press his directors for the best engineering solutions. This wasn't always easy. In the 1950s, he recalled, 'I had five designers and one engineer for the test bed. The production people said I could go ahead on new engine work but they said there must be no expense!'

This parsimony was a symptom of BMW's brush with bankruptcy in 1959. Its survival against heavy odds motivated the company's leaders to do much with little, a philosophy that soon spelled profitability. In this environment Alex von Falkenhausen flourished, for no other engineer in BMW had done as much with as little as he had in the years just after the war.

In World War II the name 'Alexander von Falkenhausen' meant not this engineer but a general of the infantry who was commander of forces in Belgium and northern France through most of the war. Described as 'a correct, chivalrous officer who disliked Nazi extremism and the methods of the SS,' he was granted clemency following his conviction in Belgium after the war. The family name meant 'falcon's house' or 'falcon's lair'.

With roots in the same noble Prussian family, our man's father was Wilhelm von Falkenhausen, a captain who died in World War I. He left behind two sons, including Baron Alexander Heinrich Ludwig Richard von Falkenhausen, born in Munich on 22 May, 1907. Brought up in Schwabing, Munich's artistic and Bohemian quarter, he had a relaxed Bavarian upbringing that was the diametric opposite of the strict Prussian code of many of his relations. Nevertheless, he would be esteemed for his distinguished bearing and correctness of thought and deed.

Fascinated by engines, Alex von Falkenhausen was riding a DKW 125 motorcycle at the age of 17. While studying for his degree in vehicle and aircraft engineering at Munich's technical institute, he rebuilt a 175 cc Villiers-powered motorcycle on his own lines, giving it the name 'ALFA' for 'Alex' and 'Falkenhausen'. In 1932, riding a British 500 cc Calthorpe, von Falkenhausen began enjoying success in races and trials. The tall, gangling rider was noticed by his home-town motorcycle producer, BMW, for whom he soon began competing. Gold medals came his way in the six-day trials of 1934, 1935 and 1937. 'I think I was the first man in Germany who did that much trial riding,' he reflected later.

Logically enough, the 1930 engineering graduate was hired by BMW. He was put to work in the motorcycle chassis department under Rudolf Schleicher, who was in overall charge of BMW development and testing, and Hans Riedel, responsible for two-wheeler design. In 1935 Schleicher introduced telescopic front forks on his latest motorcycles but was abashed when Adolf Hitler visited the BMW motor-show stand and asked, 'And when are we going to get rear suspension?' Long a feature of British bikes, this refinement hadn't yet reached Munich.

Confronting his staff with this requirement, Schleicher received a novel suggestion from young von Falkenhausen. As usual he'd been thinking ahead. He suggested sliding pillars at the rear which had the merit of maintaining frame rigidity. Tried out successfully in racing BMWs, they were introduced on production models in 1938.

Meanwhile Fritz Fiedler's cadre of BMW passenger-car engineers moved from Eisenach to Munich, bringing with them their work on the 328, the new 2.0-litre sports car that was the class of its field. Alex von Falkenhausen had already moved to cars, in 1934 acquiring one of the factory's Type 315/1 sports cars that had made a great impression in the Alpine Trials. In 1936 he upgraded to a 319/1 and in 1939 acquired his dream car, a Type 328.

'That was the real thing,' von Falkenhausen said of the 328, 'In relation to other cars of the period it had much better roadholding. It was very light and had a powerful engine with high torque.' He entered races with it and also rallies, in which he was partnered by his wife, the former Countess Katharina von der Mühle-Eckart, whose brother was an enthusiastic sporting motorist. Two years younger, Kitty, as she was known, was an enthusiastic and able navigator as well as – in due course – mother to their three daughters. They took a flat on Munich's Rappstrasse.

During the war Alexander turned to many tasks, including the adaptation to Panther tanks of a nine-cylinder BMW radial aeroplane engine and testing of an in-line six for field power whose cylinder head was air-cooled and cylinders oil-cooled. In 1942 BMW's engineers moved for safety to a castle at Berg on Lake Starnberg.

Alexander von Falkenhausen's most important job was design and testing of the 750 cc R75 motorcycle and sidecar. In the turmoil of the end of the war, von Falkenhausen boarded his experimental R75 and headed north toward the Danube and Regensburg, near which his wife and children were staying with her parents. After greeting them, his first action was to head for one of the farm buildings, where 'under junk, old horse blankets, halters, coachman's items and rusty ploughs' was his BMW 328. It stood on blocks because he'd greased its wheels and sprinkled talcum powder on its tyres before burying them in the estate's rose garden. 'The Americans were terrifically keen on these cars,' the engineer recalled, 'but without the wheels there wasn't much they could do.'

His precious 328 was the key to the post-war survival of Alexander von Falkenhausen. It meant that he could take part in the reawakening of racing in Germany. However, like other motor sportsmen he faced severe difficulties in the ruins of the defeated nation, governed as it was by the occupying victors. Fuel was in such short supply that even getting to a race, let alone practising, was extremely difficult.

The resourceful von Falkenhausen cadged extra fuel from the occupiers in exchange for schnapps until he had the help of a friend who gained access to a chemical works near Munich that still had supplies of alcohol and octane-improving tetra-ethyl lead and facilities for fuel production. 'With a little money,' said the engineer, 'I could prepare alcohol-based fuels.' These were what he wanted in any case for his engine with its 11.3:1 compression ratio. He fed it a blend of gasoline, benzol and alcohol in one-third proportions.

The occupiers frowned on motor sport, seeing it as a waste of scarce fuel. But for 21 July, 1946 a hill climb was approved at Ruhestein in the French-occupied Black Forest, the first sporting event in Germany after the war. The favourite was pre-war star Hermann Lang driving a Mille Miglia BMW coupe, but for Lang 'my most dangerous opponent' was von Falkenhausen, who 'had his open BMW correctly geared and, as usual, in first-class trim. He had to be taken seriously.'

While victory went to Lang, von Falkenhausen was runner-up at Ruhestein. He was the star of Germany's first races, held on a triangle of unused autobahn near Karlsruhe on 29 September. He was the winner of both the sports-car and racing-car events, in the latter chasing a supercharged 3.0-

litre Alfa Romeo until it faded. With the use of cars and buses banned, more than 50,000 spectators reached the races by train, bicycle and foot.

Thus 1946 was a considerable success for Alex von Falkenhausen. Encouraged, he stepped up his preparations for 1947. Seeing opportunity in the 1,500 cc class and exploiting a project he had worked on before the war, the Baron built a special short-stroke engine with a 328 head on a 319/1 cylinder block. In a 66 mm bore, its stroke was 72 mm instead of the usual 96 mm. This allowed the 1.5-litre six to rev to 7,000 and produce just over 100 bhp, exceptional for the time.

Our hero decided that the best course open to him was to become a car constructor. Although von Falkenhausen set up shop at his in-laws, he honoured the city of his birth with the name of his new productions: AFM, standing for Alexander von Falkenhausen – Munich. His first vehicle, readied during 1947, married the front frame of a 328 with the torsion-bar rear suspension of a 326.

The combination, akin to the frames of Frazer Nash's in England, proved brilliant. Made by former BMW man Willi Huber, the first AFM's narrow body of Duraluminium from a BMW hoard had cycle fenders which allowed it to compete either as a sports car or as a racing car in the new 2.0-litre Formula Two, tailor-made to German enthusiasts using BMW engines.

In the big races of 1947, in May on the fast Hockenheim Ring and in August in Hamburg's city park, Alex von Falkenhausen took the 1,500 cc sports-car class honours with his special engine in his BMW 328. In 1948 he repeated this achievement as Germany's 1.5-litre class champion using the short-stroke engine in the first of his AFMs. Von Falkenhausen's style at the wheel, said a report from Hamburg, showed 'elegance and confidence'.

For the 1949 season von Falkenhausen built his first AFM single-seater racing car. Acknowledging that against the likes of Ferrari and Maserati he would lack power, he reasoned that his car had to be as light as possible. This led him to base its chassis on one of the first true space frames, a welded network of 30 mm steel tubes 1 mm thick. The rear suspension was de Dion with step-down gearing in front of the frame-mounted differential so the driver could sit lower. Completely new were magnesium wheels with integral brake drums, eventually also with magnesium brake shoes at the front.

With its handsome body by Willi Huber, the result was a car weighing a scant 687 pounds dry and 755 pounds with fluids added. Its May 1949 debut at Hockenheim was marred by engine trouble, so Alex competed with a normal 328 engine instead of his special unit and still finished less than a second behind a Veritas after half an hour of thrilling racing witnessed by 280,000 fans.

The next race at Munich's airport in June was historic for the arrival on the AFM scene of one of the master drivers, Hans Stuck. Justly famed for his hill-climbing prowess, Stuck had been a pre-war star for Auto Union and since the war had been racing a little Cisitalia single-seater. When Stuck complimented von Falkenhausen on his car's design, the engineer said, 'Would you like to drive it?' Until its crankshaft broke, Stuck turned the fastest practice laps.

'I liked the car,' Stuck said. 'It was wonderful to control and had really incredible roadholding. I ordered another such car from von Falkenhausen, who provided me with his AFM until it was ready.' This order marked a crucial turning point for the Munich-born engineer. It meant a commitment by him to produce cars for customers and to support them at races. He took this important step with the help of his willing subcontractors plus one regular mechanic and another part-time assistant.

Free to race abroad, Stuck gained an entry for the Monza Grand Prix near Milan on 29 May, 1949. His Monza appearance was an electrifying advertisement for von Falkenhausen's engineering. Clocking the same time as Juan Fangio in a Ferrari, Hans Stuck put the German car on the front row of the grid. At the start, the combination of Stuck's reflexes and the AFM's lightness saw them rocket away from the Maseratis and Ferraris, giving the impression that they were standing still. Stuck stayed with the leaders until a broken plug wire forced a pit stop. Finally finishing seventh after 313 miles, the new marque had made its mark.

To meet the demand for his Formula Two car – Alex would build six of his new Type 50 – he simplified its design by adopting the twin-tube frame that was working well in his sports car. It was somewhat heavier than his space frame – the new car tipped the scales at 1,060 pounds – but far easier to build. Moreover, said the engineer, the space frame's high tubes interfered with driving. The Type 50 AFM had cutaway cockpit sides that allowed elbows-out motoring.

The Type 49 space-frame car was still in service on 28 May, 1950, when an entry was again made in the Monza Grand Prix. This time two 31-mile heats decided the field for the 157-mile final. Starting from pole, ahead of such crack racers as Alberto Ascari and Juan Fangio, Hans Stuck scooted off to his usual lead. This time he held it to beat the Ferrari of Ascari. A German car winning in the capital of Italian racing!

In the main race at Monza, Hans Stuck held a steady third until the BMW six's hard-pressed bearings failed at half distance. Nevertheless, the heat victory stood as a signal success for a car from a minuscule German stable against the might of Italy. This was one of only a handful of defeats suffered by Ascari and Ferrari over the entire history of the 2.0-litre Formula Two. Fascinated by the agile AFM, Juan Fangio quizzed Stuck closely about it.

Completing the last of his Type 50 AFMs in 1951, Alex von Falkenhausen was running out of customers for his cars. The Baron continued racing but less actively. He converted his faithful 328 back to road trim and entered it in the 2,000-mile Alpine Rally of 1952. He and his wife Kitty were among the demanding event's 23 finishers from 95 starters. 'Against strong competition from Jaguar, Porsche, Sunbeam-Talbot, Healey and Lancia,' wrote Rainer Simons, 'von Falkenhausen came home the winner of the event overall in addition to winning his class. This was an astonishing success in a tough rally that was anything but an "old-timer" competition. This achievement by both car and driver was one of the most outstanding in the international motor-sporting annals of that era.'

With BMW back on its feet and building its 500-series sixes and V-8s, von Falkenhausen accepted an offer to head up the Munich company's motor-sporting activities. This meant motorcycle racing at the time with BMW winning the sidecar championship in 1954, the beginning of a string of sidecar trophies that stretched to 1971. They were powered by the Baron's development of a new overhead-cam RS flat twin that laid a firm foundation for these future successes.

Alexander contributed to the design of the revised and shortened chassis needed by the two-seater BMW 507 introduced late in 1955. He also personally supervised the testing of their engines to ensure that each developed the required 150 bhp. When the BMW board demanded that their 507 demonstrate a top speed of 220 km/h, better than 136 mph, he blueprinted a test car's V-8 and closed off a section of autobahn north of Munich. Accompanied by a monitoring official, he achieved an official two-way timing of 220.1 km/h.

Engineers

A 507 prepared by von Falkenhausen took Hans Stuck to a hill-climb championship, helped by front disc brakes; the first fitted to a German road car. Stuck also raced versions of the rear-engined flat-twin 700 models, including a space-framed spyder right out of the AFM playbook. For the air-cooled twins, Alexander developed shaft-driven overhead-cam heads, a project in which Austrian engineer Ludwig Apfelbeck assisted. Apfelbeck went on to develop the radial-valve cylinder head that launched BMW into single-seater racing in Formula Two.

By 1957 Alex von Falkenhausen had taken charge of engine development at BMW, the post he held until his retirement in 1975. The early years were a struggle, he said: 'Every six months we had a new management board. Meanwhile, with a few people we had everything ready to go and just had to wait for the green light.' As usual he and his team were anticipating the future needs of BMW, whether or not anyone asked them to.

The Baron's combination of quiet confidence with immense experience gave him unrivalled authority in his discipline at the Milbertshofen factory. He was, wrote BMW historian Horst Mönnich, 'one of the "sovereigns" in development: Alexander von Falkenhausen, aristocratic, inflexible, stubborn, modest, quiet, an engineer who had already made BMW motorcycle history.'

Alex was of course behind the BMW campaign in touring-car racing with the 1800 model starting in 1964. His star driver was the mischievous Austrian, Dieter Quester, who in 1966 became von Falkenhausen's son-in-law. An important technical ally was young engineer Paul Rosche, who joined BMW in the 502/507 V-8 era. Rosche was destined to inherit the Baron's racing-engine mantle at BMW while Karlheinz Lange followed him in production-engine design.

'Alex von Falkenhausen was an excellent, creative engineer who lived his visions,' Rosche recalled. 'His character made you respect him. He was a real gentleman, very calm and a great superior who had a heart for everybody – but merciless concerning his demands. I was particularly impressed by his straightforwardness. And he had courage. I learned a lot from him.'

Rosche recalled that it was around Christmas of 1968 when von Falkenhausen called for the use of a turbocharger on the 2002 'as we won't be able to beat the Porsches in the European Touring Car Championship otherwise.' This led to a burst of turbo activity at BMW which, although necessary, was not really to the Baron's taste. 'I prefer a big engine to a small turbo,' he said. For BMW's road cars this became a guiding philosophy through the 20th century; only in the 21st did turbochargers creep back into BMW's range of gasoline engines.

In retirement von Falkenhausen enjoyed long continental drives and trail-biking sessions. He and Kitty prowled the Adriatic in their motor cruiser, 'BMW-powered, naturally.' The Falcon died on 25 May, 1989, three days after celebrating his 82nd birthday. But his nobly uncompromising spirit lives on inside every BMW.

RUDOLF
UHLENHAUT

In 1969 I photographed Uhlenhaut sitting in his office, in this case the cockpit of the C111 being unveiled at Hockenheim. I was his delighted passenger for a few laps.

A lthough Rudolf Uhlenhaut last worked on a Mercedes-Benz in 1972, the spirit of his skill and perfectionism still accounts for much of the enduring merit and reputation of the cars of the three-pointed star. When Mercedes-Benz of North America wanted to express the technical excellence of its products, it did so with a photo of Uhlenhaut sitting in an armchair. That said a lot about this man's unique contribution.

In September 1972 Uhlenhaut retired from his post as Daimler-Benz director of passenger-car development, a position he'd held since 1959. For the preceding decade he'd headed the company's experimental department. It would be no exaggeration to say that Uhlenhaut's character and personality were decisive in establishing the post-war tradition of product excellence on which the Mercedes-Benz reputation still rests today. In creating both road and racing cars, he worked with outstanding design engineers, as he was the first to admit. But if a car failed to meet his criteria in the metal it would be tested, modified and tested again until it met his exacting standards.

These were wonderful years for Untertürkheim's engineers, as Rudi Uhlenhaut said in 1969: 'In our company, the engineers who develop the car are in a strong position. The future cars are mainly decided upon by the engineers. They are shown to the sales, of course, people but at a stage where development is so advanced that not very much can be changed. Perhaps we are in a favourable position because people seem to be prepared to pay a little more for our cars. It's a very nice atmosphere. And most of our people stay with us a very long time. Of course it's *very* interesting work.'

Nothing was too much trouble for Daimler-Benz engineering in Uhlenhaut's era. He and his colleagues were driven by immense curiosity about the way cars behaved and why they behaved that way. When General Motors brought out its rear-engined Corvair, one of them was immediately shipped to Stuttgart. It fascinated the Mercedes engineers, who modified it to meet their standards. 'We made quite a good car out of it!' Rudi told an astonished group of GM stylists.

Other new cars of technical interest were acquired and evaluated by Rudi Uhlenhaut and his team. One that interested them was a Ford Taunus mounted with one of that company's first V-6 engines. 'It had scarcely arrived,' said engineer Fritz Naumann, 'when the arguments began as to whether the V-6 engine's smooth running was due to the engine or the car. We couldn't reach agreement, so we made a crossover experiment, installing the Ford engine in a Mercedes and the Daimler engine in the Ford!'

Where horsepower was concerned, Rudi Uhlenhaut seldom had enough. 'He wanted torque *and* power,' said engine engineer Kurt Obländer. 'If you made one engine that was good in power, and you made another engine that was good in torque, he would draw the curve between them and say, "*That's* the engine I want to have." He wanted the maximum at all revolutions.'

Engineers

On one crucial occasion Uhlenhaut had to make do with far less power than many thought he needed. In mid-1951 Daimler-Benz and its chairman, Wilhelm Haspel, decided to go racing again. Grand Prix entries would begin with the new Formula One in 1954, but sports cars could be raced sooner. 'We couldn't build a proper sports-racing car since we didn't have the money,' Rudi Uhlenhaut recalled. Haspel, he said, 'left it to the technicians to do something with no help from general management.'

To discuss this, a delegation of racers converged on a conference room in the passenger-car section of the central design office. Racing director Alfred Neubauer and drivers Hermann Lang and Karl Kling explained what they wanted in the way of a racing sports car. Uhlenhaut's response was discouraging: 'We shall have to use components from the production cars; we shall have to use the three-litre engine of the 300, the same front and rear suspension and gearbox – practically the whole train.' At a time when sports-racers were free to use any engine size they wanted, up to the 4.5 litres of Ferrari and Talbot and Cunningham's 5.4 litres, this imposed a handicap that many thought insuperable.

Handicapped or not, the resulting 300SL scored epic victories in 1952 at Le Mans and the Mexican Road Race plus lesser wins at Berne and the Nürburgring. In 1954 it evolved with remarkably little compromise into the production 300SL, the legendary fuel-injected 'Gullwing' that remains the iconic Mercedes-Benz automobile in the 21st century. From unpromising clay, Rudi Uhlenhaut fashioned one of the greatest sports cars of all time.

A fellow Daimler engineer, Josef Müller, paid well-deserved tribute to his colleague's achievement: 'Uhlenhaut triumphed with a rare masterpiece in his 300SL, which, with its original appearance, imprinted itself unforgettably in the history of automobiles and racing.' Although Rudi didn't personally design the 300SL in detail, conceptually it was as much his creation as any car that has sprouted from the brain of a single engineer. It was and is his living memorial.

Although engineering was in Rudi Uhlenhaut's blood, it skipped a generation. His paternal grandfather was the first academically qualified engineer at the famed Krupp ironworks, responsible for the foundry and the pouring of steel in particular. His son chose instead the career of a businessman, working for the Deutsche Bank. Posted to Britain, he met and married a native lass. Rudolf, one of the family's four children, was born at Muswell Hill, on

London's north side, on 15 July, 1906. He attended the Tollington School in nearby Highgate.

With his family resettled in Germany after World War I, Uhlenhaut gained his engineering qualifications from Munich's Technical Institute in 1931. He received an entrée to Daimler-Benz through his parental Deutsche Bank contacts. This was vital, for in the depths of the depression there was no shortage of freshly minted engineers. He was lucky to be taken on as an assistant in the experimental department. 'Experimental was a very small institution in those days,' he recalled. 'You actually did everything then. It was more transparent.'

In 1935 Uhlenhaut was made an experimental engineer in passenger-car development. His assignment was the proving of the new 170V with its cruciform tubular frame and all-independent suspension. Produced from the end of 1935 and launched at the Berlin show early in 1936, the 170V was an unprecedented success for Daimler-Benz with 75,000 built by 1942 and the model serving as the basis for the company's first post-war production.

This was the springboard for Rudi Uhlenhaut's bold leap into the uncharted waters of racing-car engineering. The public face of the Mercedes-Benz team was the rotund Alfred Neubauer, dominating the pit lane with his flags and stopwatches. In 1937, wrote Neubauer, 'a brilliant young man gave our cars a new polish. His name is Uhlenhaut and he's the only designer who knows how to drive a potent Grand Prix car at racing speeds on the track. Nobody can fool this engineer Uhlenhaut. He doesn't have to rely on the verdicts of the drivers. He knows himself what's happening. He learns from his own experience. He introduced a completely new era in racing-car design.'

Designed to meet the demands of Rudi Uhlenhaut and his newly established *Rennabteilung* or Racing Department, the 1937 Grand Prix Mercedes restored the balance against Auto Union and was the car of the season. Successful new cars for 1938-39 bore the imprint of his demands, communicated with precision through his memos and reports and those of his team. When Mercedes-Benz returned to racing in 1952–55, the W196 and 300SLR met Uhlenhaut's standards and were test driven by him personally.

Such was his team's respect for their leader that they'd cheerfully give up much of their holiday to solve a problem for Uhlenhaut. One reason why was revealed when Uhlenhaut came back from his break and read their report on the problem and a means to counter it. 'We showed Uhlenhaut that we'd found the solution,' said engine man Obländer, 'and he was very

Engineers

happy. He wrote on the test report, "500 marks" and said, "Take it to the cashier." And we got the money!'

Money alone couldn't have motivated men who would willingly work all hours for Rudolf Uhlenhaut. Their loyalty stemmed instead from the interest and confidence in their work that he expressed. 'I expect a young engineer to say what he thinks,' he said. 'I like to have his ideas. We want him to speak up. It's not like that in all companies. But in our company, at a meeting, every young engineer can state his opinion.'

Up his own chain of command, Rudolf Uhlenhaut expected his actions and opinions to be respected. He had no false modesty about his skills and views, said close colleague Erich Waxenberger: 'He knew that he was the best man for Mercedes. But he was not a diplomat. He would not always say, "Yes, yes, yes." Therefore some others resented him.'

'Uhlenhaut wasn't much interested in things other than technical,' added Obländer. 'He wasn't good at organising. He always said, "What I can do best is deal with the technical matters. We have to do our technical work as well as we can, for our customers." He didn't worry about fitting in with the higher-ups.'

Rudolf Uhlenhaut's achievements were recognised in his lifetime. He received an award from the president of the German republic and was granted an honorary doctorate of engineering by his alma mater, Munich's Technical University, on 7 December, 1972, soon after his retirement on 30 September. Although his post was filled, Uhlenhaut had no real successor at Daimler-Benz – partly because he'd failed to groom one. It wasn't the kind of task that interested him. 'When he was gone there was a very big hole,' said one of his aides.

Rudolf Uhlenhaut was a giver, not a taker. 'He was unforgettable,' said one colleague. 'He was a very modest man,' said another. 'Uhlenhaut was the best man we ever had,' added a third, 'and he was a very honorable man also.' 'He was really worshipped,' said a co-worker whose career at Daimler, like so many, was nurtured by Uhlenhaut. 'For me he was and always will be the most fascinating automobile engineer I ever met,' testified another of his many acolytes.

Consummately comfortable in his skin, Rudi Uhlenhaut left this world with few regrets. 'I had the feeling that he was never frustrated,' said Kurt Obländer. 'He lived his life!'

JOHN ZACHARY DELOREAN

John DeLorean would fit in many categories but is in the Engineers section because he made technical contributions earning 44 patents, including one for a tennis racquet.

t was too much to hope for. I had nursed the expectation that when John DeLorean died, his obituaries might give the man some credit for what he had achieved as a motor-industry executive. These were largely private achievements in the 1960s and 1970s that went some way, at least, to compensate for his very public defeats in the 1980s. The first newspaper reports I saw provided factual statements about John's death. This seemed promising. But when the *Daily Telegraph* headed its obituary 'Dodgy car manufacturer who relieved successive British governments of £78 million of taxpayers' money', I knew it was cut-down time.

I can understand why the press in Britain had it in for John DeLorean. Their enmity began long before his DeLorean Motor Company failed and John was entrapped by a cocaine sting. Though he established his car factory at Belfast in Northern Ireland, an integral part of the United Kingdom, DeLorean made no effort whatsoever to cultivate the British press. They were kept at arms' length from a project in which they were understandably very interested.

Even worse, DeLorean hired Chuck Bennington as plant manager, who had nothing but disdain for the press. This policy went hand in glove with the decision not to make the DMC-12 automobile available in the UK until well after its launch in America, thus postponing any home-country sales opportunity. So when the DeLorean plant got into trouble, John and his people had no reservoir of press goodwill on which to draw. That reservoir remained bone-dry.

The factory at Dunmurry should never have been closed. As a TV documentary showed, it made a great contribution to the area both in employment and in bridging Belfast's sectarian divide. The same documentary also portrayed the unseemly relish with which the new Conservative government smashed DeLorean's dreams. The release of some export credits could have given the plant a chance to survive but DMC was denied even this small concession.

I believe that British Prime Minister Margaret Thatcher's view of John DeLorean was coloured by her youthful recollections of a free-wheeling Grantham entrepreneur, Denis Kendall. His nascent car-building enterprise, boasting of its creation of Britain's £100 car, crashed in 1946 with debts of almost half a million pounds. Thatcher's father was the mayor of Grantham. He would have been in the midst of the fallout.

In fact a strong effort to keep the Belfast factory open lasted well after John DeLorean's personal disgrace. Suppliers rallied around to try to keep it going. Many American dealers had learned how to sell the silver sports car and were keen to get more of them, albeit not in the volumes originally proposed. Some of the dealers, to be sure, were painting their DMC-12s, a part of the process that DeLorean should never have tried to do without, no matter how environmentally friendly it was to have a paint-free plant making a car with a stainless-steel skin. Basically sound, his car was on the brink of being upgraded with a first-class turbocharging system.

No one, with the possible exception of Walter Chrysler, was better equipped to start a car company than John DeLorean. John was one of the broadest-based and best-equipped executives ever to walk the streets of Detroit. Trained as an engineer, he had been reluctant to move from little Packard to huge General Motors in 1956 'because I didn't want to be the guy who draws the fenders, or something,' he told me. 'I enjoy getting involved in marketing, in manufacturing, in engineering and what's going on in the world – and everything else.'

Although he came up the engineering ladder to head GM's Pontiac division and then Chevrolet, DeLorean fought hard against second-guessing his chief engineers. 'You really have to work hard at not being a chief engineer,' he said, 'although I'm also sure that the chief engineer doesn't try to kid me because he knows I know a little bit about it.' No area of knowledge is more important to the leader of a car company, because engineers can easily deceive a chief who isn't wise to their double-talk. With 44 patents to his name, John DeLorean wasn't easily misled on technical matters.

John made many technical contributions to General Motors. He weaned GM away from X-frames, which are hazardous in lateral crashes, to perimeter frames with torque boxes at transition points. He was the first to tool up for disc brakes at Pontiac – though the Corporation wasn't ready to use them. He found an ultra-simple way to give turn signals a lane-change feature without the integrating computers that some were proposing.

DeLorean's overhead-cam Pontiac six was America's first in the modern era and second in the world to have a cogged-rubber-belt drive. Body-coloured bumpers, now common across the industry, were a Pontiac first. John fought hard for individuality of components among GM's divisions to keep cost down, instead of knee-jerk parts sharing that meant that less-costly cars had to carry expensive parts that suited larger, heavier models.

John DeLorean was promoted from Pontiac to head Chevrolet in 1969 at the age of 44, the youngest man ever to take charge of GM's largest division. In a seven-year profitability slump at the time, Chevy was a candidate for intensive care. Its sales of cars and trucks in 1970 were less than 1.7 million after a five-year decline of 30 percent.

Back in the days when GM's general managers had real power, John revitalised the division, restoring the confidence of a demoralised organisation. Some heads rolled; he stripped three levels out of the manufacturing staff.

Inventory turns were accelerated and new sales and marketing guidelines were established.

The result was spectacular. In 1971 Chevrolet sales were up to 2.8 million and in 1972, with sales of 3,060,178 units, Chevy became the first vehicle marque in history to sell more than three million cars and trucks in a single year. It wasn't a flash in the pan; 1973 sales were 3,446,162 Chevrolets.

Greatly benefitting were the division's dealers, whose profits rose 300 per cent on average during DeLorean's tenure. This, following his successes at Pontiac, confirmed an outstanding reputation for DeLorean among America's auto dealers, who were to provide important support for his car-making enterprise.

In one of its least understandable actions, GM promoted DeLorean out of Chevrolet after only 44 months. When he first heard hints of a possible move upstairs in 1972, John said, 'I didn't want to leave Chevrolet because we still had work to do with the division. But if I had to leave, the overseas operation was where I wanted to go.' GM trailed Ford abroad, an unfamiliar position. John saw profitable opportunities in giving more authority to local staff overseas instead of the usual cookie-cutter approach of imposing American templates on decision-making in other countries.

This didn't happen. Instead John was promoted to the post in charge of the domestic car and truck divisions. His was a small and fusty bureaucracy against which he had often struggled at Pontiac and Chevrolet. He soon found that people on the infamous 14th floor of the GM Building liked it that way. Many, from finance backgrounds, were nervous in the presence of someone who knew something about cars.

This was the environment in which DeLorean grew frustrated with his inability to influence the business, frustration that led to internal dissension and his resignation from GM in April 1973. 'Looking back now to the changes that have taken place in the auto industry,' John wrote in 1979 in his excellent and enlightening book, *On a Clear Day You Can See General Motors*, 'it is even more obvious that I should have managed somehow to get the job done on The Fourteenth Floor. But I didn't do it. And I consider that to be the biggest failure of my business life at GM.'

I was an advisor to DeLorean in his immediate post-GM years, when he set up his consulting organisation and took his first steps toward the creation of his own auto company. Finding a suitable engine for his sports car wasn't easy. He had high hopes of Comotor, a joint Citroën-NSU enterprise that was to make rotary engines, but it never reached critical mass. Neither was a Citroën four – the engine in his first prototype – the answer. The PRV V-6 that was ultimately used was in fact a good solution, meeting US emissions requirements as it did in its Volvo version.

In setting up and running his DeLorean Motor Company, John made several crucial missteps. Ex-Chrysler man Eugene Cafiero wasn't the hands-on president that he needed. DeLorean struggled with his car's engineering until Lotus came into the frame. John's enterprise was scattered too widely with its factory in Belfast – which he seldom visited – engineering in Norfolk, headquarters in New York and sales operations under Dick Brown in California. Delegating, as was his style, DeLorean was too far from the crucial decision-making process in a small company that demanded – and would have benefitted from – his close oversight.

Financing his dream was a nightmare for John. 'At General Motors it was pretty straightforward,' he told me. 'If you wanted to set up a new plant you prepared the proposal, sent the authorisation around and got all the necessary signatures. Then at the end you got the money.' He wasn't prepared for the raising of money in the real world, especially in the wake of the very public 1976 failure of Malcolm Bricklin's sports-car-manufacturing venture in Canada. The memory of the collapse of that gull-winged-car company was all too recent.

Thus John DeLorean was the architect of some of the flaws in his car company that contributed to its failure. Although often criticised, the car wasn't the problem. In all, some 8,800 were made during three years. Most are giving considerable satisfaction to their owners. They gained succour from one mention in John's *Daily Telegraph* obituary: 'Meanwhile,' it said, 'his gull-winged sports car has become a collector's item, changing hands for around £18,000.' Could this mark the beginning of the DeLorean boom? After all, the explosion in Ferrari prices closely followed the death of their creator in August 1988. They don't make them like Enzo Ferrari any more – or like John DeLorean.

RACERS

JUAN MANUEL
FANGIO

*With his habitual verve and concentration and a blue skullcap Alfa
Romeo-driving Fangio won his second World Championship Grand Prix
at Spa on 18 June 1950.*

A lthough the Mercedes-Benz racing cars of 1954 and 1955 were
superb examples of the application of high technology and tradition to racing, some would suggest that their world championships in those years would not have been achieved without Juan
Fangio's skill and indeed artistry. There is some truth in this. In both years
Fangio was the undisputed team leader in the silver Formula One Mercedes.
Whenever the cars from Stuttgart were in a position to win – which was
often – Fangio was at the forefront.

As a passionate follower of Grand Prix racing from the years before there was a World Championship, I followed Fangio's career with keen interest. I remember reading in *The Motor* the remarks of British star Reg Parnell after his return from the early-1949 races in Argentina. He declared himself 'much impressed with the race fever over there...and by the determined and skilful driving of some of the local talent, particularly this Fangio who won at Mar del Plata.'

I first met Fangio in March of 1954 when he and Eugenio Castellotti came to Thompson, Connecticut, of all places, to demonstrate a Maserati and a Siata for importer Tony Pompeo. My Spanish-speaking friend Stefan Habsburg introduced me and helped me get his autograph. Several years later in New York I was on hand with a lady friend when Fangio was present for the start of a rally. A comely blonde, she told me afterwards that she'd been a weak-kneed recipient of that blue-eyed Fangio gaze that won so many female conquests. His vision was excellent both on and off the track.

My first chance to see Fangio compete came in 1957 when he was a member of the Maserati team for the Sebring 12 Hours. He handled the formidable 450 S Maserati like an agreeable toy, with Jean Behra treating it sensitively to win the race. He also memorably tested Chevrolet's Corvette SS sports-racer. He was then on the brink of the season with Maserati that would yield his fifth World Championship.

Fangio's two years with Mercedes-Benz stand out; he later said that he had expected to retire after 1955 but kept racing because he needed the money. Argentina's Peron-haters had frozen his assets there. Looking back, the combination of Mercedes-Benz and Fangio seems obvious. Of course Mercedes would build great cars and of course they would attract the best driver.

Great engineer Rudi Uhlenhaut of Daimler-Benz put it simply: 'About fifty percent depends on the car and fifty percent on the driver. We had a good look around and chose the best – and that was Fangio.'

In fact it was not an open-and-shut case. It might not have been Fangio. Daimler-Benz team manager Alfred Neubauer planned to enter his first post-war Grand Prix season in 1954 with a German driver cadre: pre-war star Hermann Lang, still quick in his day; engineer-racer Karl Kling, who knew the new car inside and out; Fritz Riess, who had been fast in the 300SL, and speedy youngster Hans Herrmann. But Neubauer and his technical boss

Fritz Nallinger knew that they needed, as Nallinger put it, a 'master driver' to lead the team and ensure success.

Though 'master drivers' were not thick on the ground, some were around. Ascari and his mentor Villoresi had been snapped up by Gianni Lancia for his new Formula One effort, and were expected to bear fruit late in 1954, the first year of the new Formula One. Nino Farina, the 1950 champion, came into consideration, although the proud Torinese had not been best pleased when Neubauer reneged (in favour of Fangio) on a verbal agreement to sign Farina when his team went to Argentina in 1951. Compensation had to be paid.

Of the Britons, Mike Hawthorn could enter the frame; his Grand Prix career had leapfrogged that of Stirling Moss and he had won at Reims in 1953, just edging Fangio out. Froilán González was another coruscating new star. But out of all these, Neubauer had set his cap for Juan Manuel Fangio. 'He knows something about sliding the turns,' he told his colleagues. 'That's our man.'

To his credit Neubauer started angling for the Argentine racing diver as early as mid-1950. He wanted him for the 1951 racing season in Argentina and later to lead the team of 1.5-litre supercharged Grand Prix cars he hoped Daimler-Benz would build. His efforts to attract Fangio to tests at the 'Ring and to a factory visit in the autumn were in vain.

Fangio, did, however, become a Buenos Aires Mercedes dealer that winter of 1950 – a clear expression of the company's confidence in him. But when the Argentine racer drove the 3.0-litre Mercedes in the 1951 winter races it did not show its best form, to Neubauer's utter mortification. This was just the opposite of what he needed to lure the cautious and canny Juan Manuel.

The stakes were raised in June 1951 when Daimler-Benz decided to build a fleet of new W165 V-8 racers to compete in 1952. Neubauer had to seduce Fangio away from Alfa Romeo, for whom he had been driving since 1950, deploying 'talents that Casanova would have envied. I had to use all my arts of enticement, pull every trick out of the box to win the confidence of the Argentine, who was as coy as a maiden before her first kiss.'

Finally, at the end of May 1951, Neubauer achieved one of his goals: a factory visit by Fangio. Accompanying him were Juan Carlos Guzzi of the Argentine Auto Club, Froilán González and Onofre 'Pinocho' Marimon, the racing-mad son of Domingo Marimon. The latter had helped the youthful Juan Manuel and raced against him and the Galvez brothers. Motoring to

Stuttgart in Juan's Alfa Romeo, they toured the famous museum and dined convivially with Neubauer.

Later that week Alfred Neubauer drove to the Nürburgring to watch the Friday practice for the 3 June Eifelrennen, a Formula Two race at which the Ferraris were expected but failed to show. Leaving the circuit, he spotted a black and red Alfa saloon by the side of the road and, kicking its tyres, Guzzi, Marimon, González and Fangio. The drivers had wanted to take a look at the 'Ring – which resulted in Marimon developing an obsession with the track – but grinding noises from the rear end meant their Alfa wouldn't go much farther.

Thinking quickly, Neubauer said he'd go at once to the Mercedes main dealer at nearby Koblenz and send back a team of mechanics to fix the axle, loan the Argentines a car so they could drive to dinner and he would even provide an interpreter. When the mechanics arrived, bringing a bearing that fit the Alfa, they found that experienced mechanic Fangio had already rolled up his sleeves and dismounted the rear axle. They were on their way again that evening, thanks to that gratis intervention by Daimler-Benz.

For the 1951 German Grand Prix in July, Neubauer made sure that Fangio had a good room in the Nürburgring's Sporthotel, a room with the bathtub in which Juan liked to have a good long soak after a tough race. He gave Fangio some of the latest German driving goggles to replace the 'welders' goggles' that he had been using. When the driver suffered a bout of conjunctivitis, Neubauer arranged for a top physician to attend him.

The relationship seemed to be warming. But when Neubauer invited Fangio to the 'Ring in September for comparative tests of Mercedes-Benz racers (his own drivers couldn't get down to pre-war sub-ten-minute lap times), the Argentine Club's Guzzi pleaded a conflict with the Paris Salon. Fangio, we may be sure, was wary of upsetting Alfa, with whom he was on the way to his first World Championship.

The pressure on Neubauer lessened in the autumn when Daimler-Benz decided not to build new 1.5-litre cars after all, but instead to plan ahead to the new Formula One for 1954. His German driver squad was adequate for his 300SLs in 1952. The only non-German to race those cars was American John Fitch. In 1953, however, with Fangio now racing happily albeit unsuccessfully for Maserati, which had an impressive new car on the stocks for 1954, Alfred Neubauer had to get busy again.

Maserati patron Adolfo Orsi was very keen to retain the services of Fangio for 1954, now that his company had adjusted to the idea of running a works Formula One team. In fact Fangio would drive Maseratis in the first two 1954 Grands Prix. Another lusting for his skills was young Gianni Lancia, for whom Fangio had just won the Mexican Road Race and was booked for Sebring in 1954.

Lancia was building a team of Grand Prix cars – the famous Jano-designed D50 models – and asked Fangio to join his squad. Pointing out that Lancia had already signed Ascari and Villoresi, Juan cheekily chided the industrialist by saying that it wouldn't be fair for him to have *all* the best drivers. But in February, the Buenos Aires newspapers were reporting that Juan would race for Lancia.

These skilled, experienced and successful teams were serious rivals to Daimler-Benz in Fangio's affections. So was Alfa Romeo, although a radical four-wheel-driven racing car that Giuseppe Busso had shown Fangio in 1952 would never be completed. Nor could Ferrari be ruled out. Enzo was in one of his sulks, threatening to abandon racing and retire to a monastery. He shrugged, telling Neubauer that he was free to negotiate with any or all of his drivers. In the autumn of 1953, Neubauer again struck up his tango with the Argentinian.

Fresh from two victories on the trot at Monza and Modena in Maseratis, Fangio granted an exceptional favour to Neubauer at the end of September. Daimler-Benz was tyre-testing at Monza with the 1952 300SL and an extensively-modified SL that had some of the features of the 1954 Grand Prix car. Fangio agreed to come along and set some bogey times. In the 1952 car he was little faster than Kling, Lang, Riess and Herrmann, but in the modified car he was a clear two seconds quicker than they were.

This was Neubauer's opportunity to make his pitch to Fangio – and he did – but he had one hand tied behind his back: incredibly, he couldn't confirm a racing programme for 1954. The new silver cars were progressing; he hoped to begin the sports-car season with the Mille Miglia at the beginning of May and Grand Prix racing in mid-year at Reims. But he couldn't commit to these dates. He said he wished there was an October Spanish Grand Prix on the 1953 calendar because he 'wanted to make a gift of a less cloudy wine' to Fangio by that time. All he could do was ask Fangio not to make any firm commitment to another team for the 1954 season.

Making firm commitments too early for 1954 was the last thing on Juan Manuel's mind when he returned to Argentina in October. Neubauer was able to communicate with this most important of his Buenos Aires dealers through a company director based there, Baron Arnt von Korff. His strong links with the Spanish-speaking countries had found von Korff first in Spain and now in Argentina on the strength of Daimler-Benz. Keenly interested in racing, the Baron was an able and appropriate interlocutor for Fangio. Another ally was the local businessman who headed Mercedes-Benz sales in Argentina, Juan Antonio.

On 27 October, Neubauer set out for von Korff the general terms of the proposition he was able to offer Fangio. The driver, he said, would receive all the starting money and prize money earned by his performance in every race, less a ten percent deduction shared among the team members. Neubauer pointed out that normal practice was to pay a driver no more than a third to half of these amounts, because teams needed the rest of the money to support their racing activities. Unlike them, Daimler-Benz would underwrite all the costs and give 90 per cent of all racing earnings, including those from accessory companies, to Fangio.

Alfred Neubauer's earnest hopes that this generous offer – communicated to Fangio by von Korff – would lead to an early commitment by the driver were in vain. Not until 12 January 1954 did the Baron come back to Neubauer with Fangio's comments on the proposed deal. He was ready to sign, said von Korff, but wanted assurances on some points. One was that no other Argentine driver would be signed. 'It is correct,' confided the Baron, 'that there are differences between F. and his countryman G.' Neubauer assured him that he would sign no other non-German drivers, let alone González, adding that there was no truth in the rumours that Mercedes was negotiating with Ascari.

Fangio asked for freedom to race for other teams outside his commitments to Mercedes-Benz. He also said he appreciated the suggestion that Mercedes would reimburse him if it failed to take part in a race but added that it was more important to him in such a situation to be free to get a ride with another team. Von Korff told Neubauer that it was vital that he provide a firm draft contract soon and, most importantly, that it specified the race programme.

'Fangio has firmly decided to join with us,' wrote von Korff early in February. 'Contractual matters are far from his thoughts and he has complete confidence that we – e.g. above all you, Mr Neubauer – will deal with him loyally and correctly. His understanding of formal matters is not great. Fangio thinks that a contract would not be so important because ours is a serious firm and it would be sufficient to have an agreement such as we have reached between us here. I take a different view and absolutely recommend a clear contract, which I explained to Fangio and to which he agreed.'

On 23 February, a Tuesday, Fangio stopped in at von Korff's office for a farewell chat before departing to Florida to race at Sebring. The Mercedes director gave the driver a set of photos of the just-completed envelope-bodied W196 Grand Prix car, which made a positive impression. Nevertheless, Fangio pressed von Korff: Why have so many weeks passed with nothing being resolved? Nothing really clarified? Was Mercedes serious or not?

Over their coffees, in this difficult atmosphere, a secretary showed the Baron the morning's mail. It included a letter from Neubauer and a draft contract – in German and unsigned. Realising that it was vital to gain a commitment from the driver before he fell into the clutches of the Lancia team at Sebring, von Korff arranged a rushed translation of the draft and reviewed it with Fangio. The driver then dated and signed its upper left corner with the word '*conforme*' – 'agreed'. For von Korff, this was a happy resolution of what had been for him, so far away from Stuttgart, a difficult task. 'You can believe,' he wrote to Neubauer, 'that all in all winning Fangio to our side was not so easy.'

On 1 March, the veteran racing director unburdened himself to the Baron on the problems he had been experiencing behind the scenes. 'If you and Mr Fangio have been wondering why a pause had seemingly arisen after last year's written preliminary discussions, there were good grounds. In fact there was hesitation on the part of the directors here to commit to a sufficient number of racing cars to secure the participation of Fangio.'

The stumbling block had been the absolute determination of technical director Fritz Nallinger that Mercedes-Benz should compete in the 1954 Mille Miglia. If this had been given priority, Neubauer explained, it would have been possible to complete only four Grand Prix cars – not enough to guarantee a start for Fangio in all six of the remaining championship races including Reims. 'Matters had almost reached the point that we were considering distancing ourselves from a contract with Fangio,' wrote Neubauer, 'because the certainty of his participation was not a given.

'It took weeks for us to be able to convince him,' Neubauer said of Nallinger, 'that we would simply not be ready' for the Mille Miglia. In fact, the sports cars were not ready to compete until the 1955 Mille Miglia. 'All these decisions had to be made,' continued Neubauer, 'and finally fell on the evening of 26 February, whereupon the already-prepared contract was signed by the management board. There was really a lot of effort here behind the fashioning of a sound support for Fangio.'

Clearly, the effort on Alfred Neubauer's side was to emphasise the company's participation in Grand Prix races in such a way that it would be possible to engage Fangio to lead the team. He prevailed against Nallinger's desire to attack across a broad front of both sports and racing cars, which would have risked the company's Formula One effort to such an extent that – in Neubauer's view – Daimler-Benz would not have been justified in asking the great Argentine to drive its cars.

Sports-car races in 1954 (Le Mans, the 'Ring and Mexico) were still foreseen in the final contract for the season, which Fangio did not sign until 30 March. In addition to the generous terms of the draft contract it assured the driver of a dollar-value fee for starting in those races, such as Le Mans and Mexico, that did not pay starting money. If Mercedes failed to start a contracted race, Fangio had the choice of a compensatory fee or his freedom to drive for another team.

According to a daily allocation, Juan Fangio's expenses were paid while he was in Europe. Although the contract didn't mention it, at the driver's request, the expenses of his lady friend 'Beba' were covered as well. In the case of 'Mrs Fangio', as she was called but was not, this was warmly agreed to by the board and himself. Neubauer said: 'We have always had the experience that especially in case of accidents, the women are very necessary because they are the only ones who take care of the injured when the racing team has to up stakes and depart.'

The contract provided for substantial amounts to be paid in the event of hospitalisation, disablement or death. It assured Fangio that no other Argentine driver would be engaged by the team in 1954. A loan car was to be provided, either a 220 or a 300. In fact after urgings from the Argentine side that nothing less than a top-of-the-range 300S would suit Fangio's prestige in the eyes of his countrymen, one of these costly custom-built cars was made available.

The car that counted, of course, was the W196 Grand Prix racer with its straight-eight engine. Fangio saw it for the first time on the Monday after his 20 June victory driving a Maserati 250F at the Belgian Grand Prix. He and the rest of the team were at Reims for two days of tests three weeks before the car's first race. 'From the very first test,' he wrote, 'I was sure that I had in my hands the perfect car, the sensational machine that drivers dream about all their lives.'

In practice, Fangio won 50 bottles of Reims champagne with the first-ever lap at over 200 km/h. 'I had not the least doubt about the race result,' Fangio said, 'a Mercedes would be first across the finishing line. Throughout the entire race, the two silver cars driven by Kling and myself ran perfectly, almost in unison. I led Kling across the line by a wheel.' Their debut victory in the French Grand Prix 40 years after Mercedes' 1914 success in the same race was storybook stuff for the sleek silver cars.

By the end of 1955, Juan Manuel had won two more World Championships with Mercedes-Benz. Neubauer could breathe easily at last. He had found and captured his 'master driver'.

PHILIP TOLL HILL

For all racing enthusiasts the combination of Phil Hill and the 'shark-nose' 156 F1 Ferrari is iconic. Their combined capabilities won the 1961 World Championship.

'Now I really feel like the world champion!' That was Phil Hill's delightful comment when he sat down to lunch in Bill Mitchell's executive dining room in GM's Styling Staff late in 1961. Enzo Ferrari cheated Phil of the adulation that was his due by withdrawing his team from the U.S. Grand Prix at Watkins Glen after the Californian had clinched the championship at Monza. To deny the Glen's spectators the chance to cheer Hill seemed cruel at best, but at the time Enzo was being henpecked by his wife Laura about expenses. He saw this as a saving that would placate her.

A tremendous racing enthusiast, GM Styling vice president Bill Mitchell extended to Hill an invitation to lunch at Styling Staff. This was always a special occasion with eight top people from Styling joining Bill and his honoured guest in his exclusive dining room, around a circular table that has a built-in lazy susan which each diner can rotate electrically to bring condiments to his place at the press of a button. The view from the window was the spectacular central lake of the Saarinen-designed Tech Center. It was an honour and a pleasure for us to lunch with America's newly minted champion, then at the peak of his powers.

At the time I was a brand-new member of GM's Public Relations Staff, just arrived from *Car and Driver*. There it had been my great pleasure to follow the progress of the 1961 season through our reports and photos from Jesse Alexander. In our January 1962 issue – my last – we published an interview I conducted with Phil about his season, accompanied by a vivid Joe Papin illustration that captured Hill's impatient urgency.

The interview turned out to be controversial because Phil was critical of his team-mate Ricardo Rodriguez. 'He's damn brave, that's all I can say,' he told me. 'I know he's a skilled driver, but to do the things he's doing you've got to be way out and if he lives I'll be surprised.'

Phil also hinted that Rodriguez had contributed to the crash at Monza in 1961 that killed Wolfgang von Trips and 14 spectators. Hill's remark fore-shadowed Ricardo's death in a Lotus only a year later when trying to seize the pole in his home-town Mexican Grand Prix. I reproduce the interview at the end of this profile.

My journalistic contacts in Europe came in handy when we organised the lunch for Phil at Styling. I got in touch with the great German photographer Julius Weitmann, who sent some of his stunning images of Hill in sports and Grand Prix Ferraris. These were vastly enlarged by Styling's experts and displayed not only in the dining room but also in the building's entrance atrium next to a chequered-flag motif with a bold number 1 in red. Mitchell's silver Sting Ray racer completed a striking ensemble.

I first met Phil Hill in 1957 when he was a member of Ferrari's sports-car team at Sebring. In 1958 I followed him as a young reporter in Europe. This was a big year for Phil with his win at Le Mans, his bravura performance in

Racers

the 500 Miles of Monza driving a rampaging 4.1-litre single-seater Ferrari against the Indy cars, and his end-of-season Grand Prix drives that helped secure the world championship for Britain's Mike Hawthorn and sealed his place in Ferrari's Formula One team.

In the early years of the Can-Am series, I reported on Hill's drives in Jim Hall's revolutionary Chaparral 2E. In 1966 Jim Hall campaigned the Chaparral 2D coupe in international sports-car races with Phil and Jo Bonnier as drivers. Their first European appearance was at the daunting Nürburgring for the 1,000-kilometre race. As usual the laid-back Texans arrived at the German track with their car on a trailer behind an unmarked white pickup truck. They went about their business with a lethargic casualness that frustrated the tightly wound Hill. 'Don't you guys realise *this is the god-damn Nürburgring?*' exclaimed the man who five years earlier was the first to lap its 14.2 miles in less than nine minutes. Hill and Bonnier went on to win sensationally with their automatic-transmission car carrying a 'Lone Star State' Texas licence plate.

When I was with Fiat in 1978, I accompanied a *Road & Track* group to Italy to drive and photograph some of our historic cars. Their team consisted of editor Tony Hogg, photographer John Lamm and Phil Hill. Phil was both congenial and professional as we inspected and drove various vintage Fiats and Lancias. That October we also did some driving around northern Italy that included a stop at a roadside restaurant, Café Milano, where Hill had dined in May of 1958. Both he and the proprietor were delighted to find Phil's 'best wishes' inscribed in the visitors' book, still vivid 20 years later.

My last personal contact with Phil was in 1997 when I asked him to write a foreword to my book about Stirling Moss. In it, Hill recalled 'that cold, blustery Easter Monday in the spring of 1950 when I first saw him race his Cooper at Goodwood.' Phil was then in England to attend service schools for British-car mechanics. Did the talented Californian come a long way from those years? Did he represent to the world the very best of American talent and sportsmanship? He sure did! And, as Phil would add for emphasis, 'You know what I mean?'

Karl: Can you follow your feelings through the 1961 season regarding your championship chances? How did the Targa and Nürburgring sports-car accidents affect you?

Phil: Those two damn accidents would make it difficult for me. They were both kind of confidence-shaking accidents. The point is, when driving is your whole career, day in and day out, you come to rely on your judgment. You don't ever mistrust anything you do.

In the Targa Florio I just plain old misjudged. You go by a point you're used to doing at 50 mph and suddenly you're going through the same point at 120 mph? Well, that's what I did. I was giving myself a pep talk. I was in good form and knew it, even at that time. But I'd had no practice in a fast car and was relying on my judgment. You can't drive the Targa on judgment.

Then at the Nürburgring sports-car race it was a combination of high-hysteresis tyres, which wore very badly, and a puddle.

The spin in the Grand Prix at Reims was just too much – horrible. It should have been a simple 360-degree turn and they wouldn't even have missed my time at the pits. If I'd been instinctive about this and just given it the gun when I was aimed right, it would have come off.

How did it happen? I knew Moss was behind me. I thought he was closer and I was sure he was closing up on the turn. My rear-view mirror was gone. It had fallen off, been blown off by the wind. So I went into Thillois, taking it easy but still avoiding Moss, and spun wide. Then without brakes he went wide too and hit me, and then it stalled.

Usually the engine would restart every time on the battery, but we had a leak across the alternator – I'm not supposed to say this, you know – and in such terrific heat, with the water temperature at 120°C, the water cooked right out of the battery. It's right behind the radiator. The car itself at Reims was great; a very nice car.

If all that hadn't happened at Reims the whole season would have been much different, much easier. I thought I had it made. If I had won then, all I had to do was stay on line with Trips in points, even finishing second or third a few times. It would have been a much better season.

At Aintree it was a simple matter of my damn near hitting a wooden post. I'd had two accidents and I was pretty sure I wouldn't have three – then this happened. We changed the front-rear braking ratio during practice on dry roads, putting more on the front. It was my fault; I requested it.

On the wet road in the race this was bad because you don't get so much weight transfer forward. Braking coming into Melling Crossing, the front

Racers

wheels went, I skated and used up all my power and at the last minute I barely made it. I thought, 'They can have the damn championship!'

Before Monza we tried a new engine that gave more horsepower at higher revs but it was no faster around the circuit. We also ran into some valve spring trouble we'd had before so we didn't use it in the race. My feelings? I was pretty determined at Monza.

Karl: What did you enjoy most this year?

Phil: Well, as a circuit I liked Spa best, but the most gratifying thing I did was breaking the record at the 'Ring, getting down five seconds under nine minutes with a litre less than we'd had before.

Karl: Did you just decide, 'I'm going to break the lap record?'

Phil: Well, no – we'd been fiddling with the car a lot; we made some adjustments and it felt so damn good that I just said, 'Let's go!' I made up the time, oh, a little bit here and a little bit there; it all adds up. Let's face it, there are hundreds of places at Nürburg where you can do it.

Karl: What was it like to change to the rear-engined Ferrari? When did you first drive it?

Phil: The first time I really drove it was at Monaco. Compared to the front-engined cars it handled much easier, lighter. Its cornering power is way up. There was no substantial difference in cockpit heat, though. In the rear-engined car it's much easier to get rid of heat but you've got to realise the radiator's still up front. Because the engine's in back everyone took a much more casual approach to insulating the cockpit this year. With hot air under pressure up front, any little hole let the heat through like a furnace.

At Monaco I drove the 65-degree [V-6 engine] car and in my opinion – and also Richie Ginther's – on slow circuits it suffered from the point of view of roadholding.

At the back its centre of gravity is 65 mm higher. The 120-degree car has a lower centre of gravity in back and on really twisty circuits, where you spend a lot of time winding back and forth, it makes a real difference.

Philip Toll Hill   159

Karl: What happened to the engines at Reims?

Phil: Heat was the main thing. It's hard cooling an engine at really high levels. The new V-8s were running into that at Monza. We're still using our big 2.5-litre radiator with 90 less horsepower!

Karl: Any changes in suspension during the year?

Phil: Yes, they tried different geometries and roll centres. We went back and forth; certain setups suit certain circuits. During the season they straightened up the rear wheels and corrected the toe-in. We gained in top speed by cleaning up this angle situation, getting less power loss through the tyres.

Karl: Does the handling change much between full and empty tanks?

Phil: There's a fair amount of difference. It's much easier to compensate, to balance between understeer and oversteer when the tanks are less full. The car's inherent understeer becomes known when the tanks are full. At the same time the increased car weight puts more weight on the rear wheels, making it more difficult to get oversteer by using power. At high speeds you're using up all your power anyhow; there's no engine power left for control so you just plain have understeer.

Karl: How about other drivers? Who's the quickest Porsche driver?

Phil: Bonnier and Gurney are both great. Gurney seems to have that good old spark. Bonnier lacks it. Sometimes when he gets passed when he shouldn't have been, he gives up. I think of all the drivers Gurney has done the best job all year long, doing an outstanding job in every race he's been in.

Karl: How's Giancarlo Baghetti coming along?

Phil: Little by little by little he might get better and better and better, you know what I mean? He lacks that certain fire that good drivers seem to have in their novice period. There's a strange thing about him: he may be slow but when someone battles with him at that slow speed he's more than willing to fight. He got a tremendous tow at Monza and then dropped back because he didn't know how to get up fast again. He was the first to admit it.

Karl: How about Ricardo Rodriguez?

Phil: He's damn brave, that's all I can say. I know he's a skilled driver, you understand, but to do the things he's doing you've got to be way out, and if he lives I'll be surprised.

By the way, you'll probably hear later on, as things come out, that there was another party involved in the Trips accident. Trips didn't just arbitrarily move over on Clark. He moved over because he had to, to avoid someone on the other side.

Karl: How was your own endurance this season?

Phil: I had a hell of a lot more endurance. I was plain running out of energy before. I learned a lot about eating, relaxing, being too keyed-up. I learned that even a cup of tea can throw you off.

Karl: How do you feel about winning the world championship this way?

Phil: Well, I'm philosophical about the whole thing. There weren't any tears at Monza. I felt sad but there weren't any tears. After all, how would you feel if you'd been through this plenty of times before? Would you burst into tears? That was just something for the press to say, that's all.

Sure, I'm happy about being champion. I haven't quite gotten used to it yet!

Karl: What are your plans now?

Phil: Just to relax. I'm not going to think about anything for a while, especially not about next year! If I do continue racing it will definitely be with Ferrari.

Philip Toll Hill   161

EMERSON
FITTIPALDI

*When my book on Mercedes-Benz racing cars was published in 1995,
Fittipaldi was using Mercedes engines so he was well qualified to join me
for its Goodwood launch.*

M y love affair with Brazil and Brazilians began at the end of
1969, when the organisers of Brazil's biennial automobile
show invited me and a few other journalists to Sao Paulo to
promote their event and display the vitality of Brazil's auto
industry and motor sports.

On that first visit I met local racing stars, the Fittipaldi brothers, Wilson and his three-years-younger brother Emerson, then 23. Their father, a famous sports broadcaster, was enthusiastically encouraging their racing efforts. Wilson had two disappointing racing seasons in Europe in 1965 and 1966. After some good Formula Two results, however, he drove in Formula

Racers

One for the Brabham team in 1972 and 1973, finishing in the points twice. In 1974 he drove the Copersucar-Fittipaldi that he and Emerson had developed, but without success.

Meanwhile Emerson Fittipaldi's career had gone from strength to strength. When I met him he had just returned from his first European sortie, which brought successes in Formula Ford and Three. Late in the 1970 season he was promoted by Lotus to Formula One.

When the Grand Prix circus came to Watkins Glen, New York, in September 1970, I naturally met up with Emerson and his charming wife Maria Helena. 'It was hard for us to believe that *this* was the track for the United States Grand Prix,' said Fittipaldi of the slippery, gloomy and cold Glen circuit. 'There was mud everywhere on the track. They let us have three or four warm-up laps and I could scarcely believe that this was America, so modern and so rich.'

This was no easy ride for Emerson. Lotus had just lost Jochen Rindt, killed in the exotic new Type 72 in a practice accident at Monza. 'It was as if the world had collapsed around me,' said Fittipaldi. 'I had learned to appreciate Jochen, as he was a real friend. It was a very sad time for everyone at Lotus.' By that time Emerson had driven the older Type 49 in three Grands Prix in Britain, Germany and Austria. For Watkins Glen he would have the new 72, with which he had only practised at Monza.

At the Glen, Lotus chief Colin Chapman gave Emerson specific instructions. Rindt could be the posthumous world champion if Ferrari-mounted Ickx, in particular, could be denied points. 'Colin came to me before the race and told me: Emerson, whatever you do you must finish in front of the Ferraris because of the championship. For me it was funny. I know my limits. I am not a *kamikaze*. I told him I would do what I could.'

Fittipaldi excelled in practice with the third-fastest lap, behind the dreaded Ickx on the pole. Emerson could do nothing about the Belgian's Ferrari but at mid-race Ickx had to stop for fuel-system repairs and Fittipaldi moved to third place behind Jackie Stewart in the new Tyrrell and the BRM of Pedro Rodriguez.

The Tyrrell retired, handing the lead to Rodriguez. 'As the Yardley BRM team prepared for its second celebration of the year,' reported *Motor*, 'the diminutive Mexican made an unscheduled stop for fuel – it was the 101st lap [of 108]. He had been told by his pit crew that his margin over Fittipaldi was 38 seconds when in reality it was more like 18 or 19. The 20 seconds consumed in the pits allowed the young Brazilian to vault into the lead as Rodriguez floundered helplessly to cross the line more than a half-minute down.'

'With nine laps to go they gave me "P1",' said Emerson. 'I looked behind me because I thought the signal must be for someone else! Then with eight laps to go they gave me "P1" again. Throughout the lap I had been thinking they must have made a mistake. I was first! I was leading the race! I could win my first Grand Prix. My mind started to work overtime. I thought of the petrol. Would there be enough? Then I thought about all the components of my Lotus. What would break?

'The last laps seemed to go on forever,' the Brazilian recalled. 'Then I saw the chequered flag. I saw Chapman throw his hat in the air. It was for me! I had seen many photographs of Chapman throwing his hat in the air in happiness, first for Jimmy Clark, then Graham Hill and Jochen Rindt. And now it was for me. When I stopped at the pit I couldn't remember a word of English!'

Emerson Fittipaldi was the surprise winner of the U. S. Grand Prix. While everyone else was saying, 'Emerson who?' I was among the very few at the Glen who had any inkling of the remarkable history of this brilliant young Brazilian. After Rindt's death, the victory was a healing catharsis for Team Lotus. Colin Chapman was literally in tears and the team's Dick Scammell was almost as speechless as Emerson: 'Winning at the Glen was just like a fairy tale…it was too good to be true…we couldn't believe it.'

When Emerson and Maria Helena came through New York on their way home, I hosted them for dinner at Le Chanteclair, the restaurant of famous French racing driver René Dreyfus. I also drove them to the airport for their departure the next day. On the way we were practically in hysterics as Emerson described the astonishing eight-cylinder VW Beetle that he, Wilson and Ricardo Divila built to race in Brazil in 1969. In one race it outqualified a Ford GT40 and a Lola-Chevrolet coupe!

Emerson continued to lead the Lotus team in 1971 and 1972, the year in which he won his first world championship with five victories, finishing his stint with Lotus in 1973 as vice-champion. He said that his 1972 success was built on the hard work of 1971: 'We spent one year developing the car and trying to work together well. From the start of the year everything worked, all the organisation, working together, the right combination between the driver, the mechanics and the team manager. And the car preparation was very good that year.

'It is very important to have the right combination on the team,' Fittipaldi continued. 'You can have a very good driver and not have a very good car. Then you don't win. You do well but it is difficult to win. Then you have a very good car and a bad driver. Or you can have a very good car and driver but no mechanics, no preparation. Then you are not reliable. The car doesn't finish the race; it doesn't handle right. You have to have the whole combination working together.'

An important advantage that the Lotus team had in 1972 was the ability to test privately, supported by tyres from Firestone, on most of the tracks used during the season. The only exceptions were Monaco and Clermont Ferrand, which were only closed to traffic on the race weekends, and too-remote Buenos Aires. They used the Race of Champions at Brands Hatch to get the settings for the race later in the year.

'Who started doing that a lot is Jackie Stewart,' Emerson said. 'With tyre testing. Now everybody is doing it. It is so important to get the right tyre for each track, for the weather conditions. Working together with the Firestone people you can set the right cambers. These days the number of options you have to change the car, to improve it, is incredible. If you give a bit more angle on the wing, then you get more downthrust. Then you have a different tyre temperature reading because the car is going to work at a different suspension height. Then the cambers are going to change. And then you have to adjust for that. One thing makes the other come together but it takes a long time and many hours of testing now to get a Formula One car to work at the limit. The Lotus 72 is a very difficult car to get on the limit. To get the right settings.

'That's why it is important to come before the official practice,' Fittipaldi continued, 'because in the official practice the driver is in the cockpit and the team manager and the mechanics are concerned about him going quickly. Everybody is looking at the stopwatch, waiting, expecting him to go quicker! The team manager is not thinking of what you can do to improve the car. He just thinks, "Oh, somebody else is going quicker!" You cannot concentrate the same way that you can in a private test, when you arrive at the track and know that you can spend nearly all day just trying to get the car right, to think about the ratios and wings and tyres.

'Throughout the year somebody has to be thinking, all the time, about where you can improve,' Emerson found. 'You can never be happy with the car. It's not only the driver, you know, it's everybody – the tyre people, Firestone, the mechanics, the team manager, the designer, the driver. That's what makes a Grand Prix car a winning car, a winning team. Because the competition is very hard. You can never be happy and satisfied with the car and say, "okay, now we did it." You always have to see where you are losing, to improve it in the right way.

'When you're having breakfast,' thought the Brazilian, 'you have to be thinking, "How was the car yesterday? How was the ratio? If somebody was quicker there, why was he quicker there?" When you arrive at the track you start talking to the mechanics and the team manager. What are you going to test? This goes on from the morning until the evening. Before you go to bed you are still thinking. And you still have to have time for press people, for your friends. It's really difficult. On racing weekends it's difficult for a person to concentrate. And you have to. Because if you don't concentrate on the racing there's just no way that you can go quickly.'

During later trips to Brazil in 1970, 1972 and 1974 – the year of his second world championship with McLaren – I visited Emerson and Maria Helena at the Fittipaldi family hideaway on the beach at Guaruja where he kept in shape with long swims. He also stopped over with us in New York. In 1980 when I came to Britain I visited his Formula One factory near Reading and joined the team at Monaco where Keke Rosberg was his other driver and Beatle George Hamilton a close friend. Ultimately this all contributed to the book I wrote about Emerson in 2002. 'You made me look good!' he told me. 'That wasn't hard!' I answered.

These happenings came to mind after the 2009 Grand Prix at Valencia in Spain, won by Rubens Barrichello driving a Brawn-Mercedes. This, it turned out, was the 100th Formula One success by a Brazilian. Emerson started the ball rolling. He hit a dry patch after the Glen, not winning again until 1972's Spanish Grand Prix. He scored five Lotus-mounted wins that year on his way to his first world championship. He won his second championship in 1974 with McLaren. In all he won 14 Grand Prix races.

In 1975, when Emerson was second in points behind team-mate James Hunt, his countryman Carlos Pace (pronounced *pah*-chay) gloriously won his home Brazilian Grand Prix in a Brabham-Ford. This was destined to be

Pace's only win in six Formula One seasons before his death in a light-plane crash. The next Brazilian to star was Nelson Piquet whose first on 23 wins came with a Brabham-Ford in 1980 and the last with a Benetton-Ford in 1991, taking three world championships along the way.

Three titles were also scored by the unforgettable Ayrton Senna, the most successful of the Brazilians with 41 wins. A long gap followed his last victory in 1993 before Rubens Barrichello could wave the Brazilian flag again at Hockenheim in 2000. He scored ten victories for Ferrari through 2004, paving the way for countryman Felipe Massa, whose first of 11 wins – also for Ferrari – came in 2006. Ironically it was a loose spring from Barrichello's rear suspension that injured Massa in the race at Hungary in 2009.

It all began on 4 October 1970 at Watkins Glen. And I was there!

MARIO GABRIELE ANDRETTI

Ronnie Peterson looked over the shoulders of Mario Andretti, left, and Colin Chapman during the 1978 season when their Lotus team swept both World Championships.

Although Mario Andretti had raced previously for Colin Chapman's Team Lotus in the odd Grand Prix, a chance meeting led the two men to team up for good in the 1976 Formula One season. With his previous team withdrawing after the race at Long Beach on 26 March that year, Mario was at liberty. 'I didn't really know what I was going to do next,' he recalled.

'On the Monday after the race I sat down for breakfast in the Queensway Hilton, near the old Queen Mary. Colin Chapman was sitting there too. He was just as unhappy as I was because his Lotuses had performed really badly in the race. He came over and we started talking. I told him that I was completely committed to F1, that I would even take a sabbatical if it meant I could get a decent drive. And he said, "Why don't you drive for me?"'

'I said I'd do it if he made me the number one driver and worked things around me,' Andretti said, 'simply because Lotus never had the resources to run equal equipment for both drivers.' In a non-championship race at Silverstone, Mario saw that the new Lotus 77 was racing decently. 'Let's see if we can help each other, Colin and I decided,' said Andretti. He was in a Lotus for the next race in Spain and all the way through the 1980 season.

I caught up with this dynamic duo at Watkins Glen, New York, for the Grand Prix on 2 October 1977. I had an assignment to write a story about Mario for a monthly magazine, so he agreed to take me into his retinue for the weekend. He was driving the Lotus 78, the first GP car to have high aerodynamic downforce thanks to the innovations of Chapman and his team. He had already won four races that season and was denied others by poor reliability.

Chapman was thrilled with his acquisition. 'It was just what we needed,' he told me. 'I'd always told Mario that if and when he ever took up Formula One full time, he was my number one. I was absolutely delighted when he came back to us. I think quite seriously that we might still be in the doldrums if he hadn't. He has this ability to get people's enthusiasm going. I know he had that effect on me and it extended to the designers, mechanics, everybody. Quite apart from his talent, he is such a genuinely nice guy that people want to do their best for him.'

At Watkins Glen he finished only two seconds behind race winner James Hunt, who was on his way to the 1977 World Championship. I had to struggle to keep up with Mario on his way back to his motor home. He didn't leave much of a wake. Only five foot six and 138 pounds, with the broad-shouldered, slim-hipped build of a welterweight, he slipped like an eel through crowds. When he started racing the big USAC roadsters in 1964, he had trouble getting rides because nobody thought he was strong enough to handle them. Now his size was ideal for the low, cramped Formula One cars.

In the back of the motor home Mario stripped down to his electric blue briefs, cleaned up and put on a long-sleeved chambray shirt and light tan corduroy slacks to meet the press. He sat down at the dinette and demolished a peach and a bunch of grapes. No grapes are safe when Mario's around. Mario replayed the events of the race for reporters from England, Austria, Germany, Italy and America.

An easy talker, Mario drawled his replies in a nasal baritone still accented by his birth in Trieste, Italy in 1940. A heavy elephant-hair bracelet hung from his right wrist and a digital Seiko from his left. He wore two diamond-studded gold rings. On the right was that of the 1969 Indianapolis 500 winner. On the left hand, next to a small wedding band, was a USAC National Championship ring. Mario won that honour in 1965 – his rookie year on the full USAC circuit – and in 1966 and 1969.

'I'm going to continue racing as long as I feel I'm enjoying it,' Mario said to an American writer. 'If I said another year in Formula One, or another three years, I'd probably be here another ten years. I'll go as long as I feel I'm competitive and I'm enjoying it.'

At 37, all but ready for pasture in today's Formula One, a sport that eats young drivers alive, Mario looked ready for ten more years. His dark, wavy hair was longer and fuller than he'd worn it in 1965 when he placed third at Indy to win Rookie of the Year honours. The distinctive face with its Roman nose and downward-sloping eyebrows was more deeply creased now, especially when he pursed his lips and frowned – a typical Andretti expression.

As he talked, Mario's moods were betrayed by his warm hazel eyes, which registered boredom and then amusement. I've looked into the eyes of many drivers, from Fangio to Foyt, Moss to Clark, and I've seen a hardness there, a shutter down, a resistance. Not so with Mario.

That morning as I walked among the cars on the rainy starting grid, their drivers shadowed by the umbrellas they were holding, I looked through the oval eyehole in Mario's silver helmet. His eyes were starkly open, hungrily vacuuming in everything beyond his immediate universe: steering wheel, cowling and, at the periphery of his vision, the front wheels of his Lotus. Those eyes were exposed, open, waiting.

I was surprised at how vulnerable Mario seemed. I felt a wave of embarrassment at having seen him that way. I thought back to the toughness, almost ruthlessness, he'd shown in some of our conversations. To a question about being used by others for publicity, he countered, 'Publicity is fantastic. I need it. But unless I can put something on the table with it, *forget it.*'

Around eight that evening after the race, we met for dinner at Pierce's, the best restaurant in nearby Elmira. The Andretti clan gathered at a big round table in the middle of the second floor. I asked Mario about his much-publicised negotiations with Ferrari for the 1978 season.

'I think if I was really 100 per cent free to to go with Ferrari,' he told me, 'I would have done it.'

I asked him to expand on that. 'Well, last summer when I was asked to sign a letter of agreement to drive for Lotus in '78, there was only one other job I'd have wanted and that was number one for Ferrari. As far as I could see, there was *no way* Niki Lauda would give that up. So I signed with Lotus, feeling I couldn't do better. Colin has treated me quite well. He *really* has. But then Niki went to Brabham and the Ferrari job was open!'

'So you went to see Mr Ferrari?'

'Yeah. And right off, instead of insisting on having all my racing time, he asked me how many of the Formula One races I could make! That really surprised me. And later, when it was time to talk about terms, I suggested he make an offer. He said, "I could not put a price on your talent." Well, that really got me. That shows you the kind of gentleman he is. Later they did talk money. I went there with a closed mind but they made me a generous offer. I had to consider it.' But he did not desert Lotus.

When Mario visited Goodyear a few days later to speak to its employees, I tagged along. Mario gave them a folksy talk about teamwork. He leaned on the rostrum and worked the microphone with skill. The crowd warmed to him when he spoke quietly of the setbacks he'd experienced.

'Out of the great joys in my career, I've probably experienced as many disappointments as anyone. In fact, I could put my disappointments and frustrations up against those of any other man in motor racing.'

Some of those who feel his frustrations most are those closest to him, he said, like his father. 'I remember when I was just a teenager I wanted to be a racer. The man who was really dead against my doing anything like this was my father. Well, all that has changed, fortunately, because he just couldn't keep on licking me for 20 years!' The line got the laugh it deserved.

On my arrival at his home in Nazareth, Pennsylvania, for an interview, I waited in Mario's panelled den while he finished a phone call. I counted 28 plaques and awards on the walls. Some testified to his recognition by civil groups for outstanding service. A huge certificate showed he was a member of the President's Physical Fitness Council under Richard Nixon.

A miniature of the Borg-Warner trophy, the symbol of victory at Indianapolis, hung over his desk. Plaques told of his nominations to the All-American Racing Team by panels of racing writers. Photos of the many phases of his career were on the wall, on the couch and on the built-in bookshelves.

We began to talk about how and why he'd gotten into Formula One racing. He didn't agree with those who had counselled him to get started in it earlier. 'I'm one of those guys who's slow in maturing, slow in having *exactly* clear in my mind what I can do. Because of that, I feel that I can peak my career between now and 40. I feel I can do a lot smarter racing now than I ever could before.'

'In terms of trackcraft? Not just how to go fast but how to beat people?'

'That's right. I feel that I don't have to do it just out of bravery. But I still have a tendency, sometimes, to let some of the young inexperienced drivers take over and it pisses me off.' He pushed himself erect, frowning and looking out into the room. 'It only tells me that, shit, I'm still a tiger in my own self.

'Just like that last race in Japan,' he added. 'I tried to take two cars in one corner, which absolutely felt feasible. The only thing that I miscalculated was that I trusted the other guy too much. I made a mistake that I would've made when I was 25 and I take pride in not making those mistakes. Yet I made it and I kicked myself all the way back across the ocean. I should have been a little bit cooler there but I wasn't.'

Yes, I thought, the electricity is still there. Andretti wants to keep that tiger caged up, that aggressiveness that appeals to Colin Chapman and race fans alike, but he can't quite do it. More and more it bugged him that he couldn't. I was also struck by his comment that he could peak his racing career between now and the age of 40 – in three years. I asked about that:

'I have the underlying feeling that you feel some of the pressure of this time passing. There's an urgency to you and your objectives.' I was thinking of the impatience I'd seen at Watkins Glen. 'Maybe three, four or five years ago, talking to you, somebody wouldn't have sensed the same feeling of the sand slipping through the hourglass...'

'Yeah,' the reply came slowly. 'I must agree with you. As a matter of fact I even find myself anticipating that a little bit too much. Because the way I feel now, I honestly feel I have a good five years in my career so, no use panicking. But then I find myself thinking, "Shit, another one went under," you know? I used to be a lot more tolerant of failures than I am now. I'd like to see that glass, the sand, still full. I've been there, you know? Sometimes I think it's more empty than it really is.'

We talked about his 1977 season, when he couldn't convert his speed advantage into a championship.

'That's bad.' He shook his head. 'That's bad. Well, I had two Formula 5000 Championships just slip right through my fingers...'

'That's right. I forgot about that.'

'There're two championships that I could've won with one hand! I didn't make a single mistake that I could have kicked myself for. Some of the dumbest things happened to the car. Those were two championships that should have been in my pocket, but like I said, you didn't even remember 'em yourself!' He flashed me a triumphant grin.

'That's right,' I answered.' 'I remember the series but I didn't remember...'

'You see how important second is? Junk. Second is nothing. It's a pacifier, you know, for a little while. You figure, "Well, at least..." But it's nothing.'

I tried to change the subject to other goals that Mario may have had in racing. He'd mentioned that he'd like to add a Le Mans win to his trophies but he wasn't having a bar of it. He kept on talking about Formula One and as he did so he sat bolt upright and started ticking off his points on his fingers.

'Quite honestly I thought I'd be in Formula One maybe a couple of years. In '75 when I got in I figured, well, I'll do '75, '76 and '77 and I think I'll have my fill. Now all of a sudden I find there's no way I could leave this for anything else! No way! First of all, I think it's more lucrative than anything else I can do. Which is important. I won't hide that. And secondly, there's nothing else that comes close to giving me the satisfaction! I mean, *not even close!*' Mario was more animated, more enthusiastic than I'd ever seen him. He was glowing.

'How long that's gonna last, I really don't know. I find that instead of losing interest, I'm *gaining* it. More. Because now I know what it's all about. I've got the feel of it. And I don't feel like I want to give it up, see?' He smiled all over. 'When you do it and you win races, and you've got the championship right' – reaching out with a grasping right hand – 'just about there, you feel you can go for it. And I don't think I'll be satisfied until I give it a valiant, valiant try.'

'So you're going to ration yourself a little more in '78? Try to concentrate on Formula One?'

'Well, I'm trying,' he shrugged. 'You know, you gotta maintain a sparkle. You gotta be able to keep looking forward to going there. And I've found – not only now, I mean back in the late 60s too – I found toward the end of the season I hated to get into the goddamn race car! And I figured, "Come on, Andretti, sit down and let's talk about it. Why? Because, too much." Too much can be too much for anybody.

'I'm scared to come to the point that I won't enjoy it anymore,' Mario continued. 'But if I don't enjoy it anymore I'm gonna look for a time, yes, to quit! Let's face it: I enjoy it if I can make a comfortable living, which I don't think I could do by doing anything else. But there's nothing, nothing in this world that would make me do it unless I enjoyed it. Because if you don't, it's way too much of a burden. But I love it, I gen-u-inely love it. I'm ready to give anything for the sport as long as I feel this way.'

As we talked we heard the doorbell and, then, Mario's wife Dee Ann talking to the kids home from school. Most like Mario was Michael, 14, while 13-year-old Jeffrey had his mum's round features. We ambled down to say hi to them and to seven-year-old Barbie, a blonde waif with the big eyes of a Keane painting.

Mario showed me out through the garage, where an Alfa Romeo roadster and a Cadillac flanked his Ferrari. A red garden tractor had a big number one painted on it and there were racing posters on the wall. A serviceman was there, getting tools from his van to work on some piece of equipment. Mario immediately became engrossed in discussing it with him. He didn't look up or wave as I walked to my car.

For 1978, Colin Chapman fielded an improved car, the Lotus 79, with which Mario registered six wins and enough other top finishes to become World Drivers' Champion ahead of his well-respected team-mate Ronnie Peterson. Their placings gave Lotus the Constructors' Championship as well, the seventh and last that Lotus would win. His final full Formula One season was 1982 with an unrewarding Alfa Romeo.

From 1983 through 1994 Mario Andretti raced at Indianapolis for the Newman-Haas team, with a best finish of second in 1985. His last full season in the Indy Car Championship Series was 1994. He persevered at Le Mans in search of a victory through 2000, frequently partnered by his son Michael. He came closest with second place in 1995. Andretti is credited with a total of 109 victories in major events.

Like Juan Manuel Fangio, Mario Andretti became a legend in his own lifetime. He never lost the tremendous enthusiasm for the sport that I sensed in my visit to Nazareth.

CAR GUYS

BERNARD CAHIER

Often managing to be part of the show, Cahier here handed a cooling bottle to BRM-driving Harry Schell while Jo Bonnier looked on. Next lap Harry returned the empty.

When I was handling public relations for GM Styling Staff in the early 1960s, Bernard Cahier posed certain problems. Bernard's friendship with design chief Bill Mitchell was such that when he visited Detroit, the genial Frenchman would stay with Bill, who would bring a swathe of his latest prototypes to his home in Bloomfield Hills for Cahier to drive and photograph. This was a PR man's nightmare – a journalist completely out of his control!

This however, was an example of the kind of intimacy that Bernard Cahier enjoyed with the luminaries of the world motor industry. He was on similarly chummy terms with BMC's Alec Issigonis, Dante Giacosa at Fiat,

Porsche's Huschke von Hanstein and Rudolf Uhlenhaut at Mercedes-Benz. Like quite a few motoring journalists, Bernard wasn't shy about accepting their favours in the form of room, board and entertainment. He was not conspicuously generous in return. When I managed to grab the cheque from him after a lunch at New York's Le Chanteclair, he was visibly miffed. "I don't often offer to do that," Bernard admitted.

You could only relax and enjoy the friendship of Bernard Cahier and his vivacious blonde wife Joan, an American whom he met and married while they were both studying at UCLA. As I found in 1958, it was an agreeable ritual for drivers and team owners to go down the coast to the Cahier home near Nice for an enjoyable reception in the run-up to the Monaco Grand Prix. The scene is well depicted in the movie *Grand Prix*. Never at a loss for a joke or amusing aside, Bernard was the ultimate in amiability as host.

How did this Frenchman with the wide-set eyes and broad grin become such a star of the motoring world? Born in 1927, Bernard travelled to California in 1948 where he studied at UCLA. He took a job as a salesman at Hollywood's International Motors, run by Roger Barlow. A fellow salesman was Phil Hill while Richie Ginther worked in the service department. John and Elaine Bond of *Road & Track* could not fail to be impressed by Bernard's enthusiasm for the burgeoning world of sports cars.

In June of 1952, Bernard and Joan settled in France, where Cahier had impeccable forebears. His father was in the French military, rising to the rank of general, while his sister was the wife of the brother of Francois Miterrand, destined to be France's president. Initially from a base in Paris, Bernard began polishing his motor-sports credentials. His entrée was his role as a photojournalist for *L'Action Automobile*. He began working for the French magazine in 1952, his first photo shoot; the Italian Grand Prix.

Soon photos and reports from Cahier began to appear in *Road & Track*. By 1954 he was listed as a contributor and in mid-1955 he was officially appointed the magazine's European representative. At the end of that year, *R&T* editor John R. Bond made his first trip to Europe. Arriving in Paris, Bond related, 'we were met by our European representative and correspondent Bernard Cahier. A wild ride from Orly field to the heart of Paris in Bernard's trusty 2CV and a taxi left us all a bit shaken, but still in one piece.' Joan and Bernard made sure Bond and his party enjoyed the best of Paris's fabled night life.

Cahier's contributions were upbeat and uncritical, which helped his currying of favour among the world's motoring elite. They could be sure he would keep their confidences. He was not terribly technical, but he had unparalleled access that gave him first crack at new models and even new companies. In 1961 he took these talents to Petersen Publishing, which was rolling out *Sports Car Graphic* as a new monthly to compete with *R&T* and *Car and Driver*, which I was editing at the time.

Waspish chronicler of the Grand Prix scene Louis Stanley called Cahier 'an irrepressible scribe,' saying that 'for years he has darted about with a foot in every pit. He represents journalism by the odd expedient of not taking it too seriously. His style is sharp and colloquial – at times he reminds me of the brilliant talker who impresses the hell out of you at a cocktail party but who, when he turns to go home, seems vaguely lost. In Bernard's case it hardly applies for there is always his Joan, a patient wife, who takes over. They make a delightful team.'

Though his road tests could be anodyne, Bernard Cahier was no slouch behind the wheel. In 1956 he joined a squad of Renault Dauphines entered in the Mille Miglia alongside such aces as Grand Prix racers Louis Rosier, Paul Frère and Maurice Trintignant. Bernard and female co-driver Nadège Ferrier were tenth in class and 154th overall in this classic race through northern Italy.

Another outing for Cahier late in 1956 was as a member of a crew of journalists recruited to drive a Bertone-bodied Abarth-Fiat at Monza to tackle records in the 750 cc class. Joining such well-known writer-drivers as Paul Frère, Gordon Wilkins and Johnny Lurani, Bernard more than held up his leg of the assignment, including demanding night-time stints during the successful run.

By far Bernard Cahier's finest motor-sports achievement was his drive in the 1967 Targa Florio, 447 miles through the jagged hills and chasms of northern Sicily. Driving a works-prepared 911S Porsche, he placed seventh overall and won the class for 2.0-litre GT cars. Sensationally, his co-driver was fellow Frenchman Jean-Claude Killy, triple-gold-medal winner in the Winter Olympics. Together they gave the then-new 911S its first important success.

Cahier was also a wheeler-dealer in motor sports behind the scenes. When Californian Dan Gurney first visited Europe in 1958, Bernard arranged the loan of a Renault Dauphine in which Dan and 1958 Indy winner Troy

Ruttman drove from race to race and practised on the Nürburgring. There, Gurney competed in a 1.5-litre Osca, a ride which Cahier negotiated from Guglielmo "Mimo" Dei's Scuderia Centro Sud in Modena. The loan of a fatigued 250F Maserati by Dei to Ruttman was less of a success.

Right up Bernard Cahier's alley was the plan of director John Frankenheimer to film a movie about Formula One racing. Making himself indispensable to Frankenheimer, Cahier became a consultant to the production of *Grand Prix*. He even had a bit part in character as a journalist. Louis Stanley recalled a filming in which Bernard was to enter a room with Juan Fangio and film star Yves Montand: 'The first shot halted when the trio jammed in the doorway; the next shot ended with a mini-struggle to get through, and finally Fangio and Montand emerged with Cahier bringing up the rear.'

This was heady stuff for Cahier, who was born in Marseilles, where he saw his first Grand Prix at nearby Miramas at the tender age of five. As a teenager he aided the wartime resistance in Brittany and toward the end of the war joined an engineering arm of General Leclerc's Second Armoured Division, attached to George Patton's Third Army. After war's end he helped with vital mine clearing.

The post-war era brought a year in the French colony of Cameroon and then Bernard's California phase and his fateful meeting with Joan Updike at UCLA. The couple often wintered with her family at Long Beach in future years. Their son Paul-Henri carried on his father's tradition, specialising in motor-racing photography and building up their formidable archive accessible at www.f1-photo.com.

With other aspects of top-line racing becoming more professional, Cahier saw the need to provide clear recognition for people who were seriously covering motor sports. In 1968 he was one of the founders of the International Racing Press Association. Its members were granted press facilities by the FIA and Bernie Ecclestone's growing FOCA. In the IRPA's early days Bernard was its president, a post he retained until he retired in 1985.

The tyre wars of the 1970s brought a new role for Cahier as a roving public-relations ambassador for Goodyear, an assignment tailor-made for his gregarious nature and love of a good cigar. He continued in this role until 1983. Thereafter, however, no race or motor show was complete without an appearance by Bernard, usually in tweeds with a new confidence or two to impart.

When I wrote my book about the career of Jackie Stewart, Bernard was very helpful with photos. I dedicated the book to Cahier, calling him 'a friend, colleague and fine photographer whose many and valued contributions to motor sports over 50 years will only be appreciated when he writes a book of his own.' He subsequently did just that, titling it *F-Stops, Pit Stops, Laughter & Tears*.

Bernard left us in 2008 at the age of 81. One often hears people bemoaning the lack of big personalities among today's racing drivers. Well, the same applies to journalists. Nowadays, people like Berhard Cahier are few and far between.

RODOLFO
MAILANDER

'm not sure when the penny dropped. I arrived in Stuttgart in February
of 1958 as a private in Uncle Sam's Army, trained to fix field radios.
My Signal Corps unit was headquartered at Böblingen, south-west of
Stuttgart, where I awaited news while those above me decided where
in Germany they would send me to carry out second-echelon radio repairs.

Needless to say, when I knew I was Germany-bound I had not been slow
to make contact with Daimler-Benz, about whose cars I had written before
my career as technical editor of *Sports Cars Illustrated* was cut short by the
draft. When I called Untertürkheim from Böblingen I was put through to the
Mercedes man who dealt with the foreign press, a fellow named Rodolfo
Mailander. We agreed to meet for dinner; he fetched me from the *Panzer-
kaserne* on a snowy evening.

I had hardly settled in his 220 saloon when Mailander asked me, 'Who
told you about the way the valve gear worked in the 1955 racing cars?' I
had written about it in *Sports Cars Illustrated* after receiving photographs of
the 1954-55 W196 GP Mercedes-Benz. He was referring to the sophisticated
way the clearances for the valve-closing rocker arms were adjusted, which
was considered a major trade secret.

I told him that I had figured it out by looking at the pictures and drawings
they provided to our European editor, Jesse Alexander.

'Oh my God,' he said. 'We have been turning the place upside-down to
find out who told you about that!'

This intimate instance turned out to be my calling card at Mercedes-Benz,
the 'open sesame' that soon had me meeting the inventor of the valve gear
and seeing his prototypes. Remarkably, only when they started checking
patents did Daimler-Benz discover that they had not invented the desmo-
dromic valve operation that did away with troublesome springs. They
discovered that many such systems had been built earlier and even raced.

*The tables were turned on Mailander at Reims in 1954 when the
Cunningham team's documentary photographer Derek Waller pictured
Rudy chatting with his wife Mary.*

Theirs was the brainchild of engineer Hans Gassmann, who conceived and patented the Mercedes system from scratch.

Mailander and I enjoyed a genial dinner in downtown Stuttgart, opposite the *Bahnhof*, and he drove me back to Böblingen. During that dinner it must have dawned on me that my host was *the* Rodolfo Mailander, the photo-journalist whose illustrated reports from Europe I had enjoyed in *Auto Speed & Sport*. In this magazine, a worthy effort by Robert Petersen in 1952 and 1953 to barge into *Road & Track* territory with a monthly for the sporty set, Mailander's material was among its strongest offerings. I had also seen the Mailander photo credit in *Automobile Year* among other publications.

Great images resulted from Rudy's initiative. His technical proficiency combined with an unerring eye achieved wonderfully consistent and image-rich negatives on Agfa, Ilford and Kodak film. With his German, French, Italian and English, he was quickly at home with all the drivers and car builders, who appreciated his knowledge and enthusiasm. Their acceptance of Mailander as part of the racing 'circus' is obvious from the warmth that many of his images display.

When I asked Rudy how he came to the profession that he pursued from 1950 to 1955 he explained: 'I was in Germany after the war but I very much wanted to get back to Italy, so I started to write for the famous editor Canestrini, whom I had come to know by chance before the war. He was interested in getting some articles about the situation in Germany and so on, so I started writing for Canestrini. No photographs yet; that came later.

'Then I decided that this was fun,' Rudy continued. 'In Stuttgart I knew a gentleman who was a German sports reporter, writing for *auto motor und sport*. So when he was to go to Italy or to Monte Carlo he said, "Right, we could do something together. You make the photographs and I write and you help me with the language and so forth." And so I started.

'Then one day at the Geneva Grand Prix, Robert Braunschweig, editor of the Swiss *Automobil Revue*, took me aside and said, "I've seen some articles of yours, some photographs. Would you like to help us? We could start with a story about the Via Emilia, which is home to Ferrari, Maserati and the other Italian sports-car and motorcycle makers." So I wrote an article and then I didn't hear anything for two months or so – or three months it was.

'In the meantime,' Mailander continued, 'I stopped every week to buy *Automobil Revue*, which was very difficult to find. Then one day when I was in Milan, Ing. Satta from Alfa Romeo phoned and said, "Congratulations!" And I said, "For what?" And he said, "For your article, of course!" I thought that because he was a high-ranking Alfa Romeo engineer, he had seen Braunschweig who had told him that I was sending an article. But he said, "No, no. It's two pages and in the next issue there is another page." So I looked and looked and couldn't find it immediately so I went to Lugano to buy one. I finally saw it. I was very happy about that.

'Then Braunschweig phoned and said he had had some very good comments on it and he wanted me to work for them. I became their travelling correspondent. The first car I had was a Mercedes 170 diesel that my father bought me and then I changed the 170 to a Porsche. I liked the Porsche very much. When I visited a girl I could take her with me – but not her mother as well!'

Rudy took wonderful pictures of Enzo Ferrari and his cars, both at the factory and on the track. I asked him how he accomplished this. 'Ferrari was a very difficult character,' he replied. 'He always gave you an appointment when he wasn't there. You had to wait and somebody took you out for lunch, waiting until he arrived. Maybe he was there, but they told you, "No, he's not here because he has other things on" and so on. Ferrari said, "Oh, let him wait, he's...not so important..." And I did this twice. The third time, after two hours I went away and left him. At that time he needed publicity for a new Ferrari automobile and Braunschweig always kept him very much involved, so Ferrari said he was very upset that I went away.

'The next morning I decided to take a chance,' Rudy added. 'I went to the barber shop where he went every morning and waited there for him. I said, "I'm awfully sorry but the last time I waited one day and then they told me, 'No, you had no time and to come the next day.'" It amused him that somebody would do that, so from then on he was always there when he asked me to call on him.'

Since 1955 the cosmopolitan and polished Mailander had been working for Daimler-Benz. Though he had sold his Leica – to his later regret – he still had his photographic archives. During my spare time from radio repair I was still writing for *SCI*, so I went through his contact prints and asked for a number of images that I needed for my own journalism.

Our relationship became more than professional. Rudy and his wife Helga visited in Munich, where I was assigned, and I saw them in Stuttgart as well. We kept in touch when I returned to the States. During these years Rudy joined Fiat, he and Helga settling in a wonderful old house part-way up the vertiginous climb to the Superga Basilica on the eastern outskirts of Turin. From 1902 to 1960 this was the venue for the 2.9-mile Sassi-Superga hill-climb. So steep was the twisting road, that the arrival of front-drive Fiats in the 1960s meant that in winter it could only be surmounted in reverse.

The Mailander house was lovely, set back into the hillside. The only problem was that it was threatening to slide down into the road and off the hill. In the early 1970s Rudy decided to fund the necessary building work by selling his photo archive. He and I had kept in touch on this topic. As luck would have it, I was able to prevent his well-ordered negatives and contact prints from joining the Kurt Wörner archive at *Road & Track*.

Rudy Mailander and I became professionally linked at the end of the 1970s when I joined Fiat Motors of North America; we had some business areas in common. By then he had risen to the top floor of Fiat's headquarters at Corso Marconi 10 and a senior role as aide-de-camp to the *Avvocato* himself, Gianni Agnelli. Thanks in part to his mastery of the principal languages, he was widely active in Fiat's governmental and quasi-governmental contacts and initiatives around the world.

In the early 1980s, Rudy and I shared similar portfolios when I moved to Ford of Europe in England to look after governmental affairs as well as motor sports. When I bought a Stratos from Lancia, he garaged it for a while at his new house in the country, not far from Fiat's proving ground at La Mandria.

Rudy's life was clouded when Helga died all too young. Their daughters, Monica and Carolina, are beautiful and brilliant reminders of that relationship. They are actively and successfully running Studio Mailander in Turin, providing marketing and public relations services to many companies.

Later Rudy met and married Carla, with whom he shared the Turin home and a flat in Nice. Our friendship was the best possible reason for my wife Annette and me to head for Turin during the autumnal white-truffle season. Rudy reciprocated by visiting London when many of his stunning images of the Mille Miglia starred in a major exhibition at leather-product maker Connolly.

The Mailander images were the core of the holdings of the Ludvigsen Library, which provided car and motor-racing images to publishers and collectors world-wide. I first started drawing on them in depth in 1997 when they richly illustrated my biography of Stirling Moss. Rudy and Moss became friends in 1950 when the young Briton was first campaigning seriously on the Continent. When Rudy asked Moss where he should position himself on a circuit to get the best photos, Stirling was quick to help. After Moss crashed two races in a row just where he had suggested that Mailander stand, he ceased providing advice!

I last spent quality time with Rudy when I was planning my book *Ferrari by Mailander*, which features 500 of his images. We had a great time looking through them while he recalled the people and events. Designed by Simon Loxley and published by Dalton Watson, the book that resulted is wonderful. In 2005 the Mailander girls arranged a fabulous exhibition of its best images at the Pinacoteca Giovanni e Marelli Agnelli atop the old Fiat Lingotto factory in the heart of Turin. The show resulted in marvellous and well-deserved tributes to Rudy.

Several years later I had planned to get together with Mailander again to review photos for the second such book, *Porsche by Mailander*, when I received news that Rudy was seriously unwell. He left hospital for his home, where he died in the early morning of 1 April 2008 at the age of 85.

When early in the 21st century I decided to part with my automotive archive, it was acquired by the Collier Collection in Naples, Florida. It is no exaggeration to say that Mailander's images represented the valuable core of my photo and negative archive. For that reason I'm pleased that they are still available to researchers who can find them on the internet at the REVS Digital Archive.

PAUL FRÈRE

Settling into his Ferrari Super Squalo at Spa in 1955, from eighth on the grid Paul Frère finished fourth behind Fangio, Moss and Farina. Not bad for a journalist!

first read about Paul Frère in the 16 June 1948 issue of *The Motor*. Two of its editors had visited Belgium to try various American cars, including the new Frazer, built by Kaiser-Frazer, for whose importer, Frère, worked as service manager. The Englishmen were important contacts for car-mad Frère, who was beginning a career as an automotive journalist while also competing successfully in motorcycle trials and races.

Born to Belgian parents in Le Havre, France on 30 January 1917, Paul Frère moved frequently on the Continent as a youth. Including a spell at school in England, this brought him the flawless command of Dutch,

French, German, Italian and English with which he communicated with people at all levels of the industry and sport. Witnessing a motor race at Spa at the age of nine attracted him strongly to the sport. Although he earned a commercial engineering degree from Brussels University, he decided that journalism was a milieu that would leave him more free time for racing.

As a Belgian citizen, young Frère managed to avoid being caught up in the devastation of World War II. He started writing for various local journals including *Belgique Automobile*. A career breakthrough came in 1952 when Frère was appointed co-editor of *Royal Auto*, the organ of Belgium's Royal Automobile Club. His joint editor was Jacques Ickx, who had an outstanding reputation as editor, journalist, historian and all-round expert.

The generous Ickx, father of future racing driver Jacky Ickx, gave the 35-year-old Frère warm introductions to leading industry figures. For almost 40 years Paul was a regular contributor to Japan's *Car Graphic* while his tenure as European Editor of *Road & Track* lasted until the end of his life. With his editing and journalism as a stable base for the first time, Paul started taking his racing seriously.

While most auto journalists fancy themselves excellent drivers, Paul Frère really was. He first raced close to home at Spa Francorchamps in July 1948's 24-hour contest, sharing the seat of the MG PB Midget of Jacques Swaters, future Ferrari importer to Belgium. They finished fifteenth and fourth in class. The winner was an Aston Martin driven by Jock Horsfall, who invited Paul to partner him the following year. They placed fourth and second in class, splitting a pair of the new DB2 Astons.

Frère rested his driving kit until 1952, when he won a production-car race on Belgium's Spa circuit driving an Oldsmobile 88. The next year he won his class in the demanding Mille Miglia. His mount, which placed 58th overall and was all but brakeless for the last 400 of the 1,000 miles, was a 1952 Chrysler Saratoga with Torqueflite transmission.

His 1952 success with the Oldsmobile led to an invitation to compete in that year's Belgian Grand Prix if he could find a suitable car. Paul approached the British HWM team, which offered him a mount for a lesser event at Chimay instead. This the journalist promptly won, setting a new lap record when taking the lead on the last corner of the last lap. This sealed a seat in the HWM team for the Spa race in which Frère finished an excellent fifth.

This remained Paul's best result for HWM, for whom he drove a few more times before switching to Gordini in 1954, when he retired in his three outings – not unusual for Gordini drivers. He did enough, however, to attract the attention of Enzo Ferrari.

Frère raced Formula One cars for Ferrari three times, placing fourth in the Belgian GP in 1955 and an excellent second in the same race in 1956. At Monaco in 1955, he shared an eighth place with Piero Taruffi, who turned the Super Squalo over to Frère after several pit stops. During practice Paul had complained bitterly about terrible understeer on the sinuous circuit, urging the mechanics to disconnect the front anti-roll bar which he knew was aggravating the problem. They couldn't do that, he was told: it was 'part of the car'.

Of medium height, sandy-haired, open-faced and very fit, Paul Frère kept in shape in his youth as an oarsman. In 1946 and 1947 he won three Belgian rowing championships in four-oared shells. He often raced cars for the Ecurie Nationale Belge, whose patron Pierre Stasse was publisher of Les Sports for which our hero was now writing.

Starting in 1953, Paul was a regular competitor at Le Mans, driving class-winning cars. Alert to new talent, Porsche's Huschke von Hanstein recruited Paul to drive one of the two new Porsche Type 550 coupes that year. He joined another driver-journalist, Richard von Frankenberg, who was expecting Huschke as his co-driver. However, Ferry Porsche felt that for such an important event, von Hanstein should be in the pits managing the team, not in the cockpit.

New to both the mid-engined Porsche and Le Mans, Paul Frère was in for a surprise. It was turning dark by the time he had a chance to drive on a circuit he needed to learn. He also assumed that the 550 'would handle better than a standard 356. On the first lap I very nearly lost it on the first left-hander after the Dunlop Bridge! Very tricky car.' Mid-engined or not, the elements that made up the 550 contributed to sudden albeit manageable oversteer. All the other drivers were already aware of this. Though both Porsches entered finished on the same lap, Frère's was ahead to take the class win.

Taken up by Aston Martin, Paul Frère won a sports-car race at Spa in 1955 and shared the second-place Aston at Le Mans that year. Frère decided to make an all-out attempt to win. This meant a Ferrari, so in 1960 he pulled some strings to wangle a seat in a Testarossa. He and Olivier Gendebien were the team's only survivors – and the winners.

After this fine result, Enzo Ferrari offered Paul a permanent post at Maranello in charge of car preparation and testing plus a regular place in the sports-car team. Frère decided against the move to Italy that the job would have required.

In 1956, Paul Frère joined the Jaguar team, which was racing its well-proved D-Type in the final year of works entries. Under the eye of team manager Lofty England, the Belgian driver got off to an awkward start. In the Nürburgring 1,000 Kilometres, he crashed a car during practice and retired another in the race with gearbox trouble. He made amends in the Reims 12 Hours, placing second with Mike Hawthorn in the middle of a trio of triumphant Jaguars.

This boded well for Le Mans, but with a full tank of petrol in the rain on a newly surfaced track, he lost control in the Esses on his second lap and retired not only his own D-Type but also that of a team-mate and a member of the Ferrari team. 'When I got back to the pits,' Paul related, 'after half an hour's walk, Hawthorn's car was standing there. All hope for a win by our team had vanished. I could find no words to explain my despair to he who had taken upon himself the responsibility of picking a foreign driver for the Jaguar team. But Lofty knows about racing, knows its risks and the fact that human beings are not infallible. Before I even opened my mouth he seemed to understand my confusion and made not the slightest reproach.'

I first met Paul Frère at the Turin Show in 1958 when we were both attending a demonstration of the latest from Carlo Abarth, a twin-cam version of his little 750 cc coupe. After then we often met at motor shows and Car of the Year gatherings to swap thoughts about the business.

Our last lengthy spell together occurred when pre-production Porsche Boxsters were being driven by journalists at what press chief Anton Hunger called 'the longest and most elaborate press event that Porsche has ever held.' Its base was the Schlosshotel Lerbach near Bergisch Gladbach, east of Cologne, where 800 auto writers from all parts of the world drove Boxsters during four weeks starting on 23 August 1996.

When on a press trip, I preferred to drive alone. With both of us assigned the same blue Boxster, Paul made no secret of the fact that he usually drove alone. Nevertheless we both got with the programme, alternating between driving and navigating. Paul was as smooth and fast as you would expect while I did my best to act like a tester, not a racer. We both formed positive views of the Boxster.

As an industry insider, Paul Frère was often asked for private opinions about new models, a role that developed into regular consultancies for a tyre maker and for Lancia, Fiat and Mazda. His close relationship with Ferdinand Piëch at Porsche led to several books about their racing cars and his stand-alone work on the 911. As well it gave him the chance to test-drive almost every racing Porsche of his era.

For a dozen years Frère was a member of the FISA Technical Commission that drew up rules for international racing. His was the idea that led to the Group C regulations starting in 1982 that controlled cars chiefly by the amount of fuel they were allowed to carry. Although Paul wasn't entirely happy with the way this was implemented, it led to a great era in endurance racing.

Paul Frère's many fans were delighted when he put his personal experiences between hard covers in three books: *On the Starting Grid; Sports Car and Competition Driving*, and *My Life Full of Cars*. I didn't hesitate to comb them for gems that could sparkle in my own works.

One that I especially remember was his recollection of Ferrari 'team manager Nello Ugolini briefing us – Farina, Trintignant and myself – on the morning of the 1955 Belgian Grand Prix and making his recommendation: "We know that the Mercedes will be very difficult to beat, but our main target is to beat the Maseratis." On that occasion we did, Farina taking third place and myself fourth.'

In 2003, at 87, Paul drove an Audi R8 during the official Le Mans test days. He was thought to be the oldest man to drive a current racing car on an official track. In 2007 he was driving a Honda Civic Type-R in a press launch at the Nürburgring when he crashed heavily. He suffered a broken pelvis, broken ribs and punctured lungs, putting him into intensive care for a fortnight.

Never having fully recovered, on 23 February 2008 Paul Frère died at Saint-Paul-de-Vence in the south of France where he had long dwelled. His was a unique and memorable career behind the wheel and typewriter. He is honoured with the renaming after him of a curve on the Spa circuit.

Bibliographic information of the German National Library
The German National Library lists this publication
in the Deutsche Nationalbibliografie; more detailed bibliographic
information can be found online at http://dnb.dnb.de.

1st edition
ISBN 978-3-667-11457-0
© Delius Klasing & Co. KG, Bielefeld (Germany)

Proofreading: Kaye Müller, Hanno Vienken
Picture credits: Ludvigsen Partners except for Stefan Habsburg from GM Media Archives,
and Phil Hill from Motoring Picture Library/Alamy Stock Photo
Cover design: Felix Kempf, www.fx68.de
Typesetting: Axel Gerber
Lithography: Mohn Media, Gütersloh
Printer: Pustet, Regensburg
Printed in Germany 2019

Delius Klasing Verlag
Siekerwall 21, 33602 Bielefeld, Germany
Phone: +49-521-559-0, Fax: +49-521-559-115
Email: info@delius-klasing.de
www.delius-klasing.de

The Alabama Gang

Cover Photo Credits
Front cover: (from left) Donnie Allison, Eddie Allison and Bobby
Allison, photo courtesy of the Allison family
Back cover: (from left) Bobby Allison, Red Farmer and Donnie Allison,
photo courtesy of the International Motor Sports Hall of Fame

Published by
THE BIRMINGHAM NEWS
Birmingham, Alabama
Division of Special Projects
(205)325-3188

ISBN 0-9635413-3-1

Book Design and Typography:
Carolyn Leath & Lori Leath-Smith

To obtain copies of this book by mail, please send $12.00 which includes shipping and handling to The
Birmingham News, Division of Special Projects, P.O.Box 2553, Birmingham, AL 35202.

Table of Contents

1

Who Are These Guys?

The old joke is that the first automobile race was run on the day the second automobile was manufactured. If it isn't true, it at least speaks volumes about men's—and women's—compulsion to test themselves and each other at mechanized speed. No one knows for certain the date of the first auto race, but it was before the turn of the century. The first one at Daytona Beach, the Mecca of stock car racing, was in 1902. Ransom E. Olds, father of the Oldsmobile, was the first man to drive on the hard-packed beach in a timed run. Minutes afterward he bubbled to his friend Alexander Winton, who also owned an automobile company: "You have no idea, Alex, what a thrill it is out there! Do you know what it feels like to go 50 miles an hour?"

The upshot was a match race in which they finished side by side, each sportsman declaring the result a tie.

A milestone in the history of automobile racing in Alabama was the opening of a speedway at the state fairgrounds in 1925. Over the years it would be known as Fairgrounds Speedway, Birmingham International Raceway, Birmingham Super Speedway and Fairgrounds Raceway, but by any name it is recognized as the mother church of the Alabama Gang. And just what is the Alabama Gang? The original Alabama Gang consisted of Red Farmer and the Allison brothers,

Bobby and Donnie. They traveled to short racks over the Southland together. To the consternation of the local hotshots, they frequently claimed the top three finishing positions. One night in the early 1960s, as they towed their racers into the pits at the track in the Carolinas, a local groaned, "Oh, no, there comes that Alabama gang," and a nickname was born.

Later the name came to embrace such stars as Neil Bonnett and Davey Allison. It applies to all Alabama stock car drivers.

No study of the Alabama Gang—narrow or broad in definition—would be complete without an overview of Fairgrounds Raceway, which is now operated by Don Leo and Tony Davis.

It is believed to be the oldest speedway in the South. Approaching 70, it is as worn as an old tire. Compared to Talladega Super Speedway, it isn't much, but it used to be viewed as a marvel, the center of automobile racing in this state, and it always will be remembered as the former "home court" of the Alabama Gang.

Horses were raced at the state fairgrounds as early as 1889, on a one-mile dirt track that ran parallel to Third Avenue West. In 1925 the present speedway opened, and visitors to the state fair gawked at a 10,000-seat covered grandstand that looked out upon a dirt half-mile track. Construction cost $200,000.

Though horses continued to run at the new facility, its appearance ushered in the era of organized auto racing. During the 1925 fair, some 30,000 spectators filled the grandstand and clustered around the track to watch an automobile extravaganza at which the Chevrolet brothers of Indianapolis showed their new Frontenac, a car designed for racing on short dirt tracks.

Word of the imposing new structure spread, and soon top drivers from over the nation were trying their skills here. Cigar-chomping Barney Oldfield raced in Birmingham, and a list of the greats who competed at the fairgrounds eventually would include A.J. Foyt, Richard Petty, Tom Sneva, Fireball Roberts, Tony Bettenhausen, Troy Ruttman, Alec Sloan, Eddie Sachs, Buck Baker, Darrell Waltrip, Fonty Flock, Cale Yarborough, Ned Jarrett and Marshall Teague.

Bill Latham was one of the big winners in fairgrounds history.

For years auto racing was basically a feature of the fair, but in the late 1940s J.P. Rotton began promoting weekly events at the track. The war was over, and folks were ready to let off some steam, have some fun. Loud cars in thrilling speed contests filled the bill.

So a new era began. The heroes didn't merely show up once a year; they were at the fairgrounds every Sunday. Men such as Bill Latham, Nero Steptoe, Sonny Black, Ed Samples, Jake Hatcher, Earl Abts, Fred Thompson, Tommy Wells, Gober Sosebee, Charlie Parrish, Joe Lee Johnson, Joe Holley, Fletcher Ford, Gene Tapia, Malcolm Brady, Charlie Griffith, Bob Reuther, Freddy Fryar and Jack Smith were weekly warriors.

Fans from over the state used up Sundays in attending the races in Birmingham. There was no air conditioning and no cable TV to tempt them to stay home, so an afternoon under the roof of the massive grandstand didn't seem so uncomfortable.

The Birmingham facility (described by Bill France, who promoted a race there in 1948, as "the biggest I had ever seen in the South") drew huge crowds. Entrepreneurs took note, and tracks began springing up at every crossroads in Alabama. They ranged from neat, paved quarter-miles to ovals scraped out of pastures with hillside seats fashioned of slabs. There would be race tracks in Montgomery, Huntsville, Midfield,

Races at the fairgrounds in the '50s were run in a cloud of dust.

Gadsden, Crystal Springs, Guntersville, Mobile, Sayre, Hollis Crossroads, Oxford, Eastaboga, Cullman and numerous other locales. In 1950 there were 17 professional baseball teams in Alabama, but that slow-paced scene would fade out, partially because of speed mania.

The hot-rodders were competitive, combative, life-loving men, blessed with that Southern knack of appreciating and telling anecdotes.

Joe Lee Johnson experienced the horror of slapping a racing opponent's eye out. He thinks it may have happened at Midfield's Dixie Speedway, which no longer exists, but he isn't sure.

"I can't hardly remember 30 minutes ago," said Johnson, who now operates a dirt track in Cleveland, Tenn.

"They had one of those pursuit races where when you got passed you dropped out," Johnson said. "His name was Joe. I don't remember his last name. But he passed me and spun me out. I came in and hit him,

and his eye fell out."

The story isn't as gruesome as it sounds. "I couldn't say anything," Johnson continued. "I didn't know what was going on. It wasn't until later that somebody told me it was a glass eye, but for awhile I didn't know what I'd gone and done. Anyway, I felt bad about it later."

Bill Latham recalls "a strange, strange thing" that happened during his racing career.

"There was a boy named Frank Reed from Murfreesboro, Tenn., and he and I were far out in front in the point standings at the fairgrounds in 1956. There was no way anybody could catch us. We'd been swapping features every week. He was one super driver.

"We'd run two days during fair week in Nashville. But this time I decided not to go. Well, Reed got killed at Nashville. He came out of turn two, and a board from the fence went through his stomach and killed him.

"J.P. Rotton was the promoter at Birmingham—the best promoter I've ever known. There was a race or two to go at the fairgrounds, and I said it wouldn't be any fun, to just declare Reed the champion. J.P. ran the races, but they didn't pay points, so Reed was the champion.

"There was going to be a Frank Reed Memorial Race on the last day. My car was skipping and everything, and there was no way I could win. But all of a sudden my car just started running perfectly, and I won the Frank Reed Memorial. I gave the trophy to his widow.

"Then, when it was time for the feature, my car just started running bad again.

"It was strange."

Cosby Hodges drove the fairgrounds, but he never won a feature. "I remember one Labor Day there was a race, and 74 cars started," he said. "Seventy-four cars on a half-mile dirt track. I qualified sixth and finished about the same position. I avoided every accident." Hodges smiles about his "career" in Grand National, now called Winston Cup, the big league of stock car racing.

"I was supposed to drive one of Jack Smith's factory Pontiacs at the fairgrounds. We worked all day on Saturday, trying to get the car to handle. I told Grayson Rose to get it out there early Sunday morning, the day of the race, because I needed practice time. I didn't want to dis-

grace myself in front of those people. I wanted to be the first in line to practice.

"Well, I waited and waited and waited. Richard Petty asked me, 'Did it tear up your car too bad to run?'

"I said, 'What in the world are you talking about?'

"He said, 'Why, they wrecked your car on the way to the race track.'

"Grayson didn't like to use a tow chain, and the trailer had hopped off the tow car where Sixth Avenue South runs into Elmwood Cemetery. It had hit a big oak tree in the cemetery. The car was beyond racing that day. So that was my Grand National career.

"Richard Petty said, 'That's probably the luckiest thing that ever happened to you.'

"After thinking it over, I agreed with him."

Mechanics, drivers and promoters were resourceful in the old days.

Rose, a mechanical genius and builder of superb race cars, learned that adding a little water to the methanol fuel would actually make a car perform better. So he sold bottles of his special "additive" to the other teams. They didn't know they were buying water.

Rose was a man who would go to outrageous lengths for a joke. In those pre-interstate days he bet a pal he could he could get a motorless car from Birmingham to Tuscaloosa. He hauled it out to the highway, flagged down a motorist, and asked for a push. When the fellow tired of pushing, Rose would beg, "Just a little more, and I think it will start." This went on through several pushers until the car was in Tuscaloosa, and Rose won his bet.

On one racing trip, Rose caught a possum and tied it under the bed in a mom-and-pop motel. He called the proprietor and complained that a mouse was squeaking under his bed. The owner came to the room with a broom, stuck his head under the bed—and bolted out of the room screaming.

Alf Knight, a figure popular in Birmingham racing circles, was promoting a race on a dirt track in Georgia in the 1940s. It was a brutally hot Sunday, so he made a huge barrel of lemonade for the concession stand.

The race started, and the cars immediately churned up a cloud of pink Georgia dust. After several laps, Knight realized he had left the barrel of lemonade uncovered, and the dust had settled on it.

So what did he do?

"I stirred it up and sold it for pink lemonade," he said. Nick Sergio remembers racing at the Iron Bowl, a Birmingham dirt track that is long gone.

"It was tough to drive," he said, "but since I was young it was a challenge. If you could master the Iron Bowl, you had a good start in racing. It was a little less than a quarter-mile, but you might call it a quarter-mile. It wasn't an oval. It was sort of triangular."

One of the curves, he said, was banked to the outside, which made it tricky to drive indeed.

B.J. Parker, a driver who later would promote races at the fairgrounds and at Dixie Speedway in the Birmingham suburb of Midfield, recalled a skirmish for the local racing dollar.

"The fairgrounds was battling the Iron Bowl after the war. One was trying to get ahead of the other, and they opened the fairgrounds on New Year's Day. It was cold, and the cars had to run anti-freeze."

Parker won some heat races, but he never won a feature at the fair-

Photo courtesy of Carl Jones

Carl Jones and his opponents didn't wear drivers' uniforms.

grounds. He may have set a dubious record, though. "I drove in a long race and spun out so many times they just blackflagged me and made me quit. It was Johnny Day's car. It handled so bad he wouldn't even drive it. But I said I would."

Old drivers have fond memories of hairy incidents at the track. "I remember one time my car caught fire," Carl Jones said, "and by the time it got to the first turn it was driverless. I couldn't get it stopped, so I just bailed out."

Bo Fields' driving career spanned the dirt and pavement days at the fairgrounds.

"I loved them both," he said. "But you felt better after a pavement race. That calcium chloride they used to keep the dust down would get in your head, and you'd feel bad for three days. It would work on your sinuses. I drove with a rag over my face."

There was a time when safety measures left something to be desired. "I remember when the guardrail was some four-by-fours in the ground with a two-by-six nailed across them," Fields said." One time I spun out, and a two-by-six came through my back window and hit my helmet and went on through the windshield. Frank Reed got killed that way at Nashville. One went all the way through him."

Calvin Cobb was the best driver on fairgrounds dirt Fields ever saw. "He was an older fellow from Anniston. He was so smooth on dirt, a fantastic driver and a good person."

The best driver on pavement at the fairgrounds? "Donnie Allison would have to take the cake," Fields said. "Donnie had a knack for handling a car. He had the most natural ability in the world."

J.P. Rotton smiles fondly when he recalls his days as promoter of fairgrounds dirt. "A crowd of 6,000 or 7,000 was just ordinary. A big crowd was 10,000 or 11,000.

"Of course, there's a lot more stuff to do today than there was then." A fellow didn't always have to have the prescribed number of wheels to win a race at the fairgrounds.

"Nero Steptoe won a race on three wheels," Rotton recalled. "He was leading, and he lost his right front wheel, the hub and everything. We gave him the black flag, but he was afraid to stop, afraid his front end would dig in and wreck him. So he drove on for two or three laps

and won the race.

"We just went on and gave it to him. We paid two first places, to Nero and the man who was running behind him. He put on such a show that everybody was on their feet."

If you could win in Birmingham, you could win anywhere, racing folks used to say. Four decades after the fact, Carl Jones' eyes dance when he recalls Rotton's importing a hotshot to challenge the locals.

"He was the Louisiana champion," the ex-driver said. "He had a black car and wore a black suit. He was supposed to really be something. But he didn't even make the slow heat. We blew his doors off."

The old Alabama drivers usually say they believe racing was more fun in their day than it is now. It was professional in that they were paid purses, but money wasn't the main lure; indeed, actually turning a profit was difficult. They battled each other in their cars and sometimes with their fists, but by next Sunday—well, maybe the one after that—they were pals again. They were opponents, but they were comrades in that they shared a marvelous experience.

It was onto this scene that three drivers from Miami burst in the late 1950s. Bobby Allison, Donnie Allison and Red Farmer were tired of the meager purses that Florida tracks paid, and they wanted some of that Alabama money. Local racing would not be the same after their arrival.

2

Red, Donnie and Bobby

Charles Farmer, who was called Red for the usual reason, was not the shy, retiring type. "We used to skip school and go to this old abandoned strip mine," he recalled his teen-aged years in Miami. "We'd climb these Australian pines that were 30 or 40 feet high and do flips off of them into the water.

"Alligators would be sunning themselves on the banks, and we'd grab their tails and try to pull them into the water."

Wasn't that, uh, dangerous?

"Well, if they were over five or six feet long, we let them alone."

Farmer was a transplanted Floridian. When he was 14 or 15 years old his parents divorced, and his mother left his native Nashville to live with her parents in Miami.

It was in the Miami area that he discovered another activity that could be even more perilous than jerking alligators' tails. He was 16 when he drove in his first automobile race. It was 1949.

The father of one of his friends had a car that raced at Opa Locka Speedway. Now, "speedway" was a stretch, for the locale was an abandoned airport, the straightaways were parallel asphalt runways, and the turns were sand.

One day the regular driver didn't show up, and Farmer pronounced,

"I'll drive that thing."

"Have at it," the owner said.

"I was coming up through the pack," Farmer remembered 45 years later, "but the car flipped and rolled four times. It was the most fun I'd ever had."

The bug had bitten. That was the beginning of a career that would lead to more than 700 victories, four NASCAR national championships and induction into the Alabama Sports Hall of Fame.

Farmer attended electrical school and became an electrician, but he raced, too.

"There weren't any divisions then like there are now," he recalled. "A guy who had never raced before started right there beside a veteran. I ran against Fireball Roberts, Banjo Mathews, Joe Weatherly, Jack Smith, Curtis Turner, the Flock brothers, Bobby Johns.

"I guess Ralph Moody was living in the Carolinas, and he came down and won eight out of 10 features. He had a red car with an X on it. He stayed half a season and won everything. He and I still joke about it when we see each other."

Farmer remembers the first race car he ever owned. "Joan and I hadn't been married long when I got an old '40 Ford. I wasn't sure where the transmission was, much less the engine. I worked on it under a mulberry tree, and my light was a bedroom lamp with the shade off. Joan held it for me."

Red and Joan Farmer (who was as redheaded as he was) married in 1950. "I met her at a skating rink," he said. "I used to be a hotshot skater. That was my hangout."

Farmer got more than a wife. "My father-in-law had a Jaguar, and I raced it on road courses for him," Red said. "He also had a hydroplane, and I raced that for him."

Though only 20, Farmer leaped into what was then the big time of stock car racing when he entered the Grand National (now known as Winston Cup) centerpiece of Daytona's 1953 Speed Weeks.

Now, the magnificent Daytona International Speedway hadn't been built, and the races were still being held on the beach-road course. It was a 4.1-mile layout. The hard-packed beach was one straightaway, and the other was a public highway.

A young Red Farmer prepares for race.

The record shows that Farmer started 41st and finished 45th in a 57-car field. He completed 12 of the 39 laps.

Fonty Flock led every lap but the last one. He had a 65-second lead when he ran out of gas as he took the white flag. His teammate Slick Smith pushed Flock's car into the pits, but it was too late. Bill Blair won the race, and Flock was second. For whatever it's worth, one Slow Poke Travis finished 25th.

"My mechanic and I drove the race car up from Miami," Farmer recalled. "It was all lettered up, and we just threw our suitcases in the back.

"We got to the city limits of Daytona and jacked the car up and took the mufflers off and taped over the headlights. We even slept in the car on the beach. It really was stock car racing back then.

"It was a Hudson, but it wasn't like the others. Herb Thomas and Fonty Flock and the other hotdogs were running six-cylinder Hornets with two carburetors. I had a straight-eight with an automatic transmission. I didn't know anything about it. I had just turned 20.

"But I did get the car qualified. In those days you drove in the gate at the Neptune Drive-In Theater and stopped at the popcorn stand. The NASCAR official would come out of the popcorn stand and inspect your car. Racers were lined up just like they were going to the movie.

"Then you went out on the beach and qualified. You never actually got on the race course itself until race day. In qualifying, you had one mile to get up speed, then they clocked you for a mile. They called it the Flying Mile."

Farmer turned some heads before his premature departure. "I got all the way up to 11th," he remembered. "I was running down some of the stars. Then the whole wheel came off. We had to repair the thing before we could drive it back to Miami."

A service stint (1953-55) took Farmer to Germany where he played end on an undefeated, championship Third Army football team. He celebrated his return to civilian life by winning the NASCAR national Modified championship in 1956, in one of the closest campaigns in the history of any division.

"The last race of the year was a 200-lapper at Concord, N.C., and the top four drivers were all there," Farmer recalled. "Any of the four could win it by finishing two positions ahead of me.

"The third- and fourth-place men dropped out by 100 laps, but the second-place man and I were still running. I tore the rear end out of my car, and that looked like it. But on the next lap he tore the rear end out of his car. He finished one position ahead of me, and I won the national championship."

In his future were NASCAR national Sportsman titles in 1969, 1970 and 1971. He would, incredibly, be a U.S. champ in three different decades.

Another family living in Miami was quite different from Farmer's. Whereas Red had only one sibling, a sister, the marriage of Ed and Katherine Allison had produced 13 children. Fifth in line was Bobby Allison, and sixth was Donnie, who would do a bit of racing themselves. In 1994, as 87-year-old Katherine "Kitty" Allison excitedly headed for Daytona's Speed Weeks, Judy Allison, Bobby's wife, marveled at her mother-in-law.

"She's the person someone should write a book about," Judy said.

"She had 15 pregnancies, with two miscarriages and two babies to die. She had a daughter to die at 16 with cystic fibrosis, who was sometimes in the hospital two or three times a year, on the critical list. During that time she had six boys and three girls, and many times she was up at 4 a.m., ironing. And they were always at mass. Another daughter died of cancer in 1988.

"She has a rod in both legs and both arms and a ball joint in both hips. She became an Avon lady when she was 50.

Donnie had a serious head injury. Bobby had a serious head injury. Two of her grandsons, Clifford and Davey, died with head injuries, and her own husband passed away. I think she's pretty remarkable."

The Allison home in Miami was old but large, with six bedrooms. Ed Allison supplied equipment to garages and service stations. The Allisons weren't poor, but with all those kids, there were few luxuries.

It was a loving family, the members sustaining each other. The pleasures were simple but solid. Saturday was the night for hamburgers and potato chips and R.C. Colas. Sunday meant a big lunch of roast beef or chicken. A birthday boy or girl was privileged to choose his or her treat—which usually meant steak (or shrimp if it was Friday).

When he was 9 years old, Bobby Allison attended a stock car race with his grandfather. He was so excited he barely slept that night, and he became an inveterate drawer of race cars on the pages of his school notebook. He believes that from that day his future was sealed.

He went out for football in high school, but he weighed just 110 pounds. The coach, fearful he would be squashed by players twice as big, influenced him to seek other extracurricular activities.

Bobby became the manager of the football, basketball, baseball and track teams. But of more importance to his future, he was a tinkerer, working on his priest's car, fixing anything in need of repair. He traded a motorcycle for a 1938 Chevrolet coupe and lavished attention upon it—and that would become his first race car.

In Bobby's mind it was a foregone conclusion that he would be a race car driver, but Donnie could just as easily have taken a different road. In fact, he was more interested in one-horsepower racing. Or he could even have become a champion collegiate diver.

Promoter Bob Harmon (second from right) congratulates young drivers (L-R)
Bobby Allison, Donnie Allison, Red Farmer

"I got into swimming when I was 12 years old," recalled Donnie, who is two years younger than Bobby. "I was on several swim teams and was even offered a college scholarship if I would go to a certain high school. But it was a public school, and I wanted to go to a Catholic school.

"We went to Tampa for the state meet, and there were 28 boys in my age group, but I won the Florida state AAU diving championship."

It was at the swimming pool that Donnie met a horse trainer who was impressed by his lack of size—and probably by his fierce competitiveness. The trainer influenced Donnie to decide he should become a jockey. He began working an apprenticeship as an exercise boy at Tropical Park race track near Miami.

Then something happened that changed the direction of his life.

Sixteen-year-old Donnie Allison was riding his motorcycle on the way to feed a horse. A truck stopped in front of him, and he crashed into it.

His left leg was mangled. The bone stuck through the skin and into the pavement.

They wanted to amputate my leg, but my dad wouldn't go along with that," Donnie said. "He told them if there was any chance to save

it, he wanted to. I think they just experimented on my leg, and it just happened to work."

Donnie, who was left with a limp and one leg that was shorter than the other, was hospitalized 13 weeks. When he entered the hospital he weighed 100 pounds. When he left he weighed 125 pounds, "and from then on I grew like crazy." So much for a career as a jockey.

Hialeah Speedway created an amateur division in 1955, and Bobby realized this was an opportunity for him to race. He promised his mother he would make good grades and would help his father at the business, so she signed a release.

He drove his school car, the '38 Chevy, to the track, removed the headlights and tail lights, strapped the door shut—and he was a race driver.

He finished seventh in a 40-car field. He was seventh again the next week. The third week, with 60 cars entered, he won.

After graduation from high school, he took a job with Carl Kiekhaefer's Mercury Outboard Motors in Wisconsin. He was testing a motor in 15-degree weather when his small runabout boat hit some waves and sank.

Bobby was dressed in heavy clothing, and he struggled toward the shore. Just as he was on the verge of giving up, his feet touched the bottom. He made it through the snow to a nearby house, which happened to be the home of a registered nurse. His pulse was weak, and he was shaking violently, but she put him into a tub of hot water and got some neighbors to drive him to the hospital, where he recovered.

Kiekhaefer not only was the owner of Mercury Outboard Motors, he had a powerful stock car racing team. His drivers included such greats as Buck Baker, Tim Flock, Herb Thomas, Frank Munday and Speedy Thompson. One day Kiekhaefer unexpectedly told Bobby Allison, "Go get your suitcase and report to the race shop in Charlotte." His life had taken another fortuitous turn, for he was now a mechanic with the most famous outfit in racing.

Kiekhaefer was a noted eccentric. For instance, he insisted his drivers stay in rooms at one end of a motel and their wives at rooms at the other end. No sex the night before a race. Bobby worked for him only

Eddie Allison (C) mechanicked while brothers Donnie (in car) and Bobby drove.

a year or so, quitting after Kiekhaefer fired three of his co-workers during a temper fit, but he learned valuable lessons from the man.

"Carl wasn't easy to get along with," Bobby said, "but he sure knew what he was doing. I learned that organization and preventive maintenance were as important to winning as a fast car. I learned that racing was a business.

"All of the mechanics worked long and hard hours. There was no specific mechanic for any car. Everybody worked on all of the cars, and you signed for your work. If you changed a rear end, you signed for it. You were awfully careful about your work.

"There was one basic philosophy with Kiekhaefer. If you're going to go racing, go to win. If he had three cars running, he wasn't satisfied unless they finished 1, 2, 3."

Bobby returned to Miami and bought a new 1956 Chevrolet with the money he had made working for Kiekhaefer. It happened to be a car in which all the elements came together perfectly in the distance between street lights—and Bobby became a noted "smoker" of other teen-aged boys, leaving his tire marks all over Miami. This led to a relationship with Red Farmer that continues to this day.

Red was a youngster who was a real hero in South Florida," Bobby explained. "I knew who he was, but I had no idea he knew me at all."

Farmer had heard of Bobby's street racing in his black and yellow Chevrolet, though. Farmer was switching from Ford to Chevrolet in his racing operation, and he figured a kid who could make a Chevy passenger car run like that would be just the man to help him to victory lane.

"I had a job, and I got off from work one day," remembered Bobby, "and here came Red Farmer with his window down and his arm waving and hollering for me to stop.

He said, 'Bobby, we're going to build a Chevrolet. Would you help me with the engine? We'll pay you.'"

Bobby still shakes his head at the memory. "Everybody thought I had souped my Chevrolet up, but I hadn't. It just ran fast.

"Homer Warren, one of Red's guys, said, 'You've been up there with them Grand National things, and they run four-barrel carburetors, and we want to run them instead of injectors, and we know you can

help.'

"I said OK. I didn't tell them I'd never even looked at a four-barrel carburetor."

Bobby bought a manual, noted that Farmer's carburetors weren't set correctly, and with no more knowledge than that afforded by the book simply set them himself according to the instructions. "I got them ready, and Homer bolted them onto the engine, and it sounded like a million dollars. We took it to the race track, and Red won easily. They thought I was the most brilliant 18-year-old kid they had ever seen."

So Bobby Allison became a member of Red Farmer's pit crew. In later years, Farmer would be crew chief for Bobby's son Davey.

Bobby resumed his driving career, too, after returning to Miami from Kiekhaefer's, at first using an alias because his mother had decided it was time to get serious about life—though she finally relented and signed for him

— 3 —

Joys and Struggles of the Early Years

The old days. Who doesn't like to remember them, talk about them? On a day during the racing season of 1994, Bobby Allison's thoughts and words traveled backward to the '50s and 60s'.

"There was a real camaraderie in racing," he said. "It took some friends along the way for you to ever make it. A couple of special ones who come to mind are Al Gorham and Bo Fields.

"Al Gorham drove a delivery truck for a paper company. He raced some on the short racks around Miami, but not consistently. He would stop by my shop in Miami and encourage me to work toward my goal, to make my car better, and if there was a race somewhere to go to it. 'Here's some money for your tow truck,' he would say.

"It was time to go back to Alabama for the opening of the 1960 season, and I didn't have any money. Al Gorham came by and laid some money on the hood of my race car and said, 'Go to Alabama. This is not a loan. It's an investment.'"

Al Gorham helped him get to Alabama. Bo Fields helped him after he got there.

"Bo said, 'Bring your racing stuff down to my house at Mud Creek,' and I did," Allison recalled.

"He gave me a place to work, but he also gave me incredible personal help. He worked at the maintenance shop for the county equipment, and he hit the floor at 4 a.m. to go to work. He'd come home after work, and Irene would have his supper ready, and he'd eat, and he'd help me on my race car until 11 p.m.

"Bo and I raced against each other a little bit, but he was quitting as a driver when I came to Alabama.

"He used to arrange for me to do repair jobs on a truck or a tractor so I could make a little money."

It was in 1959 that Bobby Allison, Donnie Allison and Red Farmer first traveled from Florida to Alabama, race cars in tow.

The short tracks in South Florida didn't pay well, but they found healthy purses over the state line. They commuted for awhile, and then they moved to Alabama.

"I dropped a transmission on my hand," Bobby recalled. "I looked up and saw the bones sticking out and my thumb turned backward. That put me out for nine weeks.

"I went to Palm Beach for my first race after that accident. Red won it, and I ran second. I finished second in a 100-lap feature and did whatever I did in the heat race—and I got a grand total of 95 bucks.

"A friend named Gil Hearn told me he had gone to Georgia and Tennessee scouting out tracks that paid good money. He said he didn't find any, but he heard there were some in Alabama."

So Bobby hooked up his race car and headed for Alabama, accompanied by his brother Donnie. Hearn and Kenny Andrews, who owned the car Hearn drove, towed their racer, too.

"I had whatever was left of my $95," Bobby said, "and I don't think Donnie had any money. This was Thursday. It was a long trip, and it was hard to even run 50 miles an hour because we had to go through every little town.

"It got to be noon time, and I said to Donnie, 'We ought to get a basket of those peaches for 50 cents. That can be our lunch.'

"Well, gas was probably 23 or 24 cents a gallon, and you got a penny or two discount if you were in a truck. But it was cutting into that $95. So we ate peaches for lunch and peaches for supper and

peaches for breakfast the next morning. We slept in the truck.

"We were really impressed by the welcome sign when we got to Alabama. And the highways actually had shoulders on them.

"We stopped at a service station in Dothan and asked where the race track was. The guy said there wasn't one there, but there was one up the road in Montgomery.

"We drove on and saw this by-pass around Montgomery. We had never seen a by-pass before.

"We came up on a service station, and there was a race car parked out front. It was a showpiece. It looked like it was ready to go to a car show. We found out people up here kept their race cars like that."

The proprietor, Bo Freeman, was a friendly sort, and he led the Floridians to Montgomery Speedway and introduced them to Harold Pentecost, the promoter. He told them there would be races at Dixie Speedway in the Birmingham suburb of Midfield that night, Friday, and at Montgomery Saturday night.

So the entourage headed for Birmingham. Eddie Wright, the Dixie promoter, sold used cars, and he lived up to his professional name of Big Hearted Eddie by letting them work on their racers right there on

Photo courtesy of Bill Latham
Donnie Allison was proud of his winning race car.

his lot.

"We went to Dixie Speedway, and there was this beautiful quarter-mile track, and we were in awe," Bobby said. "I ran fifth in the heat, fifth in the semi-feature and fifth in the feature. I stepped up to the window, and they counted me out $135.

"I said, 'Donnie, we have died and gone to heaven! Look at all this money! We can go back to that Miss Mary's Drive-In we saw and have one of those $1.98 steaks and sleep in a motel.

"We got a room near Clanton. It was $2. He and I shared a bed and got a good night's sleep."

They returned to Bo Freeman's service station, where the bench racers advised them not to try to race in Montgomery because the Cadillac-powered cars would "blow y'all off the track." Bobby told them he had been blown off the track before, and they headed for the speedway.

"I had quick time and won my heat and the semi-feature and the Australian pursuit race," he recalled. "I started on the pole in the feature, and Sonny Black started on the outside. He beat me on the start of the race and stayed in front of me for the rest of the 25 or 30 laps. He won, and I finished second. "A lot of people thought I had hard feelings about that, but I never did. Sonny Black taught me a lesson that night. He taught me to use the advantage of your equipment without being dirty."

Bobby's car handled better, but Black's was faster on the straights. And he wasn't about to give Bobby room enough to pass him in the turns.

"I went to the pay window and got a stack of money that high," Bobby continued. "I couldn't believe it. I had like $400, and I hadn't even won the race.

"All these people were saying, 'Ole Sonny Black taught you,' and 'I bet you're mad at Sonny Black,' and I was thinking, 'I ain't mad at anybody. I'm rich.'"

They stayed in Alabama for the next week's races, but after he fared poorly at Dixie Speedway, Hearn decided not to drive at Montgomery, and he caught a plane for Miami. "What am I going to do now?" Kenny Andrews, the car owner, asked Bobby.

"Put Donnie in the car," he replied. Bobby scored his first professional feature victory that night, and Donnie launched his professional career. He finished eighth, and the next night, at the Peach Bowl in Atlanta, he ran fourth.

"I went home," Bobby said, "and told my friend Red Farmer, 'Red, Alabama is beautiful, the race tracks are great, and the people are the nicest you ever met. You need to go to Alabama with us.'

"Red had won a ton of races with his Chevrolet. It was beat up but effective. He went to Alabama, and during the Fourth of July week he won seven of eight races in seven days."

The Allisons and Farmer made the trek from Miami to Alabama and back many times, frequently dusting the local competition. Disgruntled Alabama drivers began calling them "gypsies."

At one time Farmer and the Allisons and their crews rented an apartment in West End, taking turns sleeping in beds, on the floor and on the couch.

"We raced to survive," Farmer said. "We didn't have other jobs. I think we were more dedicated than somebody racing for a hobby, as most of the local boys were. If we didn't go to the pay window, we couldn't feed our kids."

They used to get tires the other drivers would throw away, sew up the cuts with wire, put boots in them and race on them.

Farmer, especially, had incentive to punch the accelerator. "I was living on unemployment checks," he said. "They had the trouble with the blockade of Cuba, and I was an electrician, and building went to a standstill. We didn't know if there was going to be a war. I had six dependents—me, my wife Joan, three kids and Joan's grandmother—and was making $33 a week unemployment. The only other thing I had was a race car."

Eventually they all moved to the Birmingham area, settling in Hueytown. Now they could use their energy driving race cars instead of tow trucks.

If someone hadn't bought a house before Bobby Allison could, Hueytown probably wouldn't have become the biggest little town in racing.

In 1963 Bobby and his family were living with Tommy Walker and

his family out in the country in Jefferson County. Walker was general manager of Birmingham International Raceway. "A for sale sign went up on the house next to the Walkers," Bobby recalled. "We really liked it, and we called the agent, but he said that one was sold.

"He had one in Hueytown he wanted to show us, but we said we'd rather be out in the country. He told us we'd like it, though, and we looked at it and bought it."

It was natural that Donnie would then move to Hueytown. Farmer said it is just coincidence that he settled there. In later years Neil Bonnett would live there to be in the center of local racing.

Someone once asked ex-driver Carl Jones if the late Grayson Rose was a great racing mechanic. "He was until those Allisons and Farmer came," Jones answered. "They upped the ante in local racing. It became a lot more serious with their arrival."

Indeed it did. But over the years many drivers would rise to the challenge, and Birmingham became recognized as the Sportsman racing capital of the U.S. Men such as Alton Jones, Ray Putnam, Jerry Lawley, Bill Sternenberg, Jimmy Means, Friday Hassler and Neil Bonnett made trips to victory circle.

"It's like a hornet's nest in Birmingham," Winston Cup star Buddy Baker said after he drove in a Sportsman race there. "If you can win in Birmingham, you can win anywhere."

A young Darrell Waltrip occasionally towed his car from his hometown, Owensboro, Ky., to race in Birmingham. "That's where the best competition was," he explained years later, "and I wanted to test myself against the best competition."

Racing at the old fairgrounds layout prospered under a progressive promoter named Tom Gloor. Gloor and his partners, Dr. W.C. Andrews Jr. and Dr. W.F. Kelley, acquired the track, paved it, changed the name from Fairgrounds Speedway to Birmingham International Raceway, and held a grand "opening" on June 24, 1962. Gloor later became sole owner and installed lights and lengthened the track from a half-mile to five-eighths.

He moved the weekly racing date from Sunday afternoons to cooler Friday nights in a time when air conditioning wasn't widespread.

Charlie Griffith won the 40-lap feature on that hot June afternoon.

Bobby Allison finished second, and Donnie Allison fifth.

Red Farmer crashed in the match race. "Ambulance, quick!" came the call over the speaker in the pits after his car smashed into the steel guard rail.

Joan Farmer and her children, Bonnie, 11, Cindy, 8, and Mike, 5, waited. And waited. And waited. Finally, Red climbed out of his racer and got into the pace car, and when it came back around he waved to his family.

"You try and keep hold of yourself for the kids," Joan told a reporter. "If I could cry, I'd feel a lot better. But you can't.

"This isn't the first time I've seen him in a wreck. I don't go expecting it to happen. You couldn't do that. And I'd rather be here watching than at home not knowing."

Farmer would suffer many injuries over the years as he followed the Alabama NASCAR "circuit" that included Birmingham, Midfield, Huntsville and Montgomery and as he raced all over the United States.

Once he listed his racing injuries as: broken right ankle, broken right foot, left leg broken on three occasions, left knee cap removed, two vertebrae in back broken, six ribs broken, cheekbone broken with subsequent loss of feeling in left side of face, burns on 40 percent of body, sufficient loss of hearing due to exhaust noise to necessitate a hearing aid.

And that was in 1971.

In 1962 he and Bobby Allison were battling for the championship of NASCAR's Modified-Special Division. Farmer crashed in practice at Dixie Speedway in Midfield and was carted off to the hospital with a broken foot.

Before the feature, a pickup truck pulled into the pits, and Farmer got out, a bright new cast on his foot. The crowd applauded. It took guts to return to the track to watch the race.

But he didn't come to watch. He came to race and pick up what few championship points he could. He borrowed a Hobby car, and tears crept from his wincing eyes as friends helped him through the window and into the bucket seat. He finished last, but it was a memorable act of courage. He drove the rest of the season with his right leg resting in a special trough that was built into the car. His mechanics coated the

trough with an oil additive so his leg would slide up and down and operate the accelerator. He couldn't stop Bobby Allison from winning the championship, but he never stopped trying.

One of Bobby Allison's early Modified-Special racers.

On another occasion, when his left leg was broken, he simply immobilized it by strapping it to the rollbar and operated all the pedals with his right foot.

Modified-Specials ran mostly in Alabama and Tennessee, and Bobby Allison took that division's titles in 1962 and 1963.

Alabama tracks switched to the standard Modifieds, and Bobby won the national championship in that widespread division in 1964 and 1965.

Farmer had won the Modified crown in 1956 when he lived in Florida, and after he finished second to Bobby Allison in 1965 he declared he would pursue no more national championships.

"It doesn't pay," he said. "We would have made more money if we hadn't been chasing points. It costs to go to Trenton, N.J., and have a

breakdown. Bobby and I caught a plane together to go as far away as Oxford, Me."

He didn't exactly live up to that declaration. He won NASCAR national Sportsman championships in 1969, 1970 and 1971.

Farmer never pursued a Winston Cup (formerly called Grand National) career, though his skills were certainly worthy of the major league. He came along a little too soon, before the big money.

"There must be, what, about 60 Grand National drivers?" he once explained. "Well, there won't be but about 10 who will make more money than a top Modified driver can make.

If we can stay on top, we'll make as much as the other 50 Grand National drivers will.

"If you can keep a Modified running in the top three two or three times a week and run within 150 miles of home, you can do OK. You aren't going to get rich, but not many Grand National drivers do, either."

But it's an iffy business. "One year I figured I made $390 profit for a year's racing," Farmer said.

That was 1962, the worst season of his racing life. First his personal station wagon caught fire from a brake malfunction while he towed his race car home from Chattanooga. The station wagon burned, and so did his tools, clothes and $400 cash he had just won. A few days later he suffered a broken foot in a crackup. The next night at Montgomery, driving with a cast on his foot, he wrecked his car. He was trying to repair the wreckage the next morning when fire broke out in his garage, and he suffered hand, leg and facial burns and a broken wrist when he fell.

The Allisons' brotherly love got strained during the highly competitive early 1960s.

"At the time we were running Modifieds, Bobby and I were our own best competition," Donnie Allison explained. "When you have competition, you have trouble.

"I think the trouble was that I wanted to beat Bobby more than I wanted to beat anybody else, and he wanted to keep me from beating him more than anybody else.

"We let things get out of hand before we finally sat down and had

a talk. We agreed it was both of our faults."

Things came to a head during a weekend of Montgomery and Birmingham racing.

"I had wrecked my car, and I was pretty broke," Donnie said. "I told a good friend I would drive his car until I got enough money to put mine back together.

"At Montgomery they made Bobby start in the rear, and he was aggravated. Bobby and I got together, and I ended up spinning and hitting the fence.

"I told Bobby, 'I'll get even with you for that.' We worked all night to get the car ready for Birmingham's 100-lapper the next day. Well, we had a caution flag about the 90th lap, and on the restart the injector sucked some air, and Bobby passed me.

"I kept telling myself if I was going to spin him out, now was the time to do it. We got the white flag, and I said to myself, 'I've only got four corners more to do it.' "I spun him, and he finished second, and I won. He shook his fist at me, but I figured that just evened the score.

"Then my father came over to me, and he said, 'We didn't bring you kids up to act like that. It's time you got together.'

" Ed Allison's intervention led to peace talks. "And from that day to this," Donnie said, "we've never had a cross word."

The appeal of the Allisons and Farmer matched their skills. Bobby was voted NASCAR's Most Popular Modified-Sportsman Driver in 1965, the Most Popular Winston Cup Driver in 1971, 1972, 1973, 1980, 1981, 1982 and 1983, the Most Popular Sportsman Driver in 1974 and the Most Popular Driver in the short-lived Grand National East Division in 1973. Donnie was voted Most Popular Sportsman Driver in 1970 and Most Popular Grand Touring Driver in 1968. Farmer was voted Most Popular Modified Driver in 1968 and Most Popular Sportsman driver in 1969, 1971 and 1973.

4

Up to the Big Leagues

In the 1960s, Cosby Hodges, a former racer who operated a used car lot, offered Donnie Allison a job. Donnie replied, "Someday I'm going to win the Indianapolis 500."

He didn't win the world's biggest auto race, but he finished fourth in 1970 and was named the 500's Rookie of the Year. He ran sixth at Indy in 1971.

Bobby had competed in four races on the big league stock car tour in 1961, driving a car owned by his brother-in-law, Ralph Stark, but the beginning of a continuous Winston Cup career waited until 1965. He drove in eight races, for teams owned by Ed Grady and Robert Harper, that year.

So in a dozen events he had driven for three owners. It was the beginning of a trend, for when a terrible crash brought an apparent end to his career in 1988 he had raced for more than 20 Winston Cup teams.

He competed in 34 events in 1966, starting the season in Betty Lilly's car. After her operation stalled, he drove one race for Smokey Yunick, and then he fielded his own Winston cupper, a homemade Chevelle.

Another Allison brother, Eddie, was a mechanic, and he and Donnie and Chuck Looney helped Bobby whip the car into existence in a cement block garage behind his house.

In those days, the rigid caste system included the rich factory-backed teams and the shoestringing independents, who won few races. And Bobby was as independendent as they came. But he had an idea. If the quick little 327-cubic-inch Chevrolet engine could power him to so many short-track victories in Modified and Sportsman racing, why couldn't it do the same in Winston Cup? It mightn't be effective against those motors of 100 more cubic inches on the superspeedways, but it might outjump them on the short tracks.

After all, under NASCAR rules, a car had to weigh 9.36 pounds per cubic inch, so he would get a weight break of more than 900 pounds.

In its fifth start, on July 12, 1966, the Chevelle proved him correct. He started on the pole and won a 300-lapper on the .333-mile track at Oxford, Me., beating Tiny Lund by a lap. It was the first of 84 victories Robert Arthur Allison would score in the big league. He was 28 years old.

Four days later, Bobby won a 300-lapper on the .2-mile track at Islip, N.Y., and on Aug. 24 he took a 200-lapper on a half-mile speedway at Beltsville, Md.

He finished the season with three victories in 34 starts, an incredible performance by an independent, but an incident in which his car was almost destroyed also captured the imagination of the public and helped earn Bobby a full-length feature in Sports Illustrated magazine. The story called him "the sport's newest hero."

On Aug. 27, 1966, the tour reached a quarter-mile track at Winston-Salem, N.C. Bobby was in his homemade Chevelle, and the legendary Curtis Turner was in a factory Ford owned by Junior Johnson.

Turner began shoving Bobby's car from the rear. Bobby let him by and began bumping Turner's car. Turner spun Bobby out. Bobby spun Turner out. Turner broadsided Bobby's car. As Turner came around, under caution, Bobby broadsided his car.

Both drivers got out of their slaughtered racers and without a word returned to the pits.

"I didn't want to do what I did," Bobby said, "but I felt I had to. I wasn't happy about it. In fact, I was nervous all the time I was doing it. We really did a job on each other."

Bobby the independent had to haul the remains of his Chevy back

Bobby Allison tells the fans how he won his second Winston Cup race, at Islip, N.Y., in 1966.

Bobby Allison's homemade Chevelle outran factory cars.

to Hueytown and rebuild it with his own muscle and money. Turner let Johnson and Ford Motor Co. worry about his car. NASCAR fined each driver $100.

Said *Sports Illustrated:*

"On the surface it was a minor incident, one that might happen half a dozen times a year in the rough-and-tumble world of stock car racing. But this one was a bit different, for it strengthened an opinion held by just about every knowledgeable observer in stock car racing—namely that Bobby Allison of Hueytown, Ala., is on his way to becoming the next superstar of the Grand National circuit, right up there with Lorenzen and Petty and Johnson and Turner and even those heroes of the past—Fireball Roberts and Little Joe Weatherly. Not because he cracked up a car, of course. Anybody can do that. But because he didn't give way, which is often what automobile racing is about."

Firestone's Humpy Wheeler, who later would become the progressive president of Charlotte Motor Speedway, ventured:

"There are so many unwritten rules, especially for rookies—like when you can bump a guy and get away with it, when you can go after the big boys and when you'd better hang back. Things like that. Bobby has broken a lot of these rules, and this is what gets him into trouble,

but this is also what will make him great."

In the minors, Bobby already had established that he wouldn't be a punching bag.

On the little quarter-mile track at Huntsville, four drivers teamed up against him. They stayed with him at all times, weaving in and out, blocking him, bumping him.

It seemed strange, Bobby told the starter, that the four qualified with 14-second laps and now they were turning 18-second laps, but the starter said he didn't see anything.

Bobby went to each of the four drivers and said, "Look, I'm not asking you to give way, but when I come up behind you pick your lane and stay there. The track's wide enough for two cars. If I can get by you, fine. If I can't, fine. Just give me room."

They said they didn't have the slightest idea what he was talking about.

They continued to block him and bump him, and finally one of them forced his car into the wall.

Bobby didn't complain to the starter. He just asked for an extra 10 minutes to get his car running for the feature.

The starter said he'd get no favor, to be ready when the green flag dropped.

The feature was into the 17th lap when Bobby got his car going, and he entered the race at that point. There were three of the four "team" drivers left, and Bobby proceeded to: Bump No. 1 out of contention. Spin No. 2 into the infield. Yank his steering wheel sharply to the right and send No. 3—and his own car—into the wall at precisely the spot where he had crashed earlier.

"I never had any more trouble with them," Bobby said.

Bobby later reflected on his days of campaigning the independent Chevelle against all odds on the Winston Cup circuit.

"Racing for yourself like I did is like trying to play a football game with one shoe off. Without superhuman efforts by everybody, you can't possibly keep up.

"Nobody except my brother Eddie and my family knew what we put into that first car as far as time and effort is concerned.

"The only thing that kept me from jumping out of my car on pit

stops and helping the crew in those days was my seat belt.

"We built every car and engine we had from the ground floor up. We never farmed out anything because we couldn't afford it. I used to work all night, tow it the next day several hundreds miles, and then try to find the energy to drive the race.

"To say we were always in a near state of exhaustion during those days is an understatement. I don't know how we did it, but I wouldn't trade the experience for anything."

Driving a Dodge for Cotton Owens, Bobby scored a popular Winston Cup victory at Birmingham in 1967, but the season was most significant for his notching his first superspeedway win. It came on Oct. 29 in the American 500 at Rockingham. Sick of the Richard Petty-Chrysler domination that was showing up its products, Ford Motor Co. assigned former driving great Fred Lorenzen to head up a team, beginning with the American 500. He could have any car and driver he wanted, and he wanted Bobby Allison.

"From the first practice lap in the car," said Bobby, "I knew I had a car I could win with. I had confidence in the car and complete confidence in Lorenzen's ability to run the crew."

Bobby lapped the field, David Pearson finishing second. Petty crashed on pit road before the midpoint.

Bobby characteristically came to the aid of a friend the next day. Driver James Hylton crashed in the American 500 and suffered a concussion and was hospitalized. Bobby flew back to Rockingham from Hueytown and then flew Hylton to his home in Inman, S.C. Hylton had

Ford Motor Co. photo

Donnie Allison and car owner Banjo Matthews found victory lane.

a commitment to drive for a movie, and Eddie Allison and Chuck Looney got his car back into shape. "James has been one person who has really, really helped me. I've used his garage a lot," said Bobby—who over the years would perform many charitable and humanitarian services that the public never knew about.

The 1967 season was key for Donnie Allison, too. Before it began he said he would race on the Winston Cup tour, and he calmly announced he would be Rookie of the Year.

Important persons were impressed when he drove the Robert Harper independent Chevrolet (on seven cylinders most of the race) to an 11th place finish in a crack Daytona 500 field. He recorded four top-five finishes in 20 races and, indeed, was named Rookie of the Year.

His performance earned him a ride in Banjo Matthews' factory Ford for 1968, and on June 16 the 28-year-old Donnie Allison scored the first of his 10 career Winston Cup victories by taking the Carolina 500 on the superspeedway at Rockingham.

Bobby ran second, two laps behind his brother. Eddie Allison was the crew chief on the runnerup car and on the machine of third-placer James Hylton.

Bobby and Donnie drove side by side through North Carolina Motor Speedway's tricky turns with only laps to go and gave each other the A-OK sign. It was the first of several 1-2 Winston Cup finishes for them.

They took $26,325 of the $78,230 purse. Donnie won $16,675, which he had to split with his car owner. Bobby, driving his own Chevelle, got to bank all his $9,650.

"When I run short I'll know where to go for a loan," Donnie kidded. "Bobby will get rich if his little car holds up like it did today."

Bobby's schedule as a Ford factory driver had been reduced in 1968. And Ford frowned on his extra-curricular short-tracking. Even when it raced, the car frequently didn't finish.

When the Winston Cup tour reached Birmingham on June 8 and he wasn't entered, Bobby couldn't stand it. He dusted off his trusty Chevelle and drove at the fairgrounds.

"I want to race," he said. "Just sitting around has driven me nuts. I want to drive in front of my hometown fans, so I quit Ford and brought

my Chevrolet out of the closet." Richard Petty won, and he finished fourth.

Driving a Plymouth owned by pal Tom Friedkin at Montgomery Speedway on Dec. 8, 1968, Bobby wrote a small historical footnote in stock car racing by spoiling Petty's last race in a Plymouth.

Petty had shocked the racing world by announcing he would switch to Ford for 1969. On a cold day at Montgomery, he had a healthy lead over Bobby when the caution flag waved with nine laps to go. Bobby pitted and took on new tires, while Petty chose to stay on the track. Bobby passed him coming off the final turn of the final lap and won by four feet.

"I ain't believing this," Bobby said. "With 10 laps to go, we were out of it. Now here I am in victory lane." It was in 1968 that country music star Marty Robbins competed in his first superspeedway event. Driving a Dodge fielded out of Bobby's Hueytown shop, he finished 12th in the fall race at Charlotte..

Robbins drove on the short tracks in the Nashville area. He took a lot of kidding—some of it fairly serious: "With your popularity and money and future, why would you risk it racing?" The question was asked even more frequently after he became a superspeedway driver.

There probably never has been a more unusual trade in sports than the one that enabled Robbins to race at Charlotte.

Bobby traded a Winston Cup Dodge Charger, a trailer to transport it, and a tow truck for Robbins' Sportsman racer and its trailer, a pickup truck, a Lincoln Continental with a "lizard skin" roof and a black Angus bull.

Donnie drove in 13 Winston Cup races and won one in 1968. He scored five top-five finishes, and Ford obviously had gotten a return on its decision to pluck him out of the ranks of the independents and assign him to the wily Banjo Matthews' team.

"Nobody thought Banjo and I would get along," Donnie said. "I had heard he was hard to get along with, but we've never had a cross word. His knowledge of racing is so much greater than people really realize. He has a hard time getting it across to people because he's so far ahead of them."

An intense Donnie Allison in the pits after being knocked out of a race.

To capitalize on the popularity of such cars as the Ford Mustang and the Chevrolet Camaro, NASCAR initiated a Grand Touring Division in 1968. Donnie's record was impressive. Though he entered just 12 of the 19 events, he won five and finished second five times. His victory total was exceeded only by champion Tiny Lund's nine.

Though Bobby Allison had become a name driver in the big league, he continued to pursue a busy Modified-Sportsman schedule. "The thing that motivates me to race is that I like to win," he said. "The thing that motivates me to race a lot is that I like to win a lot."

Early in 1969 he was at Hickory Speedway in North Carolina as a spectator, and he ended the evening driving a total stranger's car—dressed in a turtleneck shirt.

"I believe you get better at anything the more you do it," he said after returning from a Sportsman race at Jefferson, Ga. "I got out of the car after 300 laps yesterday, and the pit crew was tireder than I was. I ran over 100 races every year from 1959 through 1965."

It was a delightful situation for fans in Birmingham. A big league star was a semi-regular at the weekly races at the fairgrounds. It was like having Mickey Mantle drop in to play with the Barons.

"If I only ran for money, I wouldn't run tracks like Birmingham International Raceway," Bobby said. "There's not enough profit. I run places like that because I enjoy it, and it complements my conditioning.

"I think drivers like Cale Yarborough would be a lot better racers if they ran all the time—and he's a super-duper racer now."

5

Rising to Stardom

T he 1969 season was a feast of excitement for Alabama stock car racing fans. Alabama International Motor Speedway, the world's largest and fastest track, opened, and Talladega became a capital of racing.

Farmer won the first of three straight national Sportsman championships.

The Allison brothers continued to shine on the Winston Cup circuit, Bobby winning five races and Donnie one.

And an exciting young driver named Neil Bonnett made his debut and scored his first feature victory.

Or did he?

Biographical thumbnails on Bonnett list his first race as being on April 12, 1969, in the entry-level Cadet Division at Montgomery and his first feature win as coming on July 12, 1969, in a Cadet race at Birmingham.

But on a winter day in 1994, shortly after Neil had been killed in a racing practice crash at Daytona, Lee Hurley told of a "mystery" win by Bonnett in a Sportsman race in Pensacola in 1968.

Hurley was a Birmingham driver who had a racing shop at his house, which was a few blocks from Bonnett's parents' home. One day Bonnett showed up, saying he was a racing fan and that he had heard

Hurley owned a car and that he would like to help with his racing effort.

"I can use some help," Hurley said.

"What can I do?" Bonnett asked.

"You can sweep out the garage."

Hurley recalled his surprise when he returned home the next day. "This kid had transformed my garage into a spit-shine operation. He was that enthusiastic."

Bonnett explained that as a pipefitter he knew welding. Hurley was building a new car, and he said that skill would come in handy.

"He was at my house at least five or six nights a week," Hurley recalled. "His wife Susan and my wife Martha Jo became good friends, and they ate a lot of meals with us."

BIR closed in September, and they began taking Hurley's racer to the Sportsman races in Pensacola and Mobile. "The Pensacola promoter, Tom Dawson, would give me some tow money," Hurley explained, "but I had to start the feature to get it.

"One night I had fast time and ran second in the heat race, but I had a terrible headache. I just didn't feel like getting in the car for the feature.

"They were inverting the field, so I would be on the back for the feature. Neil had never driven in a race, but I told him to go out there and start on the back and make a few laps and come in and we'd go home."

And he did?

"Are you kidding?" Hurley said. "The next thing I knew Neil was running second to, I think, Jerry Lawley. Something happened to Lawley, and Neil ended up winning the race.

"Nobody knew it was Neil. Well, I guess a few did, but most thought it was me. Officially I won that race, but really it was Neil."

Aside from claiming the tow money, there was another reason to keep quiet, Hurley explained as he relaxed in the office of his huge HESCO automotive service in Birmingham. Bonnett was going to launch his career in the Cadet Division in 1969, and a driver wasn't allowed to step down from Sportsman to Cadet.

So in 1969 Neil Bonnett "began" his racing career. He won the Cadet championship at Montgomery that year.

Farmer, meanwhile, was perpetrating a rout in winning the 1969 national Sportsman championship. He compiled 8,276 points, some 2,700 more than runnerup Harry Gant. He competed in 83 races and won 31 of them. He was in the top three 53 times.

Photo courtesy of the Farmer family

Red Farmer won four NASCAR national championships in three decades.

"I was but one guy in a strong team effort," said Farmer. "The fellows on my crew, who all have jobs of their own and work on my cars in their spare time, are the champions. They are Bill Hamner, the crew chief, John Carter, Bobby Carter, Wimpy Cox, Lee Blakey and James Green."

Bobby Allison's five wins of the 1969 season came on short tracks, but Donnie won the National 500 in Charlotte. He beat his brother by 16 seconds as they recorded their second 1-2 finish in Winston Cup.

Their mother Katherine was in the stands, celebrating her 64th birthday and rooting impartially for both her sons.

"It's getting to be a habit, I guess," said Donnie, "but I wish it would happen more often. The money's good, and you always want to beat big brother. It's the only time I've been able to do it since we were kids."

Donnie's wife Pat, ill with pneumonia, listened to the race on the radio in her hospital room.

But the big racing news in Alabama in 1969 transcended championships and victories. Alabama International Motor Speedway was

born, and the small town of Talladega would become famous.

In fact, Ford Motor Co. named a slope-nosed car the Talladega. Residents were delighted, and they puffed out their chests. Raymond Martin, who was mayor of nearby Lincoln, got in a good-natured jab. "So what?" he said. "Ford named a car after our town a long time ago."

Enough Talladegas and Mercury Cyclones were manufactured as passenger cars to make them eligible for competition, but they clearly were designed for racing. The same was true for the even more radical Dodge Daytonas and Plymouth SuperBirds, which sported wedged noses and tall wings across the rear decks. It was a time in which the tail wagged the dog in "stock" car racing.

Donnie Allison drove a factory Talladega for Banjo Matthews, and Bobby Allison drove a factory Daytona for Mario Rossi in 1969.

But not at AIMS. They joined other top drivers in boycotting the first Talladega 500, which was contested on Sept. 14, 1969. At the new 200-mph speeds ushered in by the huge track, tires wore out quickly, and most of the stars refused to race. A makeshift field was assembled, and an unknown driver named Richard Brickhouse won the race.

Alabama International Motor Speedway (which eventually would be renamed Talladega Superspeedway) was the brainchild of William Henry Getty "Big Bill" France, the founder of NASCAR and the builder of Daytona International Speedway.

France was born in Washington, D.C. He quit high school after two years and went to work as a mechanic. There was no indication France was destined for greatness when, a few years later, he tired of the cold weather and headed South.

"I decided that if I was going to have to fix automobiles for a living, I might as well fix them where it wasn't snowing," said France, whose duties at a service station had included responding to calls from customers whose cars wouldn't start on icy mornings. "I decided I might as well do it in Florida."

He and his wife Anne and their son Bill Jr. reached Daytona Beach in their Hupmobile. They liked it, so they stayed.

"I thought it was the prettiest place I'd ever seen, and I still do," France said decades later.

And since 1902 it had been a center of timed speed runs. France

Construction crews carve superspeedway from Talladega County farmland.

International Speedway Corp. photo

Talladega Superspeedway opened in 1969 and changed the face of racing in Alabama.

himself saw Sir Malcolm Campbell set a record of 276 miles an hour in 1935 in his famous Bluebird on the hard, flat beach.

France drove race cars when he wasn't fixing passenger cars, and when the city promoted the first beach-road race in 1936 he finished fifth. The venture lost money, and so did a similar effort by the Elks Club.

France's service station on Main Street was a hangout for racers, and it was natural that the Chamber of Commerce asked him if he knew who might promote the beach-road race.

He tried to contact a promoter who lived in Orange Beach, but the man refused his 15-cent collect call, and the course of history was changed. France and Charlie Reese, a restaurant owner who also owned the race car he drove, accepted the challenge themselves. France had no money, but he said he would do the work if Reese would furnish the cash. And so a career was born. Bill France took on other tracks, and the high school dropout-filling station operator eventually became the greatest promoter the sport has ever known.

Stock car racing was a haphazard operation, but France believed it could prosper if organized. In 1947 he formed the National Association

for Stock Car Auto Racing (NASCAR). Its Winston Cup tour eventually would become the best-attended series in the world.

The first NASCAR-sanctioned race was held on Feb. 15, 1948, on the course that combined the beach and a public highway, and there was an Alabama footnote to that Modified event. Red Byron of Atlanta, formerly of Anniston, won it. France built the 2.5-mile Daytona International Speedway, and it hosted the first Daytona 500 in 1959. It was a revolutionary concept, superior in design to Indianapolis Motor Speedway, what with its steeply banked turns and a curved frontstretch "so the fans aren't looking into their next-door neighbor's ear all the time."

But Daytona International Speedway could be improved upon, and evidence of that was the Alabama International Motor Speedway that France built in sleepy Dry Valley. Measuring 2.66 miles, it was a bit larger than Daytona's. Entrance into the turns was less radical, and it became the most competitive, most unpredictable race track on the planet. Another dream of France's that materialized in Alabama was the International Motorsports Hall of Fame adjacent to Talladega Superspeedway. When 150 members of the worldwide motorsports press voted the first class of inductees into the hall of fame in 1990, Bill France received the most votes, which in effect signified that he was the most important person in the history of auto racing.

France died in 1992 at age 82. NASCAR and Talladega Superspeedway continue to prosper under the leadership of his son Bill Jr.

On Sept. 4, 1966, *The Birmingham News* broke a story that read: "A six-million-dollar automobile race track the same length as those at Indianapolis and Daytona appears to be a virtual certainty for the Birmingham area."

In that story France stopped short of saying the speedway definitely would become reality, but on Oct. 17, 1966, at a joint meeting of Talladega civic clubs, France announced that a track would indeed be built some 45 miles from Birmingham.

It would be 2.5 miles long and in the shape of a quad-oval, "sort of a rounded diamond," whereas Daytona's was a tri-oval. He hoped ground could be broken in the spring or summer of 1967 with the first race in the spring of 1969. The working name was Alabama

International Speedway Corp. photo
Bobby Allison told Birmingham TV man Tom York's audience how it was out there.

International Motor Sports and Testing Facility at Talladega.

Stock car racing wasn't on TV every weekend as it is now, and it was still an arcane sport for many Alabamians.

"I thought it was crazy to use that good old soybean land to build a race track," admitted Dr.J.L. Hardwick, who was mayor of Talladega. He changed his mind when he visited Daytona for a Firecracker 400 and realized just what France was talking about.

The Birmingham News said the speedway would "make the Birmingham-Talladega-Anniston area a United States auto racing center."

And it did, though it came out slightly different from the way France first envisioned it. Its shape was tri-oval, and it was a bit longer. Ground wasn't broken until May of 1968, and the first race wasn't run until September of 1969. It was named Alabama International Motor Speedway, though over the years most would call it simply "Talladega." Why locate the track there? "Talladega is located within a 300-mile radius of a population of 20 million people, and it's stock car country," said France, noting that the majority of the interstate highways in the U.S. would be completed by 1972.

But the first Talladega 500 became a test of wills. Members of the recently formed Professional Drivers Association announced on the day before the 500 that they would not compete because of the drastic tire wear. France contended racers should drive according to conditions,

and he said there would be a 500, with or without them.

A field of 13 Winston Cup cars and 23 Grand Touring automobiles contested the first Talladega 500. The lighter, slower GTs had competed in the speedway's first event, the 'Bama 400, on Saturday, and France opened the next day's Talladega 500 to them. Ken Rush took the 400, thus becoming the first winner at the track.

A crowd of 100,000 had been expected, but in the turmoil an estimated 62,000 showed up. Richard Brickhouse, a North Carolina farmer who resigned from the PDA, beat Jim Vandiver by 250 yards to score what would be his only Winston Cup victory.

It was obvious big league races would go on whether the stars were in the lineup or not, and the PDA eventually disbanded. The name drivers returned to AIMS in 1970, and young Pete Hamilton won the Alabama 500 and the Talladega 500, and the super track was off and running.

The Allison brothers each won three races in 1970. In one of Bobby's victories, he got an unintentional assist from Donnie. With 10 laps to go in the Atlanta 500, Cale Yarborough was ahead by more than a full lap and was extending his lead. Just as he entered the pit for a splash-and-go, Donnie Allison's engine blew, and the caution was displayed.

Bobby unlapped himself and darted into his pit for two new tires. Yarborough's crew decided against a tire change, and when the race resumed Bobby shot by Cale to win. The next week, at Bristol, the Allisons staged another of their 1-2 finishes. Donnie won by three laps, and Jabe Thomas, the Clown Prince of NASCAR, who happened to be Bobby's teammate for that race, used the big lead to have some fun in the late going.

Thomas drove down pit road, stopped at Donnie's pit, and asked car owner Banjo Matthews, "How much will you pay me not to spin Donnie out?"

Matthews waved him on, but on the next lap Matthews held up a pit board that read, "50 cents."

Thomas pulled into the pits and held out his hand. Matthews gave him two quarters, and he returned to the track to finish 12th, 56 laps

behind.

In what would be the only three-victory season of his Winston Cup career, Donnie Allison also won Daytona's Firecracker 400 and the longest stock car race, Charlotte's World 600.

Driving a Coyote Ford for A.J. Foyt, he was not competitive in the 1970 Indianapolis 500. Winner Al Unser lapped him by the 26th lap. But he drove a steady race, finished fourth and earned Rookie of the Year honors. So two famous racing families had reasons to be happy that day.

Before the 1970 season, Red Farmer said, "I've been racing some 20 years. I've won two national championships. I think I might take it easy."

Fat chance. He drove the Huntsville (Thursday), Birmingham (Friday) and Montgomery (Saturday) circuit and on Sunday competed wherever a race happened to be and took his second consecutive national Sportsman championship to go with the national Modified title he won in 1956. In 75 races Farmer scored 19 wins and 43 top-threes. He accumulated 5,516 points to Sam Sommers' 4,988.

Looking to 1971, Farmer declared, "I'll probably run three nights a week here in Alabama, and then for Sundays I'm going to buy a cabin by the river and be with my family." But, he added: "Of course, if things go pretty well at the beginning of the season, there's no telling what could happen."

—6—

Bobby Allison, Driver of the Year

The American Driver of the Year Award, motor sports' Heisman Trophy, went to Bobby Allison after the 1972 season, icing on a cake that would have taxed the capacity of any bakery.

In 1971 Bobby won 10 Winston Cup races. In 1972 he won 10 more. So nearly a fourth of the 84 victories he would compile in 25 seasons came during a two-year span.

His accomplishments over those two years are even more remarkable considering that on one occasion he almost quit Winston Cup racing, and on another he was fired.

Bobby was building and driving his own Dodges in 1971, but a plague of troubles was crippling the effort.

The Rebel 400 at Darlington on May 2 was a heartbreaker for both Allison brothers. Donnie, driving the Wood Brothers Mercury, led 250 of the 293 laps and was well in front when his engine failed 10 laps from the end, and Buddy Baker won. Bobby's engine blew after just 177 laps.

Bobby was walking through the infield to tell his wife Judy that that was the financial straw that broke his back in Winston Cup racing when Ralph Moody of the Holman-Moody team yelled at him, "Bobby, come here a minute."

"I'll be back in a minute," Bobby said, continuing his mission of delivering his grim message to his wife.

Later, Allison went to Moody's camper. "Why don't you park that (bleep) box of yours and drive for me?" Moody asked him.

"Are you serious?"

"Well, something might happen."

It did. Moody called on Monday to tell Bobby that David Pearson had quit the Mercury ride, and it was Bobby's if he wanted it.

Of course he wanted one of the better assignments on the circuit, one best known for Fred Lorenzen's stardom in the car in the 1960s. He canceled his plans to become a full-time Sportsman racer and embarked on a rewarding chapter of his career.

His first race with Holman-Moody was the Winston 500 at Talladega. Donnie scored his only victory of the season, and Bobby finished second.

Some called it the greatest auto race in history. "I guess this was the hardest race anybody ever ran for 500 miles," Donnie said. Bobby finished 20 feet behind his brother, and his front bumper was a foot ahead of Buddy baker's front bumper. There were 46 lead changes.

Donnie led Bobby and Baker into the final lap, but it wasn't because he wanted to. "I would have felt better if I had been second or third at that time," he said. He feared the other two might use the draft to slingshot past him on the final run down the front straightaway. He would rather have been in position to slingshot them instead.

But they weren't able to pull it off, and Donnie was 4-0 in 1-2 finishes with Bobby.

At Charlotte, Bobby began an incredible streak of five straight victories by winning the World 600 comfortably.

In the Mason-Dixon 500 at Dover he was the only one of the first four finishers not requiring a relief driver. "It's the toughest race I can remember running," he said. "I guess I come from farther South than most of the drivers. I guess I can stand the heat more than some of them." He lapped the runnerup, Illinois driver Lorenzen.

He won the Motor State 400 at Michigan, and when Holman-Moody didn't enter the Golden State 400 at Riverside he dusted off his own Dodge and won it. There was something new in racing technolo-

gy, and Bobby used it at Riverside.

"I was wired for sound," he said. "I had a radio hookup with my brother Eddie in the pits, and it helped a lot. There was one wreck which had the track almost blocked. The caution never came out. My crew hollered at me on the radio about the wreck, so I was on my toes. I got by without any trouble. If I hadn't known about it, I might have plowed right into it."

He drove his Dodge to victory lane in a short track race at Houston, Tex. "It's funny, earlier in the year my Dodge wouldn't finish a race. It kept breaking down. I'm not doing anything different now. Sometimes it's strange how your luck turns around."

His streak ended at Greenville, S.C. He led all but one of the first 107 laps in the Holman-Moody Mercury, and he was in front when the engine blew.

Bobby won the Yankee 400 at Michigan, then he delighted the home folks by taking the Talladega 500.

There was bad blood between Bobby Allison and Richard Petty in those days, and one of their flare-ups occurred that day at Talladega.

The last lap began with the nose of Bobby's car two feet in front of the grille of Petty's. Pete Hamilton rode on their bumpers.

Petty edged ahead of Bobby on the second turn, but Bobby regained the lead on the backstretch. In the third turn, with Bobby barely in front, Petty and Hamilton collided. Hamilton's racer spun into the infield, Petty's fishtailed, and Bobby sped to the line to win by 2.2 seconds over Petty. Hamilton recovered to finish third since he was four laps ahead of Fred Lorenzen.

"Anyone want to hear a loser?" Petty said with a grin as he entered the press box after the race. But soon the mood had changed, and no one was grinning. Accusation was matching accusation.

"Bobby was on the inside, and I was in the middle, and Pete was on the outside," Petty spoke of the late incident. "Pete was about a foot up on my car.

"When Bobby moved up, I moved up, and Pete was the one who wound up on the short end of the stick."

Petty said his car hit Hamilton's. "Once we touched, Bobby just went on."

Bobby replied: "We were coming up on a lapped car, and I had to go up. Everybody saw the lapped car. The track is four lanes wide, and there wasn't but four of us. It seemed to me there was room for everybody, and I only moved up enough to clear the slow car.

"I feel real bad Pete was the victim. Pete has suffered from lack of equipment and everything else."

Petty said: "I've been driving a race car 13 years, and the only person I ever had any run-in with is Bobby Allison. Anybody who would spin his own brother out in a 25-lap feature, you've got to watch out for them. Enough said."

Did Petty feel anything was done intentionally? "Enough said," he repeated, then added, "Everybody tries to win. Some just go about it in a different way."

Bobby retaliated: "He's had trouble with Isaac, Pearson, Paschal, anybody who has ever run against him for any time. The trouble comes in neck-and-neck competition. Anybody who is too small to realize that is hurting his own self."

Petty told writers to "go check my car. That will explain what is going on. A lot of red paint is on my car."

Countered Bobby: "I've got some blue on mine, so I imagine he has some red on his." Petty's Plymouth was blue, Allison's Mercury red.

Could Petty have won the race if the incident hadn't occurred? "It would have been a right smart closer," Richard answered.

Second-place money made Petty the first stock car driver to earn $200,000 in a season. "I want to celebrate winning $200,000," he told the press box, reducing the tension. "Somebody give me an aspirin."

Bobby won Darlington's tradition-rich Southern 500 for the first time. "I would say this has been the best day I ever had," he commented after leading 329 of the 367 laps.

He won the National 500 at Charlotte and a short track event in Macon, Ga. He had achieved a record-tying seven superspeedway victories and won what NASCAR referred to as "an amazing $236,295 in purse money alone."

And then he got fired. John Holman held the upper hand in Holman-Moody, and he and Ralph Moody struck sparks. Bobby and Moody, on the other hand, were old friends. Holman told Bobby to find

another ride.

Donnie Allison made his second Indianapolis 500 start for A.J. Foyt in 1971 and finished sixth as Al Unser won for the second straight year.

Donnie had a close call. He weaved his way through an early wreck on the backstretch, much as he had done in 1970 when several cars crashed.

"I was holding my breath," he said. "I saw a lot of oil ahead of me, and I had to go through the oil, then get out of the groove, then go back through the oil to miss everything."

His nose was bleeding because a rock flew up and hit him, almost knocking him unconscious.

Donnie's car ran out of gas on the backstretch, and he coasted all the way to his second fuel stop with a dead engine. "It might have been different. I might have finished higher except for that," he said.

"The car's back end was just too loose all day. It was wanting to spin a wheel all the time. We didn't have the wings set properly. But I did the best I could do.

"I ran a lot harder this year than last year, but I knew things were going to be stepped up."

A shower feels good after an evening of dirt track racing.

Photo courtesy of the Farmer family

Red Farmer scored the biggest victory of his career in 1971, capturing the Permatex 300, the nation's premier Sportsman race, at Daytona. So much for relaxing on the river. That sent him winging

toward the highest points total in Sportsman history, and he won his third straight national title. In amassing 9,688 points to 7,699 for Sam Sommers, he won 18 of 101 Sportsman starts and finished in the top five 56 times.

Photo courtesy of the Bonnett family

Driver Neil Bonnett and car owner Butch Nelson became a force in Sportsman racing.

On July 30, 1971, Neil Bonnett recorded his first "official" Sportsman win. It came at Birmingham.

Bobby moved to Junior Johnson's Chevrolet team in 1972, and his amazing run of successes continued. He not only won 10 races, but he finished second to Petty in points standings, and his $274,995 in earnings led the circuit.

In an interesting twist, the Most Popular Sportsman driver of 1972 was Tony Bettenhausen Jr. of Houston, Tex., son of the Indy car star. Bettenhausen drove on the Alabama circuit that year and finished second to Jack Ingram in points standings.

Bobby's first victory for Johnson's team came on March 26, 1972, in the Atlanta 500, and it was the first superspeedway win for Chevrolet since Johnson himself won at Charlotte on Oct. 13, 1963.

Bobby trailed by seven seconds with 30 laps to go, but he ran down A.J. Foyt and passed him with five laps left, winning by a fraction of a second.

"We knew all along we could win a 500-mile race," Johnson said. "Frankly, I was getting tired of everybody saying we couldn't win one. We're the only ones working on Chevrolets, and it takes us time to get everything solved."

Bobby won the next race, at Bristol, and the other drivers began grousing that the rules favored Chevrolet.

"That Chevy is supposed to win," griped runnerup Bobby Isaac. "That's the way the rules are written."

Said Petty: "NASCAR has jacked the rules around so much to help that Chevy. Just once I'd like to be even with them."

Bobby countered: "We win two races, and everybody is saying we have an advantage. I guess that's to be expected."

Bobby lapped the field in the Mason-Dixon 500 at Dover and topped that by lapping his opponents three times in the second race at Bristol. At one juncture he was five laps ahead of runnerup Petty, but he slowed his pace. "I just tried to stay out of trouble after that."

He won at Trenton and made it a sweep at Atlanta by taking the Dixie 500. The temperature was 96 degrees, but Bobby laughed it off. "It's been a hot summer, and I like the heat. Because I like it and others don't, it probably at least gives me a psychological advantage. Running a lot of short track Sportsman races helps me keep in top shape."

In his early days of racing, Bobby would drive his passenger car in the summer with the windows rolled up and the heater on to acclimate himself to the punishing conditions of a race.

After winning at Nashville, Bobby claimed his second victory in Darlington's Southern 500. He passed David Pearson with six laps to go to score his fifth win in his last seven races.

"I just flat got my fanny outrun," Pearson admitted.

Bobby took Charlotte's National 500 and Rockingham's American 500, and he had led in an incredible 40 consecutive races. The streak ended in the last event of the season as he never gained the lead.

Bobby left Johnson's team and fielded his own Chevrolet in 1973. He also made his Indianapolis 500 debut, driving for Roger Penske. His engine blew on the first lap. In his only other Indy 500 start, in 1975, a flywheel broke and sent him to the sidelines, but not until after he had

led the race.

In 1972 Donnie Allison began a streak of four straight winless seasons on the Winston Cup tour. After that campaign, he discussed his brother's single-mindedness:

"I wouldn't say he is any more serious about it than I am, but he has no interest other than racing, with the possible exception of his airplane.

"Our father used to take us hunting, but all the brothers got away from it except me. When Bobby goes, he enjoys it. But you can't get him to go.

"I think sometimes that's good, and sometimes I think it's not. He has no place to relieve the pressure of his occupation. He says the only place is flying his plane.

"But he's content. Like at night, when others might sit down and drink a beer, he's content to go to the shop and fool with his racer. It's something he has trained himself to do. That's something he enjoys doing, so he does it."

The long days and nights of earning his bread on the Modified-Sportsman circuit forced Bobby Allison to become a competent mechanic as well as driver.

"He would have to be as good or better than anybody who is a driver and mechanic," Donnie said. "He understands not just parts of the car but every part. You find a few like that—A.J. Foyt, and I figure I fall into that category, and Richard Petty.

"A lot of guys drive cars but don't really understand what makes them work. I'd say it's a very big help to be able to.

"Bobby and I did this as a living in the Modifieds. Some people who did it as a hobby might get in a bind and throw their hands up. But we couldn't afford to. I think this has helped us."

Donnie continued: "Since he was a real young fellow, he has been a very determined person. Any job he tried to do, he did some way or another, maybe not exactly like he intended to do it. He'd make some changes and get it done one way or the other, though.

"He does the same thing in a race car. If the car is not doing exactly like he wants it to, he'll make some changes in what he has to do and

maybe finish a lot better than somebody who just sits there and drives it like it is.

"This might sound cruel, but I think he enjoys catching somebody at a disadvantage and showing them he has an advantage. I feel that way myself, too.

"The most important thing is his driving ability. He has definitely got it. He has proved that time and time again. Under equal conditions, I'd say he's the hardest guy I've ever raced against. He doesn't give up. You don't beat him mentally, whereas you can beat the majority that way. Somewhere along the line you can whip them.

"The 1969 National 500 at Charlotte was an example. They were running the winged Dodges, and we were running the Ford Talladegas. Bobby was the only one who didn't give up all day. I kept beating them down, but I couldn't beat him down. Every time we'd make a pit stop it was a new race. "I'd say Bobby is a charger. I think some people unjustly accused him of being a stroker a time or two. He knows what equipment can do and can't do. He's smart enough to know better than to try to get more out of a car than there is in it.

"A lot of guys called chargers end up in the fence. This, of course, gets back to the mechanical end, knowing what it will stand and what it won't stand."

Courtesy International Motor Sports Hall of Fame
A Neil Bonnett Promotional postcard

7

Neil Bonnett - A Fearless Free Spirit

A month after Neil Bonnett's death in a practice crash at Daytona International Speedway, Butch Nelson remembered stories about his best friend. Sometimes he laughed, and sometimes he cried, and sometimes he did both at the same time.

Nelson is president of Neil Bonnett Honda in Hueytown. The mundane details of capitalism held little interest for Neil, and his role largely was to stick his head in Nelson's office door, ask, "Are we still making money?" get an affirmative answer and set off on a fishing or hunting trip.

But their relationship went back nearly a quarter-century. Though Bonnett frequently was called Bobby Allison's "protégé," and he drove Sportsman racers for Bobby, most of his Sportsman days were spent in Nelson's cars. In fact, Bonnett had won the 1972 and 1973 BIR track championships before he drove for Bobby.

"People talk about Bobby getting him started in racing," Nelson reflected, "but he was outrunning Bobby and Donnie and Red and Ray Putnam and Jerry Lawley and those boys in my car. "Neil got mad at me and drove a year or two for Bobby. One night he started 26th and finished second in my car, and he came in and said, 'Butch, if we can't do better than this, we ought to quit,' so I put Roy Milligan in the car. "But he came back and raced several years with me. We ran together

until 1978 or 1979, I guess, but he was running so much Winston Cup that we were running only eight or nine Sportsman races a year."

Nelson remembers Bonnett as a fearless free spirit. "One time at Nashville Jack Ingram told me, 'Neil said he's going to break the track record. He said he's going through turns one and two and not lift. I don't think he can.'

"Well," Nelson continued, "I didn't think he could, either.

"Jack said, 'Let's go down there in one and two and watch the wreck.'

"The car was so new that we used tape for the number, but I didn't say anything. Neil came in there, and when he hit the wall the rear tires were still digging.

"We had to take him to the hospital and he was out cold for 30 minutes. But he raced the next night."

Bonnett could, indeed, give a car owner gray hair.

"One night at Nashville we were leading a 200-lapper by two laps with 12 laps to go," Nelson remembered. "It paid about $4,000.

"Neil called on the radio and said, 'Get two right-side tires ready in case I need them.'

"I said, 'Do you have a flat?'

"He said no, and I told him there were only 12 laps left and he was two laps ahead, to just ride it out.

"But Neil said he was tired of L.D. Ottinger hitting him. He told me, 'I'm going to put him in the wall when I catch him to lap him again, and I might bust these tires when I hit him.'

Nelson was relieved when Ottinger sensed Bonnett's intention and slammed on his brakes. "Neil went on by him and won the race."

Bonnett had a way of making his point. Nelson rented a Winston Cup car from Benny Parsons for Neil to drive at Atlanta in 1975. Jake Elder was Parsons' crew chief.

"Neil passed Benny, and he was running about third," Nelson recalled. "He told me to tell Jake the car was pushing. Jake said the car never had pushed. Neil told me to tell Jake to watch this.

"He clipped the wall with his right front bumper and said, 'Ask Jake if he thinks it's pushing now.'

"Jake said, 'Bring him in, and let's take some push out of that car.'

"At Riverside, Calif., Bonnett and Nelson returned from the race track to their motel and found all the parking places taken.

"Neil said, 'Butch, is this the right Holiday Inn?'"

"I said, 'Yes.'

"He asked me about four times to check the key and be sure that was the right Holiday Inn, and didn't I think we deserved a parking place.'

"I assured him we were at the right Holiday Inn, and we

International Speedway Corp. photo

Neil Bonnett was one of those guys who usually found the sunshine in a situation.

deserved a parking place. So he just parked the rental car in the flower bed out front. He knocked down four or five bushes and locked the car, and we went to our room.

"The next morning the car wasn't there. I don't know whatever happened to it."

Bonnett's reputation as a race driver totally without fear was well founded, Nelson said.

"I had a brand new 440-cubic-inch Dodge Charger," he recalled. "We had run the Snowball Derby in Pensacola, and we were headed home. Neil was driving, and it was pouring down rain.

"I said, 'Neil, how fast are we running?'

"He said," I don't know. The speedometer only shows 160.'

"I said, 'Well, at least slow down to 120.'"

Bonnett "fished hard and hunted hard and raced hard," Nelson said. "Everything he did was with a vengeance.

"We bought this land where the dealership is, and there was an old

house on it. I was negotiating about a $3,000 deal for it. Some guy was going to buy the lumber and stuff.

"But Neil wasn't that patient. I drove up one day and the fire truck was rushing up, and the house was burning.

"I said, 'Neil, what happened?'

"He said, 'You'd be surprised what five gallons of gas and a match will do.'"

Bonnett's debut in Winston Cup racing didn't hint at the glory that awaited him. He didn't qualify for the 1973 Winston 500 at Talladega— but, as with most episodes in his life, there was a story behind the story.

Nelson bought a Dodge from Bobby Allison and an engine from Richard Petty, but Bonnett couldn't make the field in time trials.

"He had to win a qualifying race to get into the lineup for the 500," Nelson recalled. "I told him, 'Neil, we've got to win some Sportsman races and pay the bills. This Winston Cup racing is not for me. Either make the field or burn the car to the ground.'

"He came by that afternoon, and the car wasn't on the trailer. I naturally thought he had made the field and left the car at the speedway.

"I said, 'You must have won the qualifying race.'

"He was grinning, and he said, 'No, we did what you said and burned it to the ground.'

"He had gotten hold of some illegal fuel. Somebody told him to put a half-gallon in the car and he would shoot to the front. Neil thought that if a half-gallon would do that, there was no telling what five gallons would do.

"He started at the rear and passed every car in the race going down the backstretch on the first lap. Going into the third turn on the second lap he was leading by 600 yards when the motor blew and the car burned up.'"

Bonnett had a conscience that slipped into high gear one night, Nelson recalled.

"He roughed Red Farmer up bad in the first feature, and when he came into the pits he said, 'If I've got to rough up somebody like Red to win a race, I need to just quit racing.'

"I finally talked him into getting back into the car, and in the sec-

ond feature he rode on the outside of Red Farmer for 24 laps, giving Red the chance to wreck him.

"Red never touched him, and Neil won the race."

Neil Bonnett was born on July 30, 1946, in the Ensley section of Birmingham, the only child of Lawrence and Josephine Bonnett. His childhood was normal enough, as he played with the neighborhood kids, fished with his dad and, in his best clothes, went to Sunday school and preaching at Ensley Baptist Church.

He never liked school. "I think I got double promoted in the first grade, and that was my first and last scholastic achievement," he said.

He preferred drag racing his '56 Ford from stop light to stop light, and courting Susan McAdams, whom he married when they were 17.

To enable him to graduate from high school, she dropped out and sacked groceries. Four years later, she returned and got her diploma.

In school, he would gaze out the window and daydream. "I'd rather be out there digging a ditch," he thought. "I'd rather do something myself than hear about what somebody did a thousand years ago."

He got his wish when he entered the real world after high school. He got to dig ditches—and then carry his end of 250-pound pipes to fill the ditches.

"That made me better and gave me the incentive to do better," Bonnett recalled. He began taking courses in plumbing, heating, air conditioning, blueprints, etc., to get a pipefitter's union card.

Later he would say that after working on skyscrapers that were under construction, tight roping his way along girders 20 floors up, stock car racing didn't seem so dangerous.

Neil and Susan attended the weekly races at the fairgrounds in Birmingham, and they were intrigued by the skills of the Allisons and Farmer and the other stars. When Neil learned that one of the drivers, Lee Hurley, lived near his parents' home, he couldn't resist dropping in on him.

And so a career began.

Bonnett won 18 Winston Cup races, but Nelson shares a widely held opinion that 18 victories doesn't reflect his talent.

"No disrespect to the people he drove for, including the Wood

Union 76 Racestoppers demonstrated the latest in car washing techniques for Neil Bonnett.

Brothers, but he never had a winning car for a whole year," Nelson said. "Things were never exactly what they should have been.

"He always made the wrong move. A lot of people don't know it, but he turned down the number 28 car before Davey Allison got it.

"I talked him out of it. They had been blowing motors. Then when Davey got into it, they stopped blowing motors."

Nelson believes Bonnett would have won "65 or 70 races" if he could have caught teams that were at their peaks. "He should have won five Daytona 500s." Bonnett, in fact, never won more than three Winston Cup races in a season.

Bonnett's association with Bobby Allison helped him acquire something of a national reputation, though he wasn't in the big time.

Never a shy fellow, he began spending time at Bobby's shop in Hueytown when he and Nelson split. As a Winston Cup star, Bobby

could command show money to race at short tracks over the nation, so he maintained Modified-Sportsman cars.

Once in 1974 something came up that kept Bobby from keeping a commitment to race in Houston, Tex. He called the promoter and told him there was a hot young driver named Neil Bonnett in Birmingham, and if it was OK, he would send Bonnett to Houston with his race car.

"Neil who?" the promoter asked.

But Bonnett went to Houston and won the race—one of more than 50 he would win in a couple of seasons in Bobby's cars. They painted "Neil Who?" over the car door in the space reserved for the driver's name.

Bobby knew firsthand how good Bonnett was. They had met in a classic duel at BIR, running 17 laps of the 25-lap feature side by side, Neil on the outside, Bobby on the inside, metal to metal. When it was over the left side of Neil's car and the right side of Bobby's car were solid black from tire rubber.

Traveling on behalf of Bobby Allison was an educational experience. Neil learned how to quickly set up a car for a variety of sizes and styles of tracks. He learned how to drive on a miscellany of speedways. He was interviewed by an assortment of media, and he learned to charm the men and women of the press.

(Later, he would become a member of the media. He was a color man on racing telecasts, and he hosted a popular feature TV show called *Winners*. "They did those *Winners* shows in most cases on one take," Nelson remembered. "He was a natural at anything he did.")

Neil would return to Hueytown after a race and discuss the circumstances with the master. "Well," Bobby would say, "what I would have done in that case is ..."

Bonnett took Bobby's racer to a meet at the Minnesota State Fair in 1974. It was one of 176 cars there. One the first day he broke the track record in qualifying. On the second day, in a 75-lapper, he lapped the field, but when he tried to lap some of them the second time, they blocked the track. So he spun out six of them, damaging their cars and Bobby's.

After the race, the press interviewed Bonnett. They wanted to know what Bobby would think about his tearing up his car.

Bonnett replied: "Bobby told me, 'Go up there and set on the pole and blow all them Yankees in the weeds.'

"Well, so far we've set on the pole and blown a few in the weeds. Come Sunday and that 400-lapper, anybody who doesn't think I won't move them out of the way should look at the front of my race car and look at those six cars sitting over there in the garage."

On Sunday, Bonnett led the first 140 laps as the other drivers surrendered the entire track to him. When the rear end of his car failed, the crowd gave him a standing ovation.

Bobby Allison's domination of 1971 and 1972 ended as he won just two Winston Cup races in 1973 and two more in 1974. He won three in 1975 but was winless the next two seasons.

Bobby was injured in two crashes in 1976. He suffered broken ribs and lacerations in a wreck at Rockingham. He was more seriously injured in a non-Winston Cup event at Elko, Minn. There he suffered 11 broken bones and several facial cuts, including a gash near his right eye that required 40 stitches.

As he was being treated in a hospital in Minnesota, he had no feeling in his feet. He wondered if they had been cut off. He asked himself if his career would have been worth the loss of his feet. He decided it would have.

"I spent four days in the hospital in Minnesota before I could get the strength to break out of there," he recalled. "When I got back to the shop at Hueytown I had Neil and Donnie cut the cast off one leg before we loaded up the race car to go to a NASCAR race in Nashville.

"We had a motor home at the time, and that's how we went up there. They loaded me up, hitched the race car to the back, and Neil drove us up to the track."

Bonnett qualified the car, winning the pole for the Winston Cup event. Bobby started the race to get credit for the points, and Bonnett took over and drove to a seventh-place finish.

"Neil and Donnie devised a way to fasten handles on my casts so they could lift me in and out of the car," remembered Bobby, who didn't miss a Winston Cup start while he was injured.

Neil Bonnett drove Bobby Allison's cars to many short-track victories.

Donnie Allison experienced heartbreak in 1974 when, leading the Daytona 500 by 38 seconds with 11 laps to go, he ran over debris from another driver's shattered engine, and two tires exploded.

Donnie, who hadn't won a big league event since May 16, 1971, broke the drought on Oct. 10, 1976, when he drove Hoss Ellington's Chevrolet to victory in Charlotte's National 500. But he was not declared the victor until four hours after the race because NASCAR suspected the car of being a cheater and conducted a thorough tear-down.

Donnie and Elliott became a solid force. In 1977 Donnie won the Talladega 500 and Rockingham's American 500 for Elliott.

Donnie became ill on a punishingly hot day at Talladega, and Darrell Waltrip drove the final 23 laps for him. Under NASCAR rules, the starting driver gets credit for the win.

"I probably could have gone all the way if I'd had to," Donnie said,

"but if I had passed out and wrecked and hurt myself or somebody else I'd have been foolish. So I thought it was better to let somebody else have it."

A third Hueytown driver joined the Winston Cup tour on May 5, 1974, when Neil Bonnett drove in Talladega's Winston 500. His appearance was not memorable, for the record shows he started 33rd in Charlie Roberts' Chevrolet, completed 51 laps before an oil line problem, and got 45th place in a 50-car field.

In 1975, in a Chevy he built in Bobby Allison's shop, he actually led the Talladega 500 for 12 laps before his engine blew. He startled the racing establishment by finishing fifth in the 1976 Daytona 500 in his own car.

Bonnett's first Winston Cup victory came on Sept. 11, 1977, in the Capital City 400 at Richmond. He drove the Jim Stacy Dodge, with veteran crew chief Harry Hyde giving him lap by lap instructions.

"Harry was flying me by remote control," Bonnett said. "I ran on the ragged edge all day, and Harry's coaching over the radio helped. He told me what groove to take and when. This victory is as much his as it is mine."

It was only the fourth race for the new Stacy team, and Bonnett had the satisfaction of holding off Richard Petty, who had won 13 times at the Richmond track.

Back home, Susan Bonnett couldn't find the race on the radio. She usually went to the races, but with their 13-year-old son David due in school the next day, this one was too far away.

She asked Neil's cousin Larry Northcutt to call *The Birmingham News* for results. Northcutt was told Bonnett had won, and when he told Susan, she got carried away and began to pummel him.

"I beat Larry to death," she admitted. "Larry cuts up a lot, and David thought he might be kidding, so David called *The News* to be sure it was true.

"We had been sitting there during the race saying wouldn't it be something if Neil won and none of us there and we couldn't even get it on the radio."

Bonnett called his family an hour after they had heard the news. "Did you get me a trophy?" 3-year-old Kristen wanted to know, recall-

ing that he had brought her the trophy after winning a recent Sportsman race at Huntsville.

On that joyous day, Susan recalled her feelings when her husband decided to become a racer.

"I was disappointed when he first told me," she remembered. "I figured three or four laps and it would scare him to death, and that would be it.

"We went to Montgomery for his first race, and he spun out, and I thought that would scare him, but he was crazy about it, wild about it."

Eventually he became an ex-pipefitter and a full-time racer. "I was disappointed when he quit his job," Susan Bonnett said, "but he was happy. I'd be disappointed now if he had to go back to pipe fitting. I love it as much as he does."

Bonnett also recorded his second Winston Cup win in 1977. He held off Petty to take the Los Angeles Times 500 at Ontario. It was his first WC superspeedway victory.

"The track is 60 feet wide, and I must have used 62 feet in the last lap to keep Petty behind me," Bonnett delivered a typically colorful post-race quote. "I've always dreamed about running with these guys. This win is really a dream come true."

8

Troubled Times

T wo straight seasons without a visit to victory lane tore at
proud Bobby Allison. After failing to win in Roger Penske's
cars in 1976, he fielded his own American Motors Matadors
in 1977, and it was one of his most frustrating years in Winston Cup.

The man who had won 10 races and $274,995 in 1972 recorded
only five top-five finishes and earned just $87,740 in 1977.

And he had been ill most of the season. Mysterious attacks of nausea descended upon him. A five-day stay in a hospital produced a diag-
nosis of "fatigue," which was unsatisfactory to the one with the sour
stomach.

Dejected and sick, Bobby wondered what course he should take as
the 1978 season approached.

"Needless to say, both emotionally and physically, I was at a real
low spot then," Bobby said years later. "I really didn't know what I was
going to do, so I considered focusing my attention on running the short
tracks full time.

"In this business, though, things have a strange way of working
out."

He had labored in his shop all day and had just flopped in a reclin-
er in his den. Nausea was bombarding him. The telephone rang. It was
an effort to even answer it, but he did.

Photo courtesy of the Allison family

Bobby Allison (No.15, passing Neil Bonnett) won the 1978 Daytona 500.

Car owner Bud Moore was on the line. "Look," he said, "I know you've been doing lousy, and I've been doing lousy, and I think we ought to see if we can get together."

He had called it like it was. Buddy Baker had driven for Moore in all 30 Winston Cup races the previous season, and Moore's Fords hadn't won, either.

So two men who had produced only goose eggs in 1977 teamed up for 1978—and won the Daytona 500, the Super Bowl of stock car racing.

Bobby Allison's career had been bountiful, but the two premier accomplishments available to a stock car driver had eluded him—winning the Winston Cup championship and winning the Daytona 500.

He took care of one of those omissions in 1978—but he almost left Moore's team before the 500.

In his first start for Moore, at Riverside, he crashed. Then, in a Friday qualifying race before Sunday's Daytona 500, he crashed again.

He was nauseated, feeling terrible. He went to the speedway on Saturday to tell Moore he was going home to Hueytown, that he would-

n't be driving for him after all.

He entered the garage and saw the car he had wrecked. It had been resurrected. The gleaming white and blue paint was so fresh that it was still wet.

Bobby told himself that if the crew could work that hard to restore the car, the least he could do was drive it, no matter how punk he felt.

He drove it all the way to victory lane. He set a race record by charging out of 33rd spot in the 41-car field. No 500 winner had ever started that far back.

The victory came on Feb. 19, 1978, and it was Bobby's first in the big league since Sept. 1, 1975, when he took Darlington's Southern 500. Moore hadn't fielded a winner since Baker grabbed the Winston 500 at Talladega on May 2, 1976.

Bobby Allison's and Buddy Baker's fortunes were strangely entwined at Daytona.

Baker had quit Moore to drive M.C. Anderson's Oldsmobile. It was Baker who had gotten into another car's oil and triggered the wreck that sidelined Bobby in the Friday qualifier. Finally, the Daytona 500 sifted down to Baker and Bobby.

They were dueling for the victory when, with four laps to go, Baker's engine failed, leaving Bobby a free ride.

"It was ironic that it came down to Buddy and me," Bobby said. "What would have happened if Baker's engine hadn't died in the 500?"

"It looked like we were getting away from him anyway," Bobby said. "He was having to go high around the hole, and I was hooked up in a draft with Dave Marcis."

Indeed, a hole did appear in the racing surface of the third turn late in the 500, apparently the result of rain that fell during the week. Bobby described it as about three feet in diameter and four or five inches deep.

Baker and other drivers hit the hole regularly, but Bobby's car was handling superbly, and he could stay under it without lifting the accelerator. He drafted Dave Marcis, who was a couple of laps behind, and was putting distance between his car and Baker's.

Bobby conquered stock car racing's Kentucky Derby-Masters-World Series on his 15th attempt. "I saw this track in 1959 when I was

running Modifieds," he recalled. "I was so impressed by the size of it. I said, 'This is where racing is going, and I hope to be a part of it.'" It was a most welcome win. "This victory comes on the heels of a very depressing time in my career," he said. "I think maybe the impact of this one hasn't caught up with me yet. I'm not sure I'm here."

He added: "I've seen times that it looked like I couldn't win a race in an Indianapolis car against pedal cars."

Was a prayer belatedly answered?

"My oldest daughter Bonnie was upset because she said a little prayer just before the wreck Friday," Bobby said of his 15-year-old. "I told her, 'Maybe it would have been worse if you hadn't.'"

"That's the only thing that weighed on me. I hate for a child to think her prayer goes unanswered because it isn't answered right away like she wants it to be."

His poor starting position could have been a blessing. Bobby was far back when Richard Petty, Darrell Waltrip and David Pearson—who were running 1, 2, 3—crashed together.

"I missed out on that big one, and that's important," he said.

That afternoon Bobby summoned up a different brand of courage from that required to drive a car 190 miles an hour. On the cool-down lap he suffered one of the worst attacks of nausea yet. "Time to put on the best act of your life," he told himself. "When you get to victory lane, don't show these people how terrible you feel."

What he said in public was: "I'm so tickled I can't see straight."

A month later Bobby lapped the field to win the Atlanta 500. "A lot of people thought I was over the hill," he said afterward. "I hope now they think I can still drive a race car."

Bobby won the Delaware 500 at Dover and the National 500 at Charlotte, and then the 1978 season ended on a high note for the Allison brothers, for Donnie took Atlanta's Dixie 500, the next-to-last race, and Bobby won Ontario's Los Angeles Times 500, the last one.

The Dixie 500 was one of the more confusing events in NASCAR history.

At one point, Donnie had been almost two laps behind. Indeed, when he passed Richard Petty and Dave Marcis two laps from the finish, the scoreboard showed him in fifth place, a lap down. Petty appar-

ently edged Marcis for the win, but then came the announcement on the cool-down lap that Donnie was the victor.

He went to victory lane, and shortly after he concluded the traditional winner's press box interview, NASCAR said Petty had won, and Donnie was third, a lap behind.

At 7:40 p.m., NASCAR reversed itself again. Donnie was the winner, it said, after finally tracing down a scoring mix-up that had caused all the confusion. He didn't learn of the decision until the next day. It would be the last Winston Cup race he would ever win.

Bobby's fifth victory of the season, at Ontario, elevated him to second in the points standings behind champion Cale Yarborough.

And he finally learned what was wrong with him physically. He went to the Mayo Clinic in Rochester, Minn., and learned he had a hiatal hernia, which could be controlled by medication.

The 1979 Daytona 500 featured one of the zaniest endings in racing history.

Donnie was leading with two turns and a front stretch to go. Cale Yarborough tried to pass him on the inside of the third turn on the last lap, but they crashed.

Bobby, who was several laps behind, was riding in front of Donnie and Yarborough. He circled the track and stopped at the wreck scene, and Yarborough took a swing at him while he was still in the car. A national TV audience watched as they got into a scuffle that was quickly broken up.

Yarborough claimed Bobby slowed to try to block him in an effort to help Donnie. Bobby and Donnie said that wasn't true.

The benefactor was Richard Petty. He thought the race had ended a lap before it did and that he had finished third, a half lap behind Donnie and Yarborough. His crew told him to "go, go, go," and he held off Darrell Waltrip and A.J. Foyt to win his sixth Daytona 500 and end a losing streak that dated back to July 4, 1977.

Bobby snaked his way through a 17-car crash on the fourth lap of Talladega's Winston 500 and won by a lap. His 55th career victory elevated him to fourth place in all-time Winston Cup standings. Neil Bonnett led most of the race and had a 16-second lead when the engine in his Wood Brothers Mercury died with 40 laps to go.

For the second straight year, the Bobby Allison-Bud Moore marriage produced five victories.

That 1979 season was a highlight of Bonnett's career. The Wood Brothers and David Pearson parted company in April, and Bonnett took over as the famed Mercury team's driver. He won Dover's Mason-Dixon 500, Daytona's Firecracker 400 and Atlanta's Dixie 500. Only twice in his career did Bonnett win as many as three races in a season.

Bonnett beat Yarborough by two car lengths at Dover. Cale had held a lead of nearly 11 seconds with eight laps to go when a caution flag closed the field. Yarborough elected to hold his position but Neil, the only other driver in the lead lap, took on four tires and won the race.

"The Wood Brothers called the shots," Bonnett said. "I just listened and did what they told me to do. We had nothing to lose and everything to gain."

Bonnett slithered through a pack of lapped cars on the backstretch, Benny Parsons couldn't match his virtuoso driving, and Neil won the Firecracker 400 by one second. "I saw a hole that looked big enough for half a Mercury, so I decided to go for it," Bonnett said.

Neil passed another promising young driver with four laps to go and won by a car length at Atlanta. The runner-up's name was Dale Earnhardt. He was Winston Cup Rookie of the Year that season, and he and Bonnett would become fast friends.

The only victory Bonnett would score at his home track came in the 1980 Talladega 500. Anyone who didn't know him could have gotten some insight into his laid-back nature before the race.

"I was sitting in a lounge chair in the infield building, and I went to sleep and missed the drivers' meeting before the race," Bonnett admitted. "I woke up and they told me NASCAR had fined me $100 for missing it. So I went back to sleep."

"I woke up later and heard the man on the PA introducing the drivers at the start-finish line. He said, `Starting in 18th place...' and I knew I'd better get over there because it was only 16 places up to me."

Bonnett was just as cool on the last lap. He lost the lead to Dale Earnhardt on the backstretch but took it back in the fourth turn and won a thriller.

"People ask me why I've got gray hair," the 34-year-old Bonnett said after the victory. "They ought to come out and watch one of these things, then they'd know. I'd like one day to win an easy race."

But then he reconsidered and said, "No, I wouldn't, either. These are more memorable."

Bonnett had won the race at Pocono a week before Talladega, but those would be his only victories of 1980. Bobby Allison won four races, but he felt the Fords were at a disadvantage, and he left Moore and signed on with Harry Ranier's General Motors team for 1981.

Bobby won Riverside's Winston Western 500 in his first outing for Ranier. ``I want to put all the effort I can into trying to win the championship," he said after the race. "To do that, I'm going to cut down my Sportsman racing."

It was a banner year for Bobby. He won five events, including Talladega's Winston 500 and Charlotte's World 600, finished in the top 10 in 26 of the 31 races, earned $680,957 and finished second to Darrell Waltrip in points standings.

Bonnett won three races for the Wood Brothers, including the tradition-laden Southern 500 at Darlington.

But the 1981 season is best remembered for the first of the

(L-R) Donnie Allison, Bobby Allison and Cale Yarborough staged a sideshow after the 1979 Daytona 500.

tragedies that would afflict the Alabama Gang. Donnie Allison was seriously injured in a crash during the World 600 which his brother won, and though he later drove in other races, the accident marked the beginning of the end of his career.

Donnie completed 146 of the 400 laps before his car hit the wall and then hit Dick Brooks' racer. He suffered fractures of the shoulder, cheek, leg and ribs, a concussion and a collapsed lung.

John Rebhan, his car owner, immediately folded the team. After a long period of recuperation, Donnie opened the 1982 season with Jack Ogden's team—but it soon folded. He went to Bob Rogers' team—but it soon folded.

He wanted no more of under-financed, non-competitive teams just to call himself a Winston Cup driver, he declared. "I've told several people if it wasn't a good car I wouldn't drive it," Donnie said. "Both these last two times I feel I held my end up and was let down on the other end. I have no control over that. I'm not going to get involved and fall on my face." He had moved from Hueytown and become a farmer on a spread at Faunsdale near Demopolis. He did what farmers do and waited for a call from a major team, but it never came. He stuck to his word and avoided subpar cars. "I had three offers to go to the Daytona 500," he said in 1983.

"I need the money, but if I can't race the car I'm not happy. I'm very competitive and can't be a rider. I'd rather race on the short tracks than ride on the superspeedways."

He did compete on some on the short tracks. He eventually became a "coach" of young drivers hoping to make it in Winston Cup. He and his wife Pat moved to Salisbury, N.C., in the heart of stock car country.

Neil Bonnett won just one race for the Wood Brothers in 1982, but it was the longest one, Charlotte's World 600.

Bobby Allison experienced a great year. Driving the DiGard Buick, he won his second Daytona 500. He took seven other races, earned $795,077 and again finished second in points to Darrell Waltrip. Another championship had eluded Bobby. But that was about to change.

9

A Return to Form

B obby Allison had competed on the Winston Cup circuit for 19 seasons. His 73 victories placed him fourth all-time. Twice he had won the biggest race, the Daytona 500. He had earned nearly $4 million. Five times he had been runnerup for the Winston Cup championship—in 1970, 1972, 1978, 1981 and 1982. But the stock car world was beginning to wonder if he ever would win the title. Was he to be the most famous bridesmaid in the sport's history? The question was answered in 1983 when, driving DiGard Racing's Buicks, Bobby shaded Darrell Waltrip for the title. Darrell won by 4,880 to 4,827 in 1981 and by 4,489 to 4,417 in 1982. Each year the fight went down to the final race.

In addition to winning the championship in 1983, Bobby was named American Driver of the Year. It was the second time he had won auto racing's equivalent of the Heisman Trophy. The season began on a sour note for both Bobby and Waltrip. Bobby crashed a car in the Busch Clash and another in practice and finally drove DiGard's short-track racer to ninth place in the Daytona 500. But Waltrip wrecked in the 500 and got 36th place. Bobby won at Richmond the next week, and Waltrip's car failed, relegating him to 29th place. Darrell's title changes seemed to be disappearing before the headers got good and hot. Bobby scored his second victory in the 10th race of the year. He edged

Waltrip, who drove for Junior Johnson's team, by less than a car length in the Mason-Dixon 500 at Dover. The win enabled him to leap past Harry Gant to the top of the points standings. He would not trail again in 1983, though Waltrip would make it close.

Bobby's win at Pocono was his third of the season, and when the tour arrived in Dry Valley for the Talladega 500, Bobby led the standings by 202 points over Waltrip, who had climbed into second place.

After three more races, though, Waltrip had pulled to within 41 points of Bobby. The Hueytown star had enjoyed big leads in the standings in 1981 and 1982, and they had disappeared. Was it about to happen again? "I'd say we're in pretty good shape to take our third straight championship," Waltrip ventured.

Whereupon Bobby began a stunning run of three straight victories.

He survived 97-degree heat to win his fourth Southern 500 at Darlington. "If we're going to lose the championship, we're going to lose it going for the win," he vowed. "We're not going to go conservative."

He made it a sweep at Richmond by taking the track's second event of the year, edging Ricky Rudd by less than a second.

Bobby also swept Dover by nailing the Budweiser 500, and he exulted, "This is the best team I've ever driven for."

Bobby took a lead of 64 points over Waltrip into the final race of the season, at Riverside. If he could finish 13th he would win the title, no matter how Darrell fared.

Bobby drove conservatively and ran ninth. Waltrip was sixth. Bill Elliott scored his first big league victory in the Winston Western 500.

But it wasn't an easy day for Bobby. Four unscheduled pit stops for tire problems and a car that didn't want to suck fuel made things hairy.

Bobby patted his wife Judy on the back and said, "This gal here has hung around me 24 or 25 years, and I've taken a liking to her. We've had to work hard. We had a mortgaged pickup truck and a box of tools between us when we got married."

Bo Fields, who had given Bobby mechanical help and garage space when he had first come to the Birmingham area to race, accompanied his friend to Riverside. After Bobby won the championship, Fields

recalled the old days.

"There were times Bobby would go two nights in a row without sleeping," the ex-driver said. "He might wreck in Huntsville Thursday night, work on the car until Friday night when he'd race in Midfield, wreck there and work on the car until Saturday night when he'd race in Montgomery."

Fields knew the focused youngster would succeed.

"I liked him because he was the only person I ever saw with as much natural ability as Troy Ruttman," said Fields, who mechanicked a car Ruttman drove in the Indianapolis 500. "Troy Ruttman was the best race driver I had seen until then.

"I tried to contribute to polishing Bobby up mechanically, but there was nothing I could tell him about driving.

"He had to go somewhere in racing. He was too dedicated not to.

"Once he was on the Northern tour and he just drove as far as he could go. He got so sleepy he stopped on the side of the road. Wendell Scott came by and found him there, and Wendell's son drove Bobby's tow truck on in and let Bobby sleep. He wouldn't have made the race if they hadn't come along."

Fields may have helped polish more than Bobby's mechanical skills.

"He used to have a vile temper," Fields remembered. "If he had to make an unscheduled pit stop, invariably he'd tear up the clutch or the universal joint or something leaving the pits.

"I told him it was costing him too much money. He couldn't afford those tantrums."

The Winston Cup points scheme rewards consistency, and Bobby was consistent in 1983. Enroute to earning $883,009, he won six of the 30 races and finished in the top 10 on 25 occasions.

A key was the team's improved performance on short tracks. In 10 short track races, Bobby picked up 34 points on Waltrip, whereas the year before he had lost more than 200.

Neil Bonnett had a good season in 1983, too. He won Charlotte's World 600 and took the Atlanta Journal 500.

Bobby Allison and Bill Elliott had paced the Charlotte field most of the afternoon. Bobby was in front and Elliott was second with 58 laps

International Speedway Corp. photo

Talladega Superspeedway's Don Naman (R) congratulated Bobby Allison after he won the Winston Cup title in 1983.

to go when a tire blew on Sterling Marlin's car. Bobby's racer spun out, and Elliott's hit another one, opening the door for Bonnett to nip Richard Petty by less than a second and give his RahMoc team its first win.

It was a tough race, one that called for Bonnett to wring out everything that was in his car and himself.

"A couple of times I had to use the guard rail to make the second turn," he said. "Richard dictated that I drive that way. If I hadn't hit the wall I might have finished second. I was running 150 feet too far into that corner to make the turn any other way."

It was the second straight World 600 for Bonnett. "To win two of these things after 1,200 miles of racing is overwhelming to me," he admitted.

Bonnett passed Buddy Baker with three laps to go and won at Atlanta. Bobby Allison led more laps than anyone, but a blown tire relegated him to third.

The 1983 season was noteworthy in the history of Alabama racing for another reason. On April 30, Davey Allison scored his first super-speedway victory. It came in the ARCA 500, a 500-kilometer event at Talladega Superspeedway.

It was evident that Bobby Allison's son was a chip off the old engine block, for after winning at Talladega he headed for Birmingham to compete in a short-track event. "Every time I get in a race car I can learn something," he explained. "Besides, I'm racing for a living now."

Davey, 22, won the ARCA race in a Pontiac after late malfunctions benched his two chief foes, Ferrell Harris and Scott Stovall. Harris was leading on the 95th lap of the 117-lap race when his car developed an oil leak. Stovall had closed to within 100 yards of Davey, the leader, when his engine failed on the 112th lap. Davey finished a lap ahead of Marvin Smith.

"This was the biggest race I've won, probably the most important of my career," Davey reasoned.

Harris said he didn't know whether he would have won if the oil leak hadn't appeared, but he believed he had the fastest car.

"It was a good race, and I'm sure Davey is excited," Harris said. "He has every reason to be. I know I'd be jumping up and down pretty hard if we had won. If you win at Talladega in any kind of race you've accomplished a lot."

Davey was born in Florida, but he grew up in Hueytown. Bobby Allison and Judy Bjorkman were introduced at the home of her broth-er-in-law, Ralph Stark, who was, appropriately, a race car owner. They married on Feb. 20, 1960, and their first son entered the world on Feb. 25, 1961—which also was appropriate, for it was the day before the Daytona 500 and the day after his father had competed in his first Winston Cup race.

Bobby had driven Stark's car in a qualifying event on Friday the 24th, finishing 20th. (In those days the qualifying contests counted as official races). Soon after the finish he was told to rush home, for his wife was having a baby.

He jumped into his pickup truck and sped to the hospital in Hollywood, Fla., where Judy gave birth to a boy. Bobby stayed with them as long as possible and then rushed back to Daytona, where he

finished 31st in the 500 on Feb. 26.

Davey grew up in a racing atmosphere, of course. It was adventuresome to a youngster.

"Davey was always a competitor," remembered Red Farmer. "He and Clifford used to come into the shop on tricycles racing each other. We'd be there working on race cars, and we'd have to run them out....

"A few years later they'd come racing through there on bicycles."

It was a scene recalled in sadness, for in 1992 Clifford Allison would die in a racing practice crash at Michigan, and in 1993 Davey Allison would be fatally injured in a helicopter crash at Talladega Superspeedway.

Growing up, Davey swept and did other chores in his father's shop and was exposed to the nuts and bolts of racing. Eager to become a driver, he attended summer school and graduated from Hueytown High School in January of 1979, four months ahead of his class.

He and some pals built a Limited Sportsman racer, but he was a full-time employee of Bobby Allison Racing, and the focus was on fielding cars for Bobby. He wasn't allowed to work on his own car until the shop closed at 5 p.m.

He made his race driving debut on April 22, 1979, finishing fifth in the feature at Birmingham. His first victory came at the fairgrounds on May 5, the day before Bobby won Talladega's Winston 500.

Donnie Johnson, manager of Bobby Allison Racing, who is married to Bobby's sister Aggie, remembers his nephew as a precocious kid.

"He used to scare me to death," Johnson said at his office in Hueytown on a spring day in 1994. "At the pond out here, you went down to the old dam then up the hill. He had a trail bike, and he'd shoot down the hill and across the dam and up the other hill that was almost straight up. He was 11 or 12, and I didn't think he'd live long enough to become a race driver."

Johnson remembered when mechanic Grady Humphryes was driving a station wagon, and Davey, who was about 16, was riding in the back—or he was supposed to be riding in the back.

"Davey crawled out the back window and got on top of the station wagon," Johnson said. "He was just about to reach in the window on the driver's side and grab Grady. They probably would have crashed if

Young Davey Allison learned first hand that racing wasn't all glamor.

he had.

"But at that instant Bobby Allison came driving by and saw him. "Davey came back and told me, 'I'm in trouble.'

"About that time Bobby called, and I could hear Davey saying, `Yes, sir. Yes, sir. Yes, sir.'

"After they hung up Davey said, 'My daddy said I belonged in the car, not on top of it, and he'd handle it when he got home.'

"But Bobby forgot all about it before he got home."

Although some have said they always knew Davey would become a racer, Johnson isn't one of them.

"We talked about racing a lot when he was 9 or 10 years old, but I took it as boyish talk. But his senior year in high school, when his daddy told him he could build a race car after hours and race when he graduated, I saw him get in high gear.

"He worked hard to graduate early, and I guess I saw his seriousness his senior year. I knew then he would be good."

The time in the shop stood him in good stead.

"There are two breeds: race car drivers and people who drive race cars," Johnson said."Davey was a race car driver. He could come into the pits and tell the mechanics what to do to fix the car—not just come in and say fix it.

"Some just come in and say, 'It won't turn left. I'll be back after awhile.' Davey knew why it wouldn't turn left."

Obviously, having a live-in pro was a benefit. "Davey was born with talent," Johnson said, "but it had to be fine-tuned—and he had one of the best fine-tuners. Davey had opportunities because of who he was, but Bobby didn't give him anything. He made him work."

Davey made his experience count. "He could go to a race track he'd never seen and in four or five laps be within a half-second of the top qualifier," Johnson said.

"He'd look at a track and say, 'This is like Birmingham in this respect and like Nashville in this respect,' and he'd put it all together in his mind and be able to find the groove immediately.

"And he had his daddy's knack of running a 500-lap race and saying, 'On lap 246 so-and-so pulled up in front of me and slowed me,' and you could check it, and within a lap or two of that there'd be a slow lap

on the chart.

"One day in a race his daddy told the crew, 'The left rear is going flat,' and they checked it, and it had lost five pounds. It was going down, but it had lost just five pounds of pressure, and he knew it. Davey had the same ability."

Davey became a more reflective person after he was injured in a wild crash at Pocono in 1993, Johnson said.

"His desire didn't change after the accident, but he changed the way he looked at life. He set aside more time for his family and his religion.

"He saw that he wasn't invincible. He could get hurt. He rearranged his priorities. They didn't need a lot of rearranging. They needed adjusting more than rearranging."

Johnson recalled the day Davey was fatally injured in the helicopter crackup.

"Three hours before the crash he stuck his head in the door and said, 'Where's my dad?' I told him he was at the airport, and he said, 'I'm going to Talladega, and I thought he might want to go with me.' That was the last time I saw him alive, or at least when he knew me."

Johnson reflected, "I can't say that when I lost Davey I lost a son, because I don't know what that feels like, but I can say I lost one of my best friends."

Davey swept both Talladega ARCA events in 1983. He beat Red Farmer by 75 yards in the ARCA 200 in July.

Davey took the lead on the 34th lap of the 76-lap race and never surrendered it. In the closing laps he was able to draft Billie Harvey, who was a lap behind, and pull away.

"Thanks to Billie Harvey for coming up there and helping me get away from Red," said Davey. "If he hadn't it would have been awfully close."

Farmer was perched on the fender of his car as his crew pushed it toward the garage, past victory lane where his young neighbor was being crowned the race's champion.

"Way to go, Davey," he said, though he couldn't be heard above the din. "At least he kept it in the Alabama Gang."

Bobby Allison once said a chart of his racing career would look like the peaks and valleys of Arizona. That was evident as he followed up

his championship season by winning just two races in 1984, none in 1985, one in 1986 and one in 1987. A highlight of 1984, though, was his becoming the first race driver ever inducted into the Alabama Sports Hall of Fame. Red Farmer became the second, and only other, in 1990.

Neil Bonnett was winless in 1984. He won twice in 1985, once in 1986, and didn't find victory lane in 1987.

But there was a new Alabama Gangster on the horizon. David Carl Allison was coming fast, guns a'blazing.

10

A New Star Is Born

H ueytown will never be mistaken for Hollywood, but the 1988 Daytona 500 resembled something out of a movie script.

An in-person crowd of 135,000 and millions more in front of TV sets watched as 50-year-old Bobby Allison edged his 26-year-old son Davey to win stock car racing's premier event.

As if that weren't enough to brand the race as especially memorable, Richard Petty's car crashed spectacularly on the front stretch, standing on its nose and damaging the catch fence. Spectators wept openly as they feared the worst, and a TV announcer speculated that Petty finally would retire, but Richard wasn't seriously injured.

Davey came a long way in a short time to be in a position to challenge his dad in the Daytona 500.

The lad who started racing in 1979 was ARCA's Rookie of the Year in 1984, winning at Atlanta, Talladega and Macon, Ga. He and Buddy Baker were the only men who had taken three consecutive events at the world's fastest speedway. Could Davey break the tie in the second Talladega ARCA race of '84?

Nope. He won the pole, but Red Farmer won the race. "At least we kept it in Hueytown," Davey said.

Davey's popularity (he ran just a few NASCAR Dash series races in

1983, but he and Michael Waltrip were voted the division's co-Most Popular Drivers) did more for Saturday preliminary races at Talladega than anything else. Fans had been indifferent before, but they got into the habit of going when Davey was winning, and attendance increased dramatically.

In 1985 he won ARCA races at Talladega and Atlanta and Indianapolis Raceway Park. When the season ended he was ARCA's all-time leader on superspeedways with six victories.

His Winston Cup career began in 1985 as he finished 10th to Hoss Ellington's car in the Talladega 500. He had eight Winston Cup races under his safety belt when Ranier-Lundy, the team that later would be owned by Robert Yates, hired him as its driver for 1987.

International Speedway Corp. photo
Davey Allison drove a Ford to Rookie of the Year honors in 1987.

It was obvious immediately that the move was a wise one. Davey was the No. 2 qualifier, at better than 209 miles an hour, and he became the first rookie to start on the front row of the Daytona 500.

Rookies aren't supposed to win poles or races, but he won five poles and two races in 1987. No rookie had ever won two Winston Cup events, and he was an easy choice for Rookie of the Year.

Davey's first Winston Cup victory was achieved in the Winston 500 at Talladega on May 3 in just his 14th WC start. Two races later he won the Budweiser 500 at Dover.

His father figured prominently in both events.

On the 22nd lap at Talladega, Bobby's Stavola Brothers Buick became airborne after a tire blew. It wiped out 35 yards of the front stretch catch fence and fell back onto the racing surface.

"My heart sank," Davey said after the race. "That was the most scared I've ever been. I looked up in the mirror and saw Dad against the fence, and that probably was the lowest emotionally I've ever been.

"I came back by and saw him getting out of the car, and that lifted my heart back where it should be."

The race was red-flagged for two hours, 38 minutes and 14 seconds while the fence was repaired.

Davey dominated the 500. He would open a lead, a caution flag would close the field, then he would open a lead again. That became routine. He led 101 of the 178 laps and beat Terry Labonte by less than a second.

"To get my first Winston Cup win at Talladega is fantastic," Davey said. "I saw the fans standing in the grandstand, waving me on. I couldn't hear them cheering, but I knew they were cheering for us, and it gave me cold chills. I always wanted to win my first one here."

In 1986 Bobby Allison had won Talladega's Winston 500 at age 48, becoming the oldest man ever to take a Winston Cup event.

Now, through his 26-year-old son, youth was having its day at the same track.

At Dover, Bobby led 147 laps before his engine failed on lap 362. He and Davey had dueled, but his departure made it easier for his boy, who beat Bill Elliott by seven seconds.

"It was a thrill to run with my dad," Davey said. "I've learned a lot from him about this place. I've run some Sportsman races here, and I've listened to what he told me."

The 1988 season produced an incredible high and an even more incredible low for the Allison family.

Bobby and Davey ran 1-2 in the Daytona 500 on Feb.14, but on July 19 at Pocono, in the Miller High Life 500, a race named for his sponsor, Bobby was in the most serious crash of his career. Though he hasn't declared himself retired, he has driven only in an exhibition race since.

Bobby Allison had been following the siren song of unmuffled exhaust since he was a teen-ager, but he didn't have to ponder to name his biggest day in racing." You'd sure have to say this was it," he told the press after beating Davey by 2 1/2 car lengths at Daytona.

It was a dream come true for Davey—almost.

"I've dreamed about this for years," he said. "Since I was a kid I've dreamed about a down-to-the-wire battle with Dad.

"But in my dreams I won."

Phil Parsons finished third and Neil Bonnett was fourth, in the lead draft.

"If Neil had been third, they would have burned down Hueytown tonight," said Red Farmer, who was crew chief on the Grand National car Davey had driven to sixth place in the Goody's 300 the day before.

Davey faked to the outside and tried to pull to the inside coming out of the fourth turn of the last lap, but he didn't have the horsepower to seriously challenge his father.``My only hope was to get alongside and beat him by two inches because I don't think I could have ever gotten all the way around him," Davey said. "I couldn't do it."

Said Bobby: "I saw the nose of his car out of the corner of my eye, but I really thought I had enough suds to beat him."

Davey said he gave it all he had and wasn't content with being the runnerup. "I definitely don't settle for second place any time in this race, and I never felt I didn't have a chance to win it or my chances were slim."

It was the first 1-2 finish by a father and son in Winston Cup history since pappa Lee Petty beat Richard Petty on a short track in Pittsburgh in 1960. Lee beat Richard at Lakewood Speedway in Atlanta in 1959 in the only other one.

Daytona 500 finishes can get nasty, but neither Allison considered the possibility this time.

"I've seen over the years how fair he is," Davey said.

"I knew if I had the car to beat him, I'd beat him, and he wouldn't do anything out of the way."

Said Bobby: "I've always played it straight, and when I'm racing against the best youngster to come along I wouldn't do anything different."

International Speedway Corp. photo

Neil Bonnett sparked Hueytown surge in 1988.

After Bobby's car hit the catch fence at Talladega the year before, NASCAR mandated carburetor restrictors to slow the cars at Talladega and Daytona. That made passing difficult, but not as difficult as many drivers had predicted. There still were 26 lead changes among 12 competitors.

Bobby didn't play games. He went to the front and stayed there when circumstances permitted.

"It was important to get the lead so I didn't get hung up with somebody with a fairly good car who was willing to bend up sheet metal," he said. ``It was really good being in front today."

"And it was a great feeling looking back there and seeing somebody you really think is the best driver coming up and knowing it's your son. It's a special feeling, hard to put into words."

Bobby's car was indeed able to pass with relative ease as it carried him to his third Daytona 500 victory.

"It wasn't a no-passing situation," he said, "but it was difficult to pass. We worked the chassis out, and that's where our ability came from—also, your willingness to stick your neck out."

Reporters kidded Bobby about winning the biggest race at age 50.

"What it proves, maybe, is that I'm a late bloomer," he said.

"What it proves," Davey interrupted, "is that he's a winner."

Bonnett's fourth-place finish represented a nice comeback. He suffered a shattered leg in a crash at Charlotte in 1987, missed the final three races, and underwent grueling therapy.

"I'm tickled to death," said the Pontiac driver, who passed Terry Labonte near the finish. "The guys worked their rear ends off all winter. That made all the therapy work worthwhile.

"Coming down at the end, I couldn't plan anything. I had to wait for the car in front of me. When Terry moved outside, I went around him.

"My leg hurts like heck, but I couldn't care less."

In taking the Goody's 300 Grand National the day before, Bobby had tied Cale Yarborough as the winningest driver at Daytona International Speedway. His victory in the Daytona 500 was his 16th at the track, and it broke the tie.

"That makes me feel real good," he said. "I didn't win a major event here until way late in my career, and that makes it especially nice."

It was the biggest day in racing for Judy Allison, too. But Bobby's wife-Davey's mother had a favorite as they roared toward the checkered flag.

"I was pulling for Bobby," she said.

Why?

"I knew him first."

The blonde housewife smiled and added, "And he still pays the bills."

It was a nerve-wracking day for her, of course. "I was biting my nails without biting my nails," she said. "I was hoping nothing would happen. I've seen so much happen on that last lap."

What better Valentine's Day present than seeing your husband earn $202,940 and your son $113,760?

"It's got to be neat for both of them," Judy said. "You think about a finish like that happening some day, but when it does you don't believe it."

Fans of the Alabama Gang were beaming early in the 1988 season. Bonnett took the second race of the year, at Richmond, to end his 16-month winless drought. He overcame a two-lap deficit in the last 175 laps and beat Ricky Rudd by one second.

International Speedway Corp. photo

Davey Allison followed his dad's footsteps to many victory lanes.

The third event was in Australia. It wasn't an official Winston Cup event, but it had the blessings of NASCAR, and it was the first WC-type stock car race outside North America. Bonnett won it, and Bobby Allison finished second.

The fourth race was at Rockingham. Bonnett edged Lake Speed by less than a second to take the Goodwrench 500.

Four races, four winners from Hueytown. Who could have dreamed that Bobby Allison and Neil Bonnett had scored the final victories of their careers?

Another Hueytown high occurred at Talladega in April of 1988 when Red Farmer scored one of the biggest victories of his career by winning the ARCA 500k. Grant Adcox had taken four straight ARCA events at the world's biggest track, so he owned the longest winning string in the speedway's history.

Farmer was leading with Adcox on his bumper when another car hit the wall in the fourth turn on the 115th lap of the 117-lapper to bring out the caution flag. Farmer held off Adcox in the dash back to the finish line, and the race ended under yellow.

It was the 707th victory for Farmer, who drove a Chevrolet fielded by Davey Allison. "The car was just beautiful," Red said. "I couldn't have asked for more. Every time we'd make a pit stop Davey wanted to know if the car was working good. He'd ask, 'Do you want to change the handling? Do you want to change the wedge?' I said, 'Don't touch it. Just put in the gas and wipe the windshield and send me back out.' We didn't touch a jack bolt all day. We never even changed left-side tires."

But disaster was just up the high-banked road.

On June 19, 1988, the cars rolled off to start the Miller High Life 500 at the triangular, 2.5-mile Pocono International Raceway. Bobby Allison was making his 717th appearance in a Winston Cup race.

The green flag waved, but Bobby immediately realized something was wrong. "I think I've got a right rear tire going down," he told his crew over the radio. "Get one ready. I'm coming in."

But he didn't make it in. As he drove into the second turn his car broke loose and smacked the outside wall.

Bobby looked to the left and spotted a racer's worst nightmare—another car about to hit his in the driver's-side door. Jocko Maggiacomo's Chevrolet T-boned his Buick.

When the Motor Racing Network cut to a commercial, turn announcer Alan Bestwick confided in anchors Eli Gold and Barney Hall: "That was the hardest hit in a race car I've ever seen in my life. Allison is not moving. It looks pretty bad."

Davey Allison drove under the caution flag and over his radio asked Robert Yates, "Robert, what's going on? Is Dad involved?"

Yates answered: "Davey, it's your dad, and I've got to tell you it doesn't look good."

It wasn't good. Bobby had suffered a broken leg, broken shoulder, broken ribs and a cerebral concussion. Doctors drilled a hole in his skull to relieve pressure that could have caused death or permanent brain damage.

Bobby stayed in Lehigh Valley Medical Center in Allentown, Pa., until July 31 when he was transferred to Lakeshore Hospital, a rehabilitation facility, in Birmingham. His recovery would be a slow, ongoing process, requiring years.

On Sept. 27, 1988, in his first interview since the crash, he told *The Birmingham News* he believed he would race again but that he could live without it. He felt he would be in the 1989 Daytona 500.

That night he went out with Judy and friends to a restaurant and ate a steak, potato, salad and cheesecake. He told a reporter he had eaten in restaurants three times recently and had been to church twice. He said he hoped to be dismissed from Lakeshore soon.

He said he had lost 30 pounds but regained 12. "I don't recommend this as a way to lose weight, though," he joked.

Bobby discussed candidly the possibility of his driving again.

"I think I'd really love to do that. But I'll say to you right now it's not a requirement from where I stand. My vision has to heal all the way. My broken bones have to heal up properly.

"I'd love to get back in a car, but I don't think that's a total necessity for me to continue living a happy life."

One of the immortals of auto racing was asked if his career had been worth all this.

"I don't know why it had to happen," he answered. "I don't know why it had to happen the way it did. But my racing career has been worth it.

"I'll say this: if I had gotten killed right there, my racing career still would have been worth it."

He was dismissed from Lakeshore in October, and though he did not return to the driver's seat, he was fielding his own Winston Cup team in 1990.

Davey Allison won two races in 1988, at Michigan on Aug. 21 and at Richmond on Sept. 11.

He had trouble containing the tears when he went to Michigan's victory lane. "I dedicate this race to my father, my family, and all those loyal race fans who are the reason we keep racing every week," he said.

Davey earned $57,800 for winning at Richmond and set a record for the fewest races required to reach $1 million in Winston Cup earnings. He had done it in 52 starts.

But he got a boost that day that couldn't be gauged in money. Over the phone and the PA system, his father, back in Alabama, gave the ceremonial command for the gentlemen to start their engines.

"I was kinda prepared for it," Davey said, "so it didn't catch me off guard as bad as it might have, but it still sent cold chills down my spine."

There would be blank spots in Bobby Allison's memory over the years. Perhaps mercifully, he wouldn't remember the race in which he was so grievously injured. But, sadly, neither would he remember the 1988 Daytona 500.

11

The Gang Faces Trouble, and Expansion

nother tragedy struck the Alabama Gang in 1990. Neil Bonnett was involved in a 14-car crash in the TransSouth 500 at Darlington on April 1, and he suffered a head injury that produced temporary amnesia.

A month later, in his first interview since the wreck, he told *The Birmingham News* he would be sidelined for at least the rest of the season. He said he didn't know if he ever would race again, but that he had no retirement plans.

"I can do virtually anything I want to do, but I can't drive a race car."

For the most part his memory had returned, and he knew everyone he was supposed to know, he said, but he couldn't recall the crash in which he was injured.

The old trademark Bonnett humor surfaced. "Hey, it gives you a heck of an excuse when there's something you don't want to remember."

Now Davey Allison was the only active member of the Alabama Gang who had ever won a Winston Cup race. Though 1990 wouldn't be one of them, he had a couple of dream years ahead of him as driver for Robert Yates' team. Yates built the engines that Bobby Allison used when he won 10 races for Junior Johnson in 1972. He built the engines

that Bobby used while winning the Winston Cup title for DiGard in 1983. He built some of the engines Davey Allison used in winning ARCA races.

The driving Allisons and the mechanicking Yates obviously were a winning combination.

Yates acquired Harry Ranier's team in 1988. A teacher had once predicted Robert wouldn't amount to anything because he wanted to be a mechanic, but now he owned his own Winston Cup outfit.

Davey had been a sensation as Rookie of the Year in 1987, winning two races. But he also won only two races each of the next three years, and the team's great potential seemed to remain just that—potential.

"From 1988 through 1990, we just flattened out," Davey put it.

But then came the 1991 season, "the first one where we made significant improvement. It was the most incredible season I ever dreamed of."

In 1991 he won five races, plus The Winston, the sport's all-star event, earned $1,732,924, finished third in points standings, and led more races (23), more times (73) for more miles (1,879,129) than any other driver.

The first four events of 1991 indicated no such banner season. He finished 15th, 12th, 16th and 40th and was in 21st place in the standings. But when the season was over, simple arithmetic showed that if he could have erased those first four races he would have been the champ.

After those four events, Yates hired Larry McReynolds as crew chief. McReynolds was a Birmingham product who as a boy had watched the races at the fairgrounds. According to Davey, he became the straw that stirred the drink: "His personality and style fit our team perfectly."

Davey's charge began in Charlotte in May. He won The Winston and followed that success with victory in the Coca-Cola 600, leading 264 of the 400 laps.

He notched his first road course victory at Sears Point, and then he took the Miller 400 at Michigan, beating out Hut Stricklin, who was driving for Bobby Allison's team. Bobby watched with mixed emotions. "We're looking forward to the day when we can get our Buick in

front of that darned old Ford of Davey Allison," he said. "Really, this outcome today is a neat deal."

Harry Gant dominated Rockingham, but a long pit stop decked him and gave the victory to Davey. The next event, at Phoenix, was Davey's too. The team won two of 1991's last three and took momentum into the off-season.

The Alabama Gang, expanded version, made news at Michigan International Raceway in 1991 as Maylene's Dave Mader III and Chelsea's Stanley Smith swept the super speedway's two ARCA events.

Mader probably is the state's foremost victim of the Winston Cup numbers game. He is an excellent driver with 185 short track victories to his credit, a man once called "the best young driving prospect in America by Donnie Allison, but he has not been able to secure a regular ride on the top circuit. Five Winston Cup events is the most he ever has driven in a year. On a given Sunday there are 1,200 persons playing NFL football and 600 playing major league baseball—but just 40 playing Winston Cup.

Asked if not being able to land a WC ride eats at him, Mader, on an April day in 1994, replied, "In a way it has. I look at people like Davey Allison and Hut Stricklin that made it. They were kids in the grandstand when I started.

"For a lot of years it was very hard, but now that I've lived it being so hard... Yeah, it's been hard, but I don't feel the way I did six years ago. I'm not so bitter about it any more.

"Six years ago I was about to have ulcers and a heart attack because I wanted to do it so bad and just couldn't beat the numbers game. It's hard to get one of those 40 spots.'

Mader, 38, hasn't given up hope. He has even moved to Mooresville, N.C., to be near the hub of stock car racing where perhaps some team owner will give him a chance.

Meanwhile, he smiles at the memory of winning on the big track at Michigan in 1991 in Clint Folsom's car. "It was great," Mader said. "The car was so fast. We qualified like 21st, and I passed everybody and went to the front. It rained, and they called it a race. But we had the fastest car."

Alabama drivers all: (L-R, front) Davey Allison, Dave Mader III, Donnie Allison, Neil Bonnett; (L-R, back) Hut Stricklin, Bobby Allison, Red Farmer, Stanley Smith, Mickey Gibbs.

Davey Allison wouldn't make a prediction before the 1992 season, but he did say, ``I feel 1992 will be our best chance ever to win a Winston Cup championship.''

He didn't win the title, but it was another banner season. In 1992 he won five races, plus The Winston, earned $1,955,628, finished third in points, led more laps (1,362), more miles (2,315), more times (tied at 50) than any other driver and scored the most top-five finishes (17).

One of his 1992 victories came in the Daytona 500. The lad whose father had captured the Great American Race three times had now won it himself.

Davey reached the throne room by surging past a midpoint crash that banged up 14 cars, including those of a half-dozen leading contenders. He dominated the last half of the race, leading 98 of the final 102 laps and beating Morgan Shepherd by two car lengths.

He wouldn't cite that victory as the greatest thing that ever happened to him, though. He mentioned the 1988 Daytona 500 in which he

ran second to his father. "That day was such a special day," he said. "I don't think anything will ever replace it."

He reflected on being the son of Bobby Allison: "I never had a burden on my shoulders because of my dad's name. That's the greatest advantage a kid like me could ask for.

"I don't want to be as good as my father. I want to be as good as Davey Allison can be. Whether that's better than him or not as good, I don't think it matters as long as I do the best job I can."

He crashed at Bristol but, driving with injuries that included fractured ribs and torn shoulder muscles, he won at North Wilkesboro. A wreck at Martinsville reinjured the ribs, but he led 110 of 188 laps to win Talladega's Winston 500. He won The Winston at Charlotte but crashed at the finish, suffering a concussion and other injuries.

Davey was involved in a spectacular wreck at Pocono that left him with a broken arm, wrist and collarbone, but he started the car at Talladega the next Sunday before handing it over to Bobby Hillin.

On August 13, 1992, Davey's younger brother Clifford Allison was killed in a Grand National practice crash at Michigan International Speedway.

Just before he pulled onto the track, the 27-year-old Hueytown driver told his father Bobby, "We're gaining on them, Dad. We're getting there." But as he was zooming down the backstretch of the two-mile track, the car broke loose, and while he was fighting to regain control it hit the wall head on. Efforts to revive him failed, and he was pronounced dead in a nearby hospital. He left a wife, Elisa, and three children.

Clifford hadn't pursued racing with the intensity of his father and older brother, but he was beginning to be serious about the sport. Though he had raced for a number of years, he hadn't developed the ambition to be a top driver until the last two or three years or so of his life, said his uncle Donnie Johnson.

"I was beginning to get close to Clifford," Johnson said. "He had always agitated me because he was so carefree. He didn't seem to have a worry in the world. Maybe I was even a little jealous of someone who was so carefree about making a living.

"But Clifford grew up the last two or three years before his accident. He was going to make another race driver.

"When Clifford was starting to get serious about his racing, Davey stood beside my desk and said, 'Clifford Allison has more raw talent than I had at his age.' I thought that was quite a compliment."

Johnson remembers Clifford as a fun-loving boy who would rather drive around with a carload of girls than aid in the family racing effort. "It was more fun to get on a motorcycle at 14 without a license and try to get to Virginia Mines without getting caught than to sweep the floor of the shop.

"He was the world's best at taking things apart and the world's worst at putting them together. I remember he took his daddy's riding lawnmower apart, and it never got put back together.

"I thought he had killed himself here one day. he came around the shop on a go-cart, and there was a truck, and he hit it. 'I didn't know that truck was there,' he said. Of course, he hadn't bothered to look."
Bobby and Clifford had planned to take a Winston Cup car on that ill-fated trip to Michigan for Clifford to drive, Johnson said.

"They had worked on it, but Bobby said, 'Son, we need to leave that car at home. We don't need to go up there half ready. We're trying to upgrade your career.'

"Clifford said, 'OK, Dad.'

"I knew that day he had grown up. Used to, he would have argued about it or maybe taken it anyway."

The day after his brother was killed, Davey qualified third for Michigan's Champion Spark Plug 400. He finished fifth in the race.

Davey won at Phoenix and took a 30-point lead over Alan Kulwicki into the final race of the season, the Hooters 500 at Atlanta. He led Bill Elliott by 40.

Elliott won the race, and Kulwicki finished second. Davey was running sixth on lap 253 of the 328-lap event when Ernie Irvan's car spun and crashed into his. Davey returned after 45 laps of repairs, but the championship had escaped. Kulwicki finished with 4,078 points, Elliott with 4,068 and Davey with 4,015.

Davey didn't blame Irvan. "It looked like Ernie must have had a flat

tire or something," he said. "The car just got away from him."

Davey won the third race of the 1993 season, at Richmond, but it would be the last of his 19 Winston Cup victories.

On July 12, accompanied by Red Farmer, he flew his helicopter to Talladega Superspeedway, where David Bonnett, Neil's son, was testing his car. As the helicopter was landing, it suddenly shot into the air and then fell to earth. Davey died the next day without regaining consciousness. Farmer was injured but dismissed from the hospital on July 15. Davey left a wife, Liz, and two children.

Bobby Allison had been gravely injured in a racing crash in 1988, his son Clifford had been killed in a racing wreck in 1992, and now his son Davey was fatally injured in the crackup of a helicopter in 1993.

The news of Davey's death seemed unreal.

"God has really asked a lot of them," Robert Yates, owner of

Country Time photo

The prospect of driving again brought a smile to Neil Bonnett's face.

Davey's race team, said. "I guess sometimes life is not always fair, but it seems like with Bobby and Judy Allison it's just more than not fair."

But the Hueytown horrors were not over.

Neil Bonnett hadn't raced since his crash at Darlington in 1990. He had developed into a polished TV color commentator who had his own show, *Winners*. He had tested cars for his friend Dale Earnhardt, but he

wanted to drive again.

On the day of Davey Allison's fatal helicopter crash, Bonnett had held a press conference at Talladega Superspeedway to announce that he would race in the July 25 DieHard 500. He would be in a car fielded by Richard Childress, owner of Earnhardt's team.

"I know I told you I wouldn't drive again," Bonnett told a reporter before the press conference, "but when I said that I thought I couldn't. Now I think I can."

He said he had no plans to race beyond that one event. "Hopefully, I can have a good racing weekend and that will be it," Bonnett commented.

It wasn't a good racing weekend, and that wasn't it.

Bonnett's Chevrolet flipped spectacularly on the front stretch during the DieHard 500, but his injuries weren't serious and, characteristically, he was joking about the crash minutes later. Chelsea driver Stanley Smith was gravely injured, though, in a wreck that sent Jimmy Horton's racer over the first-turn wall and down a seven-story embankment. Bonnett's teammate, Earnhardt, won the 500.

Bonnett resumed his racing career in 1994. It was announced that he would drive in six events for Country Time Racing, including the Daytona 500.

"You can't just walk away from the sport you've spent your entire life around," Bonnett said. "Television was a good avenue for me to get involved in racing again. It opened the door to come back and be around all my friends. But it also stirred up that interest to get back inside of a race car."

Though he had crashed, the race at Talladega had fueled his desire to compete again. Explained Bonnett: "I got out of the car and said to myself, 'Hey, I can drive one of these things again.' It may have looked negative to a lot of people, but I had a real positive attitude when everything was over."

But on Feb. 11, during a practice run, Bonnett lost control, and his car hit the wall at Daytona International Speedway. The 47-year-old driver died from massive head injuries.

He left a wife, Susan, and two grown children.

Butch Nelson, Bonnett's best friend and president of Neil Bonnett

Honda, reflected on his ill-fated return to racing.

"He couldn't sit still. He would get antsy at a red light.

"He came in one day and shut the door and said, 'What do you think about me racing again?'"

I said, 'You don't need to.'

"He said, 'It's my life.'

"I asked him if he was going to continue to test Earnhardt's cars, and he said yes.

"I said, 'You might as well race as do that. What kind of money are you talking about?'

"He said, 'We haven't talked about that. What they don't know is that I'd do it for free.'

Nelson said he feared Bonnett might be injured, but he wasn't afraid he might be killed because it just didn't happen to the top men. Indeed, among the top 50 winners in Winston Cup, Bonnett became only the third to be killed racing or practicing. The others were Fireball Roberts and Joe Weatherly.

Neil's son David, 29, decided to continue with his racing career. He was scheduled to compete on the Grand National circuit in 1994.

"I thought about it long and hard," he said. "But I have put too much into it to just quit. I've been racing six years now."

The winner of 25 short track races in 1991, David reflected, "When you crawl in that window you know it can happen, but it always happens to somebody else."

Did he want his father to return to racing? "Truthfully, no," David answered. "But that was his life. He enjoyed the TV stuff, but he wasn't happy."

The 1994 season began with one member of the original Alabama Gang still racing. Red Farmer, who makes a joke of never revealing his age, continued to drive on the dirt tracks.

A lot had happened since 1949 when, as a 16-year-old, he had flipped a borrowed car at Opa Locka Speedway to begin a love affair with racing and a career that would touch six decades. He had witnessed more of triumph and tragedy than most men ever would.

The Alabama Gang Grows

12

Steve Grissom

It was supposed to be fun. Neil Bonnett, race driver turned TV commentator turned race driver, was interviewing Steve Grissom as the subject of an episode of his show, *Winners*.

Grissom was flattered. After all, when he was a boy in Gadsden, Ala., Bonnett was one of his heroes.

"When I was 4 or 5 or 6 years old, almost every Friday afternoon we'd get out of school and leave at 4 or 4:40 in the afternoon for the fairgrounds in Birmingham," Grissom remembered.

"The interstate wasn't complete, and I guess it was a two-hour drive, fighting the Friday afternoon traffic in downtown Birmingham. But we always went to the races."

Now one of those stars he had admired at the old speedway wanted to interview him for a television program. But why not? In 1985 Grissom had been the All-Pro national champion, and in 1993 he had been NASCAR's Grand National champ. Now they were in Daytona for the opening of the 1994 season, and Grissom was tackling the Winston Cup series, and Bonnett was beginning a comeback after being injured in 1990.

"It was Thursday, and Neil and I went over to a golf course in Daytona to do some taping," Grissom remembered a month later. "We spent all morning together. We raced golf carts, and we putted some–and

we talked.

"Then we went back to the race track, and our cars happened to be parked side by side in the garage area."

The early part of Friday morning, Feb. 11, was devoted to getting the race cars through inspection. Bonnett told Grissom they needed to do some more camera work that day, but he realized everyone was busy, and if it wasn't convenient they'd shoot later. They left it at that, and they drove onto the track to practice.

Grissom returned to the garage, and when he looked out onto the racing surface of Daytona International Speedway he saw no cars. He asked what caused the caution flag.

"A wreck," someone said.

"Who?" Grissom asked.

"Neil," came the answer.

"It's bad," someone else said.

It was the worst. Bonnett's car had hit the concrete retaining wall, and the crash cost him his life.

Grissom reflected on Bonnett's ill-fated comeback and on this dangerous sport for which they shared a passion.

"People said they didn't know why he got back into a car, because he didn't have anything to prove. But when we were talking off camera, Neil told me, 'It's something I've got to do. It's something I want to do.' Neil died doing something that made him happy, and that's something a lot of people don't do."

Grissom understands the attraction. "Pretty much the first race I went to, I knew racing was what I wanted to do."

He was a star football lineman at Gaston High, and he got plenty of letters from college recruiters, letting him know they were interested in him. "I never gave them a second thought," he said. "Half of them I never opened. I knew racing was what I was going to do. I knew my heart wouldn't be in football. The ones I talked to on the phone, I told them to give a scholarship to somebody who would want it."

He wasn't hesitant to get back into his race car after the accident that killed a man he had been chatting with minutes before.

"You have to blot it out of your mind," Grissom said. "I've had wrecks that tore up my car, and you're sore, but when you get back into

the car you don't think about it."

Now Grissom and Hut Stricklin are left to carry the banner of the Alabama Gang in Winston Cup racing. Grissom is driving a Chevrolet for Diamond Ridge Motorsports.

"I had three other offers," he said, "but I wanted to go with Diamond Ridge. This is a new team, but it is committed, and it's the best for Steve Grissom. Their goals and mine are the same."

Gary and Carolyn Bechtel own the team.

Diamond Ridge photo

Steve Grissom hopes for stardom.

"They realize it's not going to be easy, that it's not going to happen overnight," Grissom said.

Though just 30, Grissom has accomplished much. The home folks recognize it, too, for March 9, 1994, was Steve Grissom Day in Etowah County.

Gov. Jim Folsom Jr. hailed him as "a local hero and fast-rising star in the motorsports world." There's a "special place in Alabama for football players and stock car drivers. Alabamians love football and motorsports."

"It's pretty neat to have a day for you," Grissom said at a luncheon in his honor. "It kinda blows you away."

Grissom started racing when he was 15. His debut on dirt at Talladega Short Track was unremarkable. "I got lapped in the heat race," he said, "and the feature wasn't anything to write home about either."

Among the spectators that night was Susan Frazier, who not only was his high school sweetheart but his grade school sweetheart. "All of

our dates were at race tracks," explained Mrs. Steve Grissom. "I was 16, a year older than him."

"She drove on our dates before I could drive on our dates," chimed in her husband.

Racing even figured into naming their little boy. He is Kyle—because they liked Kyle Petty's name.

The Grissoms are a racing family.

Wayne Grissom, Steve's father, sells Oldsmobiles, Mazdas and Hondas in Gadsden. He has owned most of the race cars Steve has driven. "I loved racing growing up," the ex-farmboy said, "but I couldn't afford to buy a ticket."

But in later years he purchased half interest in a $1,300 street stocker, and he was hooked as a car owner.

Steve's older brother Phillip was the first Grissom boy to drive for Pop. Another son, Bobby, enjoyed working on the cars. Phillip enjoyed some success, finishing third in NASCAR's All-American Challenge series national standings in 1979, but he eventually stopped driving.

"Trying to run two cars was taxing on everybody," Phillip, 34, explained. "Steve didn't have that much interest in the car business, so

Diamond Ridge photo

Diamond Ridge is a young racing team.

Bobby and I focused on the car business, and he raced.

"I pulled out some old newspaper articles the other day. My kids have a hard time believing I raced against Bobby Allison and Donnie Allison and Davey Allison and Neil Bonnett."

Does he miss racing? "When I go to the race car shop or to races I think about what might have been," Phillip said, "but then I go back to selling cars and to reality."

Watching sons race is "a thrill," Wayne Grissom said. "It's full of fear and full of excitement both. My wife Mary Sue and I trust the boys' driving, but some races you're keyed up with butterflies, and some you're not.

"It was totally their idea to race. I never really wanted them to race, but since they've gotten into it I would encourage my grandsons to race. If I live, I'm going to try to get those boys to give those grandsons an opportunity. I hope you'll be writing about Grissoms for years to come."

Mary Sue Grissom teaches home economics at Gaston High School. There were times she left in a car after school, arriving at a race location at 2 a.m.

"It's not the profession I would have chosen for them," she said of racing, "but it's an honorable profession, and I've always supported them in it."

Steve scored his first superspeedway victory in 1990, winning a Grand National at Rockingham, and that's the event that sticks out above all others in his father's mind.

"Winning Rockingham, beating Dale Earnhardt and Mark Martin," Wayne answered the question. "When Steve passed him with two laps to go, it made Mark so mad he couldn't see. Steve could drive right under them that day."

Steve raced on dirt at Talladega Short Track and in Rome, Ga., his first season, but in 1980 he switched to asphalt and ran at Birmingham, Nashville and Montgomery.

He drove in four All Pro races in 1980, and then tackled that demanding circuit with all guns blazing in 1981. But it wasn't until 1985 that he scored his first feature victory of any kind, at Sayre, Ala. He won at St. Petersburg, Fla., too, enroute to the national champi-

onship. That was his break-out season.

Steve advanced to Busch Grand National in 1988, and his first victory on the second most important circuit in stock car racing came in 1990. In fact, he won his first two events and his last two events that year, at Pulaski, Va., Indianapolis Raceway Park, Rockingham and Martinsville.

In 1993, victories at Hickory, N.C., and Rockingham helped him to the Grand National championship.

"I didn't think that much about winning the championship at first," Steve reflected. "It wasn't what we started out to do. We started out to win races. But around the first of May we had the lead, and we never fell back farther than second."

Butch Lindley, a driver who would be fatally injured in a crash during an All Pro race, had a big effect on his career, Steve said.

"He helped me in 1984 and 1985. He more or less took me under his wing. At Huntsville in 1985 he won and we finished second. It was the race before he got hurt.

"Probably the most important thing he told me was to always be able to change with the times. It didn't make sense at first, but going from All Pro to Busch was a big change, going from bias tires to radials was a big change, going from Busch to Winston Cup was a big change. I think about it all the time."

At 6-foot-3 and 220 pounds, Steve looks the part of a former football star. He is one of the bigger Winston Cup drivers. Is his weight a handicap?

"Well, it's not an advantage," said his father. "Some of those guys, like Mark Martin and Jeff Gordon, look pretty small. A hundred pounds in a restrictor plate race is a lot to give up. But a plus is that Steve has the stamina to handle a tough race."

Although Steve is currently living in Trinity, N.C., for racing purposes, he said Gadsden and Alabama "will always be home," and now he is one of the front-line lance bearers for the Alabama Gang.

"That's an honor," Steve said, "but there's also some awfully big shoes to try to fill. You take Bobby Allison's wins and Donnie Allison's wins and Davey Allison's wins and Neil Bonnett's wins, and that's a lot of wins."

13

Hut Stricklin

"I always wanted to be the leader of the Alabama Gang," Hut Stricklin said. "But never this way." Injury and death decimated the Gang, and Waymond Stricklin Jr. and Steve Grissom have emerged as the only two Alabamians driving regularly on the Winston Cup circuit.

"I hope and pray we can get our program turned around and Steve and I can get things going to where we'll make everybody proud for Alabama, like Davey and Bobby and Donnie and Neil and those guys did," Stricklin said.

As Stricklin entered the 1994 season, his six-year record showed 141 Winston Cup starts without a victory. He had just five top-five finishes.

The pattern of his career is not unfamiliar. Drivers reach the Winston Cup circuit by winning regularly on the short tracks, but then they find themselves in a league in which only the few have keys to victory lane.

In 45 seasons of Winston Cup racing, just 142 drivers have won—and only 86 of them won more than once.

"It's tough to take," Stricklin said. "When you're used to winning, and all of a sudden you get to the place where you don't win—or I haven't won yet—that's hard." His prescription for that ailment? "I

McDonald's Racing photo

Stricklin's ride with Junior Johnson produced no victories.

occasionally go run other types of racing—go back to my roots, I guess you'd say—and win races, and it kinda renews your confidence.

"I felt that was one thing that always helped Bobby Allison. When he was having some tough times in Winston Cup, he'd go run short track races over the country and win some of those races. It helps keep your confidence level up."

There hasn't been a new winner on the Winston Cup circuit since 1991. "The driver has to do his part all day, the engine builder has to do his part, the crew has to do its part on stops, everybody has to do his part for a win to come together," Stricklin said. "You almost have to have a perfect day. In this game, so many of the teams already are close to perfect, and you're trying to outrun them."

Stricklin is driving Fords for a new team owned by veteran mechanic Travis Carter, R.J. Reynolds' Camel brand is the sponsor.

"I think this is probably the best situation I've been in," the 33-year-old Calera driver said. "If not the best, one of the best. We're starting off kinda on the bottom, but I see this as the type team that can build our way to the top. It's something we can build into something good."

Like so many other drivers, Stricklin is a second-generation racer. Waymond Stricklin Sr. ran the Alabama short tracks, with his admiring son as his No. 1 fan.

"I'd clean his windshield, sweep up, do anything that needed

doing," Hut said. "When I was 10 or 11, I started going with him to the races, sneaking in the pits. You had to be 16 to get in the pits, so I'd lie down in the floorboard."

He was 5 or 6 years old the first time he saw a race, at old Dixie Speedway in Midfield. He decided then he wanted to be a driver. "I thought it must be the biggest thrill anybody could ever have," he said. "Other than working in a junk yard, pulling parts, driving a race car is the only thing I ever did. I was fortunate to be able to do something I love doing."

Stricklin is related to a second racing family. In 1986 he married Pam Allison, daughter of former driver Donnie Allison, first cousin of the late Davey Allison, niece of sidelined driver Bobby Allison.

At first, Pam wasn't one of his fans.

"He beat Davey all the time, and I was pulling for Davey," she explained.

"After graduation, all the seniors went to Panama City. A girlfriend and I ran into Davey, and Hut was with him. I wondered why he was with Davey.

"Davey told Hut I didn't like him. Hut said, well, he didn't like me either."

But Stricklin called her—she thinks it may have been on his 19th birthday—and they talked, and in a couple of weeks they went to the movies. "I think from that time on neither one of us saw anybody else," she said.

They were wed on Nov. 7, 1986. "I got married on 11/7 because I'm a gambler," Stricklin said. They have two children.

Though her father was nearly killed in a racing crash in 1981, Pam had no qualms about marrying a stock car driver.

"I don't guess I ever thought about it," she said.

When her husband is involved in a wreck? "I try to stay as calm as I can until I know the facts," Pam answered. "I've seen people jump up and down and cry, but nine times out of ten it's not as bad as it looks. I try to get the facts before I get upset. Sometimes I get nervous after it's over."

She was a teen-ager when her father was injured at Charlotte. Her mother Pat didn't let her and her brothers know how critical the situa-

tion was.

"She didn't tell us how very serious it was until it was all over, until he was in the clear and back on the road to recovery and we knew he was going to make it," Pam said. "I'm thankful. For awhile it was just touch and go.

"When it happened I was sitting on the floor at Hut's house, watching the race on television. I said, 'Take me home. My daddy's dead.'"

Hut Stricklin and Davey Allison, kid race drivers, not only were fast friends, they were each other's best competition on Alabama short tracks.

"It got to where I'd win at Birmingham, and Davey would win at Montgomery," Stricklin recalled, "and then Davey would win at Birmingham, and I'd win at Montgomery. It got to be an ongoing thing.

"I started racing a year before Davey did," he continued, recalling the Limited Sportsman days at Birmingham International Raceway. "And for the first year we raced together it seemed like every time he'd get the lead I'd be running behind him, and he'd blow up one of those motors that he was building out of a junkyard."

They grew to be friends because they had cars that were alike, that featured a type of suspension system developed by Davey's father Bobby Allison. "We were the only ones who had those cars," Stricklin said. "Nobody else could make them work.

"I said I started racing a year before he did. Well, Davey would watch me in that type car and tell me things about it. The next year he wished he hadn't helped me like he did."

Stricklin realizes that if he hadn't been taken ill, he could have been in Davey's helicopter that crashed on Monday, July 12, 1993.

They had raced on Sunday in Loudon, N.H., and Stricklin was invited to fly back home with Davey on Davey's plane.

But Stricklin suffered from a stomach virus before and during the race, and when it was over he went to a hospital near the race track. He flew home via commercial airliner Monday morning.

"If I hadn't been sick I probably would have flown back with him," Stricklin reflected, "and he probably would have said, 'I'm going to fly over to Talladega in my helicopter, do you want to go?' And I probably would have gone."

Davey's death affected Stricklin profoundly.

"It was so hard to stay focused on everything I had to stay focused on, losing somebody like that who was so close to me," Stricklin said.

"Every Saturday evening after the last practice, he and I would compare notes on our cars. He'd tell me what his was doing, and I would tell him what mine was doing, and he'd tell me something he had done, and I would tell him something I had done.

"We were honest with one another, and that meant a lot.

McDonald's Racing photo

Hut Stricklin working hard to win again.

He was always somebody I could go to.

"I give him more credit than anybody for helping me get into Winston Cup. He always told me if he made it to Winston Cup he'd do all he could do to get me in, too.

"He got there, and he held true to what he had said, and I was always grateful for that. When car owners like Rod Osterlund would talk to him he'd say, 'Here's the driver you need to get. This guy beat me at Birmingham.' He'd throw my name into the hat."

He doesn't pattern his driving after Davey's or Donnie's or Bobby's, though. "If I had to pattern after anybody, I always liked Red Farmer's style," Stricklin said. "He could get a lot out of a car. He was always driving a car as hard at the end of the race as at the start. He always had a knack for staying out of trouble."

His father, Waymond Sr., was a junkyard owner who raced mostly for fun. He didn't encourage or discourage his son from driving. He gave Hut the hulk of a 1964 Chevelle and said he could restore it to life if he was willing to work.

"It needed a bunch of work," Hut remembered. "I told him I wanted to drive, and he left it up to me to show I had the determination. I was helping him on his car, and it was a matter of how much I could work on mine. But it got done."

He started racing in 1977, winning the first two Limited Sportsman races in which he competed, at Sayre Speedway near Birmingham. The next year he won the state Limited Sportsman title and 15 features.

Grand American, All Pro and All-American Challenge racing were his fare before he won the national championship in NASCAR's Daytona Dash series in 1986.

He drove in three Winston Cup races in 1987, and in 1989 he became a regular, driving for Rod Osterlund. He raced for Bobby Allison's team in 1990, 1991 and 1992 before realizing the dream of every driver and moving to Junior Johnson's organization in 1993.

He ran fourth in the Daytona 500, but the bright promise just fizzled, and after that his best finish was 10th.

Stricklin won't get into specifics about the failure of that team, but it was a tremendous disappointment. "All I can say is it just didn't work. I felt like it would, and it just didn't."

Bill Elliott drove Johnson's other racer, and he wasn't competitive, either. It was the first time since 1966 that a Johnson car failed to win a Winston Cup race.

14

Jimmy Means

Tortoise and hare races make great fables, but in the real world of Winston Cup competition it's speed that wins and money that buys speed.

Jimmy Means never had the money to buy the speed, so as he entered the 1994 season he had driven in 455 Winston Cup races without a victory. Or a second. Or a third. Or a fourth. Or a fifth. Or a sixth.

Yet, he remains a popular figure in Alabama racing. B.J. Parker recalls Means being more in demand than the celebrated Rusty Wallace to sign autographs at his Southern All-Star races at Talladega Short Track.

The Huntsville product was a bullring star, holding his own against Bobby Allison, Donnie Allison, Red Farmer, Neil Bonnett and the other top dogs, but when he went to the big league in 1976 the winning stopped. He never acquired the big-bucks sponsor who could buy the golden key to victory lane.

Means used to say it hurt, having been a winner and then knowing he didn't have a chance to win, but eventually that ceased to irritate him. "I'm resigned to the fact I had to do what I had to do to make a living," he said. "My ego is not that big. People would ask, 'Why do you keep doing it?' For the same reason you're writing—it's what I do

Young Jimmy Means starred in Sportsman racing

for a living."

He added: "I have no regrets. I'm just sorry I couldn't run to be more competitive. I knew I could have run if we had had the equipment and tires to run."

Means fielded his own cars, learned all the cost-cutting tricks and became the definitive independent.

"We couldn't buy a set of new tires," he said. "I ran a motor longer

than others did. We didn't have the personnel. I had one guy working with me.

"The big teams would run 10 or 15 laps of practice, and I'd buy their tires. The cost of a set of scuffs might be anywhere from them just giving them to me or me paying $50 to $100. A set would have been $500 if I had bought them new. Now a set of new tires costs $1,240. I did what I had to do.

"People would say, 'Why don't you gamble and put on new tires?' But I couldn't gamble on a $5,000 tire bill."

On race day the car is serviced by a volunteer, unpaid crew. "I've got a loyal group from different parts of the country who come to the race on weekends," Means said. "One guy comes all the way from Dover, Del., every race. Some just come to the Northern races; some just to the Southern races."

The day of the shoestring operation in Winston Cup is drawing to a close. Jimmy Means and those like him are facing the prospect of being shut out. There are so many well-funded teams now that even high-dollar cars routinely are failing to qualify for races.

"When I started Winston Cup there were 25 guys like me," he said. "Now there's not. There are no more little guys to outrun."

Means, 43, admits he is weary of the uphill fight. His driving days may be over. In the early races of 1994 he was putting other drivers in his cars, "using first this one and then that one."

His team itself appears headed for the history book of racing "unless we can find some talented driver with a sponsorship. If I continue on, I'll lose everything I've got. I'm just going at it one race at a time."

He could make a living, perhaps in "something to do with racing engines," or a similar endeavor, Means said. "I see there are other things out there. This is not the whole world. In the past I thought it was."

He rented two cars to a driver before the last race of 1993, at Phoenix, and the fellow wrecked both of them. Then, as he was preparing his cars for the 1994 opener at Daytona, it hit him that he didn't want to go. "I'm burned out," he realized.

But he did go, and there was a hassle in getting the cars through

inspection. Then he saw Neil Bonnett's fatal crash. "Man, why was he doing this?" Means asked himself. "He didn't have to do this."

Still, he planned to drive. But then Rodney Orr was killed in practice. And instead of being a driver-car owner, Means became simply a car owner. It wasn't that he suddenly was overcome with fear. (``I never go out in a race car expecting to get killed.")

It's just that he took a long look at his situation. It's one thing to be a high-salaried star driving a car that has a chance to win, he reasoned. It's something else to be a fellow who is just out there making a living.

Jimmy Means believes his interest in racing stemmed from seeing a Huntsville Speedway program at a house on his newspaper route when he was a carrier boy of 13 or 14.

"I looked at that program, and then I wanted to go see the race cars. When I saw them, I wanted to be around them. When I was around them, I wanted to work on them. When I worked on them, I wanted to drive them."

He took a class in mechanics in school. Eventually he helped a Huntsville driver named Tommy Andrews, and that earned him trips to Baton Rouge, La., and Jefferson, Ga., and even Daytona, and he was having a ball.

He paid $225 for a chassis, and then he bought an engine for $325 at a wrecking yard, and he and Andrews souped it up.

"I worked at a machine shop 16 hours a day to get the money for that motor," Means remembered.

He put the engine on the chassis, and he begged cut tires from racing teams and sewed them up with wire and put boots in them and in 1970 became a driver in the entry-level Cadet Division at the quarter-mile Huntsville Speedway.

He won a race that was rained out at halfway. "I remember it well, because I didn't have a windshield," Means said. Then he won the last four of the season.

The next year he borrowed a truck and a trailer, and a fellow let him have two tires off a dune buggy, and he and pals Bill Gray and J.D. Smith hauled the Cadet car to the fairgrounds in Birmingham. They stood at the back gate of the 5/8ths-mile speedway and watched the

Sportsman racers zoom by in practice and said, "We're in the wrong place."

But they weren't in the wrong place. They won one of the two features—without brakes. "The brakes went away," Means remembered, "but I said, 'I'm not going to park this thing.'" And he didn't.

The status of the dune buggy tires changed with his unexpected success. "The fellow was going to give them to us," Means remembered, "but after we won the race he charged us $50."

Means won the state Cadet championship and scored some victories at Birmingham and Huntsville that year and figured it was time to graduate.

"Ever since I've raced, the race car has paid for itself," he said. "It paid its way or I couldn't have done it. I made money the first year in Cadet, and I made money the second year in Cadet. I sold the car and built a Sportsman car."

It was a strong racer from the start, and Means was a worthy new entry in the Sportsman mix.

"I remember the first Sportsman race we won at Birmingham," he said. "I spun out Red Farmer to win it. It was like a Fourth of July weekend, and we were going from Birmingham to Montgomery to Opp to race. Being young, we thought there was nothing else in the world but racing, and I thought the whole town of Birmingham knew I spun out Red Farmer. So we were scared to spend the night in Birmingham. We went on to Montgomery."

Means idolizes Farmer. "I didn't mean to spin him out," he said. "I went over and said, 'Red, I didn't mean to do it.' He said, 'I know you didn't.'

"As far as I'm concerned, Red Farmer is it. He's the best sportsman I've ever seen. I love that old man. As far as I know, he never touched me on a race track."

Means quickly established himself as a star on the Alabama circuit. "I don't know how many races I won. All the trophies and things are in the attic of my house in Huntsville. Every time we'd go to the track we had a shot to win, and that's what we were shooting for." He was the state Sportsman champ in 1973.

Birmingham occasionally hosted triple features, and he always

wanted to win all three, but he never did. "One night I won the first one and had a straightaway lead in the second when another car blew its motor and was sitting in the first turn. Instead of the caution flag, the flagman gave the car I was lapping the move-over flag. There was no caution flag and no caution light, and I hit the one that had stopped on the track. It totaled my car. I think I had a good chance at winning all three that night."

Means recalls those days fondly. "I think at the time that was the best Sportsman racing in the country," he said. "I know we always beat those guys who came down from the Carolinas."

Incidents that are funny now weren't funny then.

Once he hauled his Sportsman car to Daytona and failed to make the field. He started home, and he was on the interstate near Lake City, Fla., when the motor of his pickup blew.

A fellow in a passenger car came by and said he would give him a lift to the next exit, and Means hooked his trailer to the man's car.

"We heard something, and we looked back, and the race car had come off the trailer," Means remembered. "We had forgot to tie it down.

"That race car went across the two lanes on our side and across the median and across the two lanes on the other side. It was just lucky nobody was coming. It never even bent the race car."

Means remembers a particularly hairy moment in his Sportsman days.

"We had a brand new car, and they were going to run a race at Huntsville on Sunday. Me and Bill Gray and my wife Marsha—we weren't married then—went out on Saturday night to practice.

"I borrowed the keys to the track and turned the lights on and started driving. The throttle hung, and the car went out of the race track. It tore down the billboards, and everything was pitch black, and I said, 'Well, I guess this is it.'"

It was 11 o'clock at night, and the car was upside down outside the speedway. But the only lick I got was when I undid the seat belt and fell on my head and jammed my neck.

"I got another car and came out the next day and won the race. The fans sat there and looked at that tore-down fence and my other car out

there upside down. Every time I came by I saw that gap in the fence. "Those were the good old days. We had fun back then."

But the circumstances of short tracking changed. There was a technology explosion, and suddenly the cost of Sportsman racing was soaring. It became unprofitable, and Means moved into Winston Cup, where he thought he could make a living.

NASCAR records show that entering the 1994 season he had earned $1,937,240 in Winston Cup racing. That sounds like a lot until you

International Speedway Corp. photo
Jimmy Means, the Winston Cup veteran.

consider it came over a period of 18 years and he was fielding his own team.

It has been a long, hard road for the man who was owner-driver-crew chief-everything. Making a living as an independent was tough enough when everything went right—and it didn't always go right.

Once he was making the 17-hour trip from Pocono, Pa., to Huntsville, and he was near Knoxville, Tenn., when the motor in his transporter blew.

He took the motor out of his race car and put it into the truck. But it was set for up for racing, and it would pull the big rig only 35 miles an hour. That's how they puttered in to Huntsville. "But a wrecker bill would have been $200," the cost-conscious Means said.

He relocated to Forest City, N.C., in 1982, but he still has a house in Huntsville.

"That was the best move I ever made," Means said. "Most of the races we were traveling to were eight or 10 hours away. We'd get back

at 6 or 7 on Monday morning after racing on Sunday and driving all night, and then we'd have to leave again on Wednesday or Thursday. I was out of the hub of racing, and it was killing me. "If I had done it the first few years I would have been a lot better off." His best finish in a Winston Cup race came, appropriately, before the home folks. He ran seventh in the 1983 Winston 500 at Talladega, finishing in the same lap with winner Richard Petty. "Luck was with us that day," he recalled. "Every time they'd get within 100 yards of me to lap me the caution would come out. "I didn't even qualify for the race. I had to use a provisional, and I started 41st. Considering that, I thought it was an accomplishment."

15

John Ray

Wrote the poet: *Of all sad words of tongue or pen, the saddest are these: it might have been.*

John Ray will never know whether he would have been a successful Winston Cup driver, for on Feb. 15, 1976, in the Daytona 500, a crash ended his career and nearly claimed his life. He was left with thoughts of what might have been.

Yet, few persons have had as varied a sojourn through racing as has Ray. He has been a motorcycle racer, a sprint car racer, a stock car racer, a builder of Indianapolis cars, a stand-in for movie actor Paul Newman, a Winston Cup team owner and a world-record speedster in, of all things, an 18-wheel truck.

"I think I could have been a good, consistent driver," the Eastaboga resident said. "But I've never been bitter about it. That's just part of racing. Those things happen.

"I guess our Maker has reasons for things happening. It's probably turned out for the best for me as a husband and a father."

Ray competed on the Winston Cup circuit in 1974 and 1975, and in 1976 the plan was for him to drive his own Chevrolet on the superspeedways and Bill Champion's Ford on the short tracks. Ray hadn't compiled enough starts to affect his eligibility for Rookie of the Year. They thought they had a good chance for rookie honors, and they were

Photo courtesy of the Ray family

John Ray, son Johnny (now 21) and John's first Winston Cup ride.

anticipating a rewarding season.

But the dream ended in a wreck that broke 52 bones in Ray's body. It broke his neck in three places, fractured his skull and tore his heart and kidneys loose. "I was in the ambulance with him on the way to the hospital," recalled his wife Kay, "and he quit breathing three times."

"I don't even remember being in the race," Ray said. "I've seen films, but none of it ever comes back. I can remember before the race started, but I don't remember anything about the race.

"What I have been told was that Ramo Stott blew an engine, and I got in his oil and spun and hit the wall and stopped between the first and second turns. Skip Manning lost it in the oil and T-boned me."

While John Ray was fighting for his life, the most famous Daytona 500 of all was unfolding. It was the one in which David Pearson and Richard Petty crashed on the front stretch on the last lap, and Pearson coaxed his battered car across the finish line to win while Petty's sat stalled in the infield, 300 yards from the stripe.

Ray lost more than his memory of the race. "I came to a month later," he said. "I was in the hospital at Daytona for three months and then in the hospital in Birmingham for three weeks.

"But I don't really have any disability from it. In rainy weather or cold weather I ache all over, but it's nothing I can't live with."

He also has lived without driving a race car since, but not by choice.

"All I wanted to do was drive again," Ray said, "but the doctors said no way."

"I bought another car, but the doctors said they wouldn't give me a release. They said my neck could easily be broken again, and that would be it."

Another young driver dreamed the same dreams that John Ray had dreamed. He had competed in only two Winston Cup races, one in 1975 and one in 1976. His third start, in the 1976 Dixie 500 at Atlanta, came in Ray's car.

His name: Dale Earnhardt.

"The Frances had helped me get the car," Ray said, speaking of NASCAR founder Bill France and his family, and different people had driven it, like Johnny Rutherford.

"Jim Foster wanted me to put Rutherford in it for Atlanta, but I told

him I wanted to put Earnhardt in it. He said, 'Who in the world is Dale Earnhardt?'"

It was natural that the NASCAR executive would prefer the gate appeal of the Indianapolis 500 winner to that of an unproven youngster, but Ray knew Earnhardt, and so he picked him. Dale also drove in a few USAC races for Ray.

Earnhardt's career zoomed. He became the first man ever to be Rookie of the Year (1979) and Winston Cup champion (1980) in successive seasons.

Remembered Ray: "After he won the championship, I said, 'Foster, who in the world is Dale Earnhardt?'"

But Earnhardt's Atlanta drive ended in a violent crash.

"He was running like fifth late in the race," Ray remembered. "Dick Brooks was down on the apron, just trying to finish. Something broke, and he went right, and Dale hit him.

"I still had my neck brace on, but I ran down there, and I just knew Dale was dead.

"I went to the infield hospital, and they said, 'You can't come in here,' but I said, 'Yes, I can.' I went in and Dale was sitting up, and all he had was a cut finger.

"He said, 'I tore your car up, didn't I?'"

That he had. The racer had flipped end over end several times."

"I had had enough," Ray said. "I couldn't drive, and it wasn't any fun being a car owner." He fielded a car for a few more races and became an ex-WC owner.

Ray got considerable recognition when he fielded cars for Rutherford. The handsome, popular star eventually won three Indianapolis 500s, but he enjoyed little success in NASCAR.

"Rutherford was good in Indy cars," Ray said, "but he never could really adapt to stock cars. He never had a feel for them, I guess you'd say."

Despite some nightmare episodes, Ray, 57, recalls his racing days with fondness. "I've had a good life," he said, looking out over acres of rolling land at Eastaboga on which is located a beautiful home and a thriving trucking business, John Ray Enterprises. From a shop on the property he fields a race car for his 16-year-old son Kevin.

John Ray (44) was a star bike rider before tackling stock cars.

He has never quite conquered the urge to race again himself. Why would a man who was almost killed wish to return?

"I don't know," Ray said, "but I thought life couldn't go on without me driving a race car, and I'm sure Neil Bonnett felt the same way."

Is it an addiction?

"I think it's worse than anything a man can get into, as far as getting away from it," Ray said. "I'm sure Bobby Allison would have gotten back in a car if the doctors would have let him.

"I was at the hospital after Davey Allison's helicopter crash, and I heard somebody ask Neil, 'Why in the world would you want to get back into one of those things?' He said, 'You can go hunting or fishing or do anything else all you want to, but nothing takes the place of driving a race car.'"

Ray was born and raised in Eastaboga. He was captivated by the sport early on. As a boy he traveled to races with Eddie Martin, a noted short-tracker.

He joined the Air Force and was stationed in California. He discovered the California motorcycle scene, and soon he was racing bikes. He was good enough that he rode for the Triumph factory team

for five years.

"I got my legs broken up bad about three times and finally had to quit," he said matter-of-factly. A motorcycle racer is more likely to get "broken up" than a stock car driver, Ray explained, but a stock car driver is more likely to get killed. "Motorcycle racing is rough on legs."

But he didn't quit racing when he abandoned the bikes. He became a sprint car driver. "I never won any championships," Ray said, "but I won some races in California and Arizona."

While in California he took a job building Indianapolis cars. He was with Jerry Eisert, who fielded a racer for Rutherford.

During his California days, he did the driving for Paul Newman in the movie *Winning*. "He's a lot of fun, a nice guy," Ray said. "But they lead a terrible life. They can't go anywhere. They can't even go out and eat in a restaurant without people hounding them."

During filming, Ray drove a car that had been built for Mario Andretti. The builder, he recalled, had insured the car for $1 million.

"I demolished it at Elkhart Lake, and the insurance company had to pay a million dollars."

Gene White hired Ray to build Indy cars for his Indianapolis-based operation, which featured Lloyd Ruby as driver. He later switched to White's Atlanta base and built Trans-Am racers for Ruby and Pete Hamilton.

Ray moved to Anniston in the late 1960s, continuing to race sprint cars in Anniston, Rome, Ga., Memphis and other locales.

"I flipped a sprint car one night at Anniston Speedway and broke my neck," he said. "It landed on its wheels, and it was still running wide open, going around and around. My brother Macon got to it, and about the time he hit the kill switch a tire got him. They brought the calf muscle of one of his legs to the hospital in a shop rag."

In 1974 car owner Charley Roberts gave Ray a ride in a Sportsman racer at Daytona. "The engine blew, but it felt good," Ray remembered. "I really liked it."

It was his first superspeedway start, and it whetted his appetite for Winston Cup, the big league. "Bob Davis gave me a ride in a Dodge at Talladega in 1974, and I drove his car several times that year," he said. His stint as a Winston Cup driver had begun, though it would be brief,

ended by the 1976 crash at Daytona.

Ray's racing career was marked by injury, but there were many good times, he stressed. "I won at least 100 motorcycle races and around 50 in sprint cars. You always want to win, but I enjoyed working on them and building them and just being around race cars."

He made the record book by driving one of his 18-wheelers 92.083 miles an hour around Talladega Superspeedway during a festival of speed several years ago. Spectators held their breath, hoping the tall rig wouldn't topple over as it negotiated the 33-degree banks.

Ray's friendship with Earnhardt and Earnhardt's team owner Richard Childress continues. When James Cline drove a Ray-owned racer on dirt, they used the operation to test engines for Childress .

"And Dale gave Johnny his first race car," Ray said, referring to a son who is now 21. "He drove five or six times, but he would rather work on them."

Kevin Ray, 16, would rather drive them. He started racing quarter-midgets, moved to mini-sprints, and for 1994 he planned to race a street stock car.

John Ray said his wife Kay never liked for him to race, but that she is more comfortable with Kevin driving. "Of course," he pointed out, "he isn't on 200-mile-an-hour tracks. But that's where he wants to go."

"On certain days it makes me more nervous than on other days," Kevin's mother said. "But Kevin is going to race no matter what."

__16__

Stanley Smith

Race drivers think it can't happen to them. Stanley Smith knows better now, for on July 25, 1993, it did happen to him. A crash in the DieHard 500 at Talladega left Smith teetering on the brink of death. He spent 40 days in the hospital, and he still hasn't completely recovered—but he already has the itch to race again. It's an itch he may not scratch. On an April day in 1994, he considered the question.

"My desire to race is still there," Smith said. "The wreck didn't scare me or kill any desire. I'd like to go to BIR or Montgomery. I'd like to go back to Talladega.

"But I don't know whether I'll drive or not because of all I put other people through. For me to get back in a car at Talladega and know they were thinking about it...

"But Delphia said if I want to it's fine."

His wife and their three children, sons Brett and Scotty and daughter Autumn, suffered mightily through the ordeal, Smith realizes, and he worries about dredging up all the old memories and creating new anxieties.

And another incident increased his hesitation to race again. "I had breakfast with Neil Bonnett on the morning he was killed at Daytona," Smith said. "I told him I was working toward running Talladega in July.

I had talked to a couple of sponsors about it, and they were behind it.

"Three hours later, Neil was dead."

Smith, who was timing Bonnett with a stopwatch when Neil crashed fatally on Feb. 11, 1994, said, "Do you really want to put your people through that? I had just eaten breakfast with him, and now he was dead. I could just see Delphia saying, 'I just kissed him this morning. Is he really dead?'

"I'm about 50-50 wanting to race again and 50-50 not racing again."

Perhaps in 1995, the 44-year-old Chelsea driver said. Perhaps never.

This from a man who admits his first outing in a race car "scared the heck out of me."

The proprietor of Stanley Smith Dry Wall, a prosperous sheet-rocking business, was raised in Hueytown. He moved to Chelsea when he was 15, but the racing bug already had planted its incisors in his psyche.

Smith would drop by Red Farmer's and Bobby Allison's garages and gaze at the men and the machines. "That turned me on to racing," he remembered. "Seeing those cars in Hueytown and wondering how it would be to race made an impression."

In 1972 he bought a racer to drive in the entry-level Cadet Division in Birmingham. "For $2,500 I got a car, a motor and a trailer, the whole nine yards," Smith remembered.

"The first time I went to the fairgrounds, if I could have sold it for $1,000 I probably would have. It scared the heck out of me. I learned in a hurry it was one thing to sit up there in the stands and talk about what the drivers should do and quite another thing to be in the middle of it.

"I ran dead last in my first feature. I got lapped one or two times in a 20-lap feature. The second week I got lapped, but I made up my mind that if I was going to do this I was going to run with them. The third week I finished in the top five, and that gave me a fever that has never left."

The knowledge that racing was more than simply putting the pedal to the metal came hard to Smith.

"I should have won four or five or six races in 1973," he said, "but patience wasn't my guide. I remember a kid came down from the grandstands after a race and told me he had nicknamed me Wild Man."

Smith recalled in one race trying to pass the leader on the inside, failing and zooming to the outside. He hit the wall so hard and stopped so suddenly that his goggles kept going before they snapped back on his nose.

Photo courtesy of the Smith family

Stanley Smith teetered near death after crash.

He advanced to Late Models in 1975 and spent the rest of the '70s driving at Birmingham, Montgomery and Mobile. He gave All Pro a shot but was stung by the high cost. Then he discovered a home in NASCAR's hot All-American Challenge Series.

"They competed with All Pro, but you were at a race only one day instead of three as you were with All Pro, so the cost wasn't as much," Smith said. He finished third in the standings in 1986, fifth in 1987, third in 1988—and in 1989 he captured the national championship.

"I won five races that year," Smith recalled. "I had a 150-point lead, but the last two races were nightmares. I had a flat in one, and then I went into the last one needing to finish 10th or better to win the championship. It was at St. Petersburg, Fla., and a local guy spun me out early, and I went back to about 25th.

"I said it was over. Then I said no, it wasn't over. I began passing cars like it was life or death and finished seventh and won the championship."

Interstate Batteries noticed and decided to sponsor him in the

All-American Challenge Series for three years. But dealers began clamoring for the company to go Winston Cup, so in 1990 Smith rented a car to drive in Talladega's DieHard 500.

He stunned everyone by qualifying 12th, but his Winston Cup debut was a mess. As he drove down pit road during the race, another car pulled out of its pit and struck his. Smith's hit a third car that was stopped for service, scattering the crewmen.

"I thought I had hurt some people bad, so I just parked it," he said. "But actually I think only one guy stayed in the hospital overnight."

Interstate wasn't daunted, though, and it told Smith it wanted to sponsor him on the Winston Cup circuit in 1991.

He got $450,000 for 12 races. He asked David Pearson about providing a car. Pearson said that was enough money for just eight races.

"You must be planning on me wrecking every race," the shocked Smith said.

Photo courtesy of the Smith family

Stanley Smith (49) had high hopes for a Winston Cup career.

"I'm not planning on you ever wrecking," Pearson replied.

So Smith decided to field his own team. He bought five new cars and went to work—and soon realized just how expensive Winston Cup is.

"David was right," Smith said. "It costs money to do it. There was no money for testing because it costs $10,000 or more to go testing. I got into my own pocket to help the deal along.

"I had a $21,000 tire bill at Rockingham—and one time I didn't pit because I knew the race was about over. It costs $6,000 to freshen an engine that originally cost $30,000. There's motel bills and food and travel and all the rest. The race paid me $6,700. That was when reality set in."

The biggest win of his career occurred in 1991. Driving for Bessemer car owner Clint Folsom, he took an ARCA race on the super-speedway at Michigan. "I nearly lapped the field," Smith remembered. "It was nice just to worry about driving and not whether we had used all the tires. When you're the owner, too, you start worrying about that kind of stuff instead of driving."

Interstate began sponsoring Joe Gibbs' team in 1992.The Washington Redskins coach was a natural to garner publicity. Its Armitron brand backed Smith, though. He never recorded a top-10 finish in Winston Cup, but his best chance came that year.

"We were running ninth at Dover with 50 laps to go," he recalled, "but I got carbon monoxide poisoning. The pavement looked like it was rocking. Donnie Allison was my crew chief, and he called me in and just reached in and shut off the switch. He could look at me and see that I shouldn't be out there."

The 1993 season dawned with Smith's Interstate Batteries sponsorship ended. "We had the shop and the equipment, and we were trying to find a sponsor, but we had no credentials," he said. "It's hard to get somebody to give you $2 million or $3 million."

Kresto, a hand cleaner, gave him $50,000 for one race. Unfortunately, it was the DieHard 500 in which he was so seriously injured. ``We went up to Talladega to try to impress them," Smith said. "Well, we impressed them. We turned them off to racing."

Smith remembers everything about that day up until race time, then

his memory is blank. He recalls starting the car and sending his son Brett to fetch a different helmet. "That's the last thing I remember."

He has watched the tape of the crash many times. He said it was triggered when his car and Kenny Wallace's touched. The chain reaction sent Jimmy Horton's racer over the first-turn wall, and Ritchie Petty's car hit Smith's in the driver's door. "That moved the roll cage over seven inches, and I hit the wall head-on," Smith said.

He believes quick transportation via helicopter to Carraway Methodist Medical Center in Birmingham saved his life. "I had a cracked skull, and it tore a hole in an artery in my brain," Smith said. "That was what I nearly died from, the artery being torn." Incredibly, he suffered no other broken bones.

"I woke up on Friday after the wreck on Sunday," Smith said. "I didn't know why I was there. The only reason I'd ever been in a hospital was for kidney stones, and I thought it must be that."

Forty days in a hospital provides a man with plenty of time to think. "People take so much for granted," Smith said. "I didn't have tears for three or four months. I didn't have saliva until November. People say, 'Big deal,' but it is a big deal when you have to put stuff in your eyes and spray stuff in your mouth all the time."

His daughter Autumn was Miss Teen Alabama, and while Smith was hospitalized she was in the Miss Teen USA pageant in Biloxi, Miss. "I guess they didn't give me my painkiller, and I woke up for about 30 minutes and watched it on TV," he said. "When she didn't make the top 10 I went right back out."

Bobby Allison, the hero of his teen years, visited him weekly, Smith said. "I know it was tough on him to go through those doors into a place where his son had died a week before."

17

Don and Mickey Gibbs

D on Gibbs can tell you about a drought. "I won the first race I ever drove in," he said. "Nine years later I got my second victory."

He also can tell you about winning. Gibbs estimates he won 250 main events, 90 percent of them on dirt. "Once I started winning features it stayed with me," he said. "I won 20 in a row in 1980 at Hokes Bluff."

Don and Mickey Gibbs are one of the better known father-son teams in short-track racing. As a little boy, Mickey watched in awe as his pop churned up the clay. Then they drove together. Now Don is retired from driving, and Mickey is a star of the bullrings.

No one denies that Mickey is blessed with talent, but he is caught in the numbers game that makes Winston Cup racing one of the most exclusive sports in the world.

On a given Sunday there are 600 men playing major league baseball, 1,200 playing NFL football, but only 40 competing in a big-league stock car race.

To compound the problem, a fellow with skill and a cheap glove can make it in baseball, but a fellow with skill and a cheap car can forget Winston Cup.

Mickey got his shot at the big league, but it didn't work out. At 37,

Mickey Gibbs posed before a race at Daytona.

he isn't old for a race driver, but there is no Winston Cup opportunity on the horizon. "But who knows?" he said philosophically. "Strange things happen in life."

He and his father formed their own Winston Cup team, right there at their shop near Glencoe, in 1988. "The first thing I did was go to Daytona and win the ARCA race," Mickey recalled. "I thought, 'Boy, we've got it made.'"

But it turned out to be a bittersweet Speed Week. The Gibbses were building their own motors, but then they got talked into buying a supposedly mean one from another company. "We put it in and slowed down six miles an hour, and I didn't even make the show for the Daytona 500," Mickey said. "I was a hero one day and a zero the next. If we had left it like it was we would have made the show without a problem."

The season wasn't spectacular, but it was promising. "I think we

ran five Winston Cup races or something," Mickey said. "In all the races we finished, we were in the top 20. The first time I ever went to Charlotte in my life I qualified 13th. At the end of the year I won the ARCA race at Atlanta, so I was two for two in ARCA."

He got noticed, and another team hired him to drive for 1989. The sponsorship it expected didn't materialize, and it folded soon after the season began.

Another team hired him in 1991, but again sponsorship problems prevented its finishing the season.

He drove a few races for a part-time team, but that led nowhere, and he returned to the short tracks. In 1993 he competed in 19 dirt races at such locales as Green Valley and Fyffe and won 15 of them.

He and his father can't afford another venture into Winston Cup, neither can other wannabes who would be proud to have him as a driver, so Mickey Gibbs follows his dream on the short tracks.

"Not many people can reach into their pocket and pull out $3 million," Mickey said, "and that's the least it takes in Winston Cup. Some of those teams have a $4-million budget. It's not only money, you have to have help from the factory. You can't outrun the technology with just money.

"It's a team effort, but it's a very big team. You have to have 15 guys in the pits and another 15 back home in the shop, and anyone you can get to do some R&D for you," he continued, stressing the importance of research and development to keep in step.

"I'll always have hope," Mickey said, "but if you can't get in a Winston Cup car that has a chance, it's just like a Sunday drive. I drove in about 35 of those races, and I think my highest finish was 13th.

"It makes you feel less of a man, knowing you're out there and you don't have a chance."

On a gorgeous Sunday in March, Fairgrounds Raceway was launching its 1994 season with a Southern All-Stars circuit 100-lapper. Mickey Gibbs was transporting his racer from Glencoe to Birmingham and listening to the broadcast of the Winston Cup race that was being contested at Richmond.

"I used to couldn't even stand to hear them on the radio," he said, recalling the disappointment of his bobtailed Winston Cup career. "But

I'm a lot better about it now."

He was running second midway of the 100-lapper when a spark plug malfunction ended his charge. "I think we would have won," Mickey said defiantly.

And he has won, many times. One doesn't have to be in Winston Cup to be a star.

"I have no idea how many races I've won," Mickey said. "Between 100 and 200. I wish now I had kept up with it, but I was too busy trying to keep the car going to keep up with it. But the little races don't mean that much to me. I like the big races with the big heroes in the lineup."

His first big hero was his father. At 56, Don Gibbs is a tall, lean, distinguished looking man with iron gray hair. He quit school in the ninth grade and began selling used cars. The automobile business, coal mining and sales of heavy road-building equipment made him a millionaire.

"I've been crazy about it since I was old enough to remember," Mickey recalled. "My dad wasn't just a race car driver, he was a winner. The excitement and competitiveness of it got in my blood, and as a boy I never missed a race I could get to.

"For a long time it was just me and him. He would be out of town in the car business, in Chicago picking up cars, and I'd be packing wheel bearings, things like that. I was 10 or 11 years old. I didn't build motors or anything big, but I'd clean up the car and the trailer.

"When I was 15 I got a driver permit, and I'd meet him at the race track with the race car. I probably had somebody with me—but they were probably 14."

A friend of Don Gibbs was a driver, and Don caught the fever from him.

"In about 1954 I went with Charles Bradberry to see him race at the old Anniston Speedway," Don said. "He let me drive it a lap.

"He gave me an old car he had, and I rounded up a motor and started racing. I qualified and made the slow heat and won it. I won the first race I ever drove. Nine years later I won my second one.

"I ran at the fairgrounds in Birmingham when it was dirt and ran third three weeks in a row. I used to tow my race car up here with the

family car and take the carburetor off the family car and put it on the race car. I used to really think I was doing something. Well, I guess I was; I ran third against some of the best in the world."

Don Gibbs said he simply didn't have the money to race properly during those nine years. Once his pockets began to jingle, things changed.

With Mickey pit-crewing, Don drove at Attalla and Albertville and Gadsden and Pensacola and Mobile and other tracks and piled up victories. Then Mickey made his debut as a driver in the mid-1970s.

Photo courtesy of the Gibbs family

Don Gibbs once won 20 features in a row.

Ray Putnam, another driver, called Don Gibbs on a Saturday and told him he knew of a superb race car that was for sale. It was built to run on asphalt, but Don told him if he could get it there in time for them to put dirt tires on it and get it to Gadsden Raceway for the night's competition, he would buy it and let Mickey drive it.

"I won the first heat in my car, and I drove the second heat in Mickey's new car and won it," Don recalled. "I told him, 'There's you a proven winner.' Then I won the feature, and he finished second."

(As Mickey remembers it, the feature was rained out, and his actual debut didn't come until the next season.)

Don had some coal mines in Kentucky to see after, and Putnam and the Gibbses raced as a team in Don's cars in the Bluegrass State, frequently running 1, 2, 3.

But they couldn't race in the dark.

"One night in Corbin, Ky., they waved the starter's flag, and everybody stood on the gas," Don remembered. "We fell in Putnam, Mickey and me. Then the lights went out. We just sandwiched Mickey's car and tore it all up. But Ray did go on to win the race."

Don loved Gadsden Raceway, a high-banked, super-fast dirt track. "I got shook up pretty good there one night," he said. "I did 11 end-over-ends and was laid up for a month.

"Then one night Mickey and his older brother said they were going to Gadsden Raceway, and they asked if I wanted to go. I said I didn't know whether I could or not.

"But I went, and I was sitting up on a hill watching when the Blackburn brothers said their driver didn't show up. He thought the race was rained out. They asked if I'd drive their car.

"I was hurting so bad I didn't know if I could, but I said I would, and everybody just stuffed me into the car.

"When the race started, I just forgot all about how I was hurting. Then when it was over I got out of the car and fell flat."

It was at Gadsden Raceway that popular driver Harold Fryar lost his life in 1970. A driveshaft came off another car and hit him.

"I was right on Harold's back bumper the night he was killed," Don said. "You couldn't have stuck a finger between our cars.

"They inverted the field that night, and Harold and I started on the rear. We talked about which way we'd move to get up through the field, because it was always between Harold and me anyway.

"We agreed that whichever one a hole opened in front of would let the other one in, and we'd go to the front.

"The hole opened in front of me, and I let him in. Then he was passing the lead car, Henley Gray's, and I was right behind him. Henley Gray's driveshaft twisted in two and came back and hit him in the head. We didn't have windshields.

"I didn't know what happened. I thought his throttle hung. He shot out of there and went into the top of some pine trees outside the track. I stopped and got out of the car, but one of my sons said, 'Dad, don't go over there. He's dead.'"

The best Don ever saw on dirt?

"Harold Fryar and Tootle Estes, and they both raced there at

Gadsden Raceway with me. Tootle started coming to Gadsden Raceway after Harold got killed.

"Tootle stepped out of his race car in Knoxville, Tenn., after he had won the race and had a heart attack and died."

Don preferred dirt to asphalt. "The dirt was just me," he said. "I liked the asphalt, but dirt is it."

That's one of the few things he and his son disagree about. "I like asphalt better," Mickey said. "The dirt cars are as much fun as you can have. They are light and overpowered. It's like a 700-horsepower go-cart. But the asphalt takes a little more team effort in the pits, a little more finesse. Asphalt is more of a challenge."

As a driver, Don went out in style. "I never raced full-time, like Bobby Allison and Donnie Allison and those boys," he said. "I worked six or seven days a week. My last five years Mickey kept my car running. In 1981 I won my first four races and just turned it all over to Mickey."

About The Author

Clyde Bolton

Clyde Bolton is the sports columnist for The Birmingham News. He has covered automobile racing for the paper since 1962. Twice his stories on the sport have been recognized as the best in the nation.

Bolton is the author of four novels and nine other non-fiction books, including three on racing: Bolton's Best Stories of Auto Racing, Remembering Davey and Talladega Superspeedway.

Bolton and his wife Sandra live in Trussville. They are the parents of three sons.